LITTLE, CRAZY CHILDREN

ALSO BY JAMES RENNER

Nonfiction

True Crime Addict: How I Lost Myself in the Mysterious Disappearance of Maura Murray

Amy: My Search for Her Killer

It Came from Ohio: True Tales of the Weird, Wild, and Unexplained

Fiction

The Man from Primrose Lane

Muse

The Great Forgetting

LITTLE, CRAZY CHILDREN

A True Crime Tragedy

JAMES RENNER

CITADEL PRESS
Kensington Publishing Corp.
www.kensingtonbooks.com

In memoriam, Rob Lucas

CITADEL PRESS BOOKS are published by

Kensington Publishing Corp.
119 West 40th Street
New York, NY 10018

Illustrations by Todd Jakubisin

All Kensington titles, imprints, and distributed lines are available at special quantity discounts for bulk purchases for sales promotions, premiums, fund-raising, educational, or institutional use. Special book excerpts or customized printings can also be created to fit specific needs. For details, write or phone the office of the Kensington sales manager: Kensington Publishing Corp., 119 West 40th Street, New York, NY 10018, attn: Sales Department; phone 1-800-221-2647.

CITADEL PRESS and the Citadel logo are Reg. U.S. Pat. & TM Off.

ISBN: 978-0-8065-4255-3

First Citadel hardcover printing: July 2023

10 9 8 7 6 5 4 3 2 1

Printed in the United States of America

Library of Congress Control Number: 2023933471

ISBN: 978-0-8065-4257-7 (e-book)

We are what we always were in Salem, but now the little, crazy children are jangling the keys of the kingdom, and common vengeance writes the law!

—ARTHUR MILLER, *The Crucible*

Lee Rd.
Sedgewick Rd.
S Woodland Rd.

Shaker Heights
Arabica Cafe
2940 Lee Rd.
Station
RTA
S Woodland
3387 Norwood Rd
Shaker Square
Van Aken Blvd.
Lee Rd.
N

CONTENTS

II. Trial

III. Judgment

PROLOGUE

THE DETECTIVE EYED THE YOUNG man sitting beside him. The boy's hair was freshly buzzed on the sides, but up top it was long and messy. He had a friendly face and looked a bit younger than the other juniors from Shaker Heights High. It was late for the kid—nearly 4 A.M. But none of this could wait.

"Are you presently under the influence of any alcohol or drugs?" the detective asked.

"No," the boy replied.

The detective's name was Thomas Gray. His messy hair days were long gone. He was balding up top and what was left was not long at all. He was thirty-four years old, but looked older. He'd been around, spent some years in the Big Easy as a short-order cook before returning to Ohio and becoming a cop. Detective Gray didn't know it yet, but the mystery that began that early Friday morning in 1990 would become the biggest case of his career. In fact, it came to define the rest of his short life. Did Detective Gray feel a prickle of apprehension at that moment? Could he sense the subtle pivot of his fate? Impossible to say. All we have are his notes and this interview, snapshots of the past.

It was good that the boy was talking. He hadn't lawyered up. That was a mark in his favor. But Gray was smart enough to know that the lawyers were coming. Oh yes. The best lawyers in town would be lining up come first light. Half the kids in town might need one. So it was vitally important that he get the boy's statement down while he still could.

The boy's name was Dan Dreifort. He lived with his parents in a mansion at the corner of Lee Road and South Woodland. Any other Friday morning, Dan would still be sleeping, resting up for another day of school. But it was a good bet that Dan wouldn't make it in for classes today. It was possible the boy would never go back. A lot depended on how Dan answered the detective's questions.

The routine process of a homicide investigation is designed to be impersonal. Emotion, sympathy—all that stuff distracts from the truth. Routine provides momentum when things would otherwise grind to a halt. It also gives the detective permission to ask upsetting questions without feeling guilty about it—it's the job, nothing personal. Routine separates us from the stark fear of a traumatic event—from what they'd found hidden behind the bushes next to this boy's house, for instance. When faced with life-altering events, it's best to rely on routine to get you to the next day and the next, until you find your footing again. So, in a way, the detective was doing the boy a favor.

"To the best of your knowledge, were Lisa's parents aware that Lisa was coming to visit you?" asked Detective Gray.

"No, they were not," the boy said. Already the boy had been caught in a lie. He'd said something altogether different when he'd called 911.

"Could you describe the clothing you were wearing at the time the police arrived at your house?"

"I was wearing brown moccasins, a black bathing suit with flowers on it, and a T-shirt from a Unitarian Youth Conference in Toledo."

The detective held up a shirt.

"Showing you a white T-shirt, brand name Fruit of the Loom, size large, with an insignia on the front in purple-and-black letters stating, 'Spring Conference 1988. Toledo—Maumee Valley,' and also containing the words 'The Search for Self,' and the initials 'Y.R.U.U.' on the front. Is this the shirt that you described?"

"Yes, it is."

"Could you describe the Converse All Star shoes that you were wearing?"

"Size nine, Chuck Taylor's, tie-dyed, high top."

The detective considered his words, then began, "Could you describe what you remember of the screams?"

Part One

INVESTIGATION

Chapter One

ON SHAKER HEIGHTS

TO THE EAST OF CLEVELAND, just past the ghetto, is a town with a lot of trees called Shaker Heights. Its side streets meander around gardened ovals full of hostas and it's easy to get lost if you've never been here before. The paved throughway that cuts east/west across the middle is called South Woodland. The bigger mansions are here. Homes of Cleveland doctors and lawyers, entrepreneurs and politicians. Farther east is the town of Beachwood, a Jewish enclave full of high-end department stores and kosher restaurants. To the north is Cleveland Heights, a liberal, postcollege community with garage-rock venues and Irish pubs. And to the south you have your workaday suburbs full of too-close homes and postage-stamp lawns. Shaker Heights is its own universe in the middle of it all: separate and weird.

Shaker Heights was a planned utopia. The town was plotted out, parcel by parcel, by two eccentric brothers who never married and shared a bedroom in a fifty-four-room estate they named Roundwood Manor. Oris and Mantis Van Sweringen were real estate prospectors, and in 1905, they started buying up land to the east of Cleveland that was owned by the United Society of Believers in Christ's Second Appearing, a religious sect that came to be known as the Shakers, on account of their habit of convulsing during church services when the Lord came into their bodies. The Shakers prohibited sex and so their ad hoc communities seldom lasted longer than a single generation. The Cleveland commune was on the way out when Oris and Mantis found them and recognized an opportunity.

The Vans, as the brothers were known around town, wished to create a new neighborhood for the city's elite and the plan was wonderfully Disney-esque in its audacity. There was this societal movement at the time, a reflection of the opulent wealth made possible by the industrial revolution, a mission to design communities around nature and not be concerned about how long it might take residents to get to the factories—this elite class had no need to punch a clock anymore. So the Vans made their parcels over large, with wide, tree-lousy lawns. And while the Vans were alive, nobody could move into Shaker Heights unless both brothers approved.

And then the Great Depression happened. The Vans, at one time worth over $3 billion (which, adjusted for inflation, was stupid rich), were wiped out. Their legacy, the town, like Ozymandias's trunkless legs, is all that remains. And because the dapper and dainty brothers were so very ruthless with the city zoning statutes, Shaker Heights looks pretty much as it did a hundred years ago.

But slowly, all through the 1960s and 1970s, real Clevelanders creeped in from the west and the Waspy aristocracy inside their tony mansions were forced to make room for African Americans. To this day, integration in Shaker Heights is treated as a science, something that can be tabulated, controlled. During the '80s, the city offered rock-bottom loans to whites who moved into the Black sections of Shaker Heights and to the Blacks who moved to the white streets. On the surface it appeared to be an enlightened bit of social engineering—a way to guarantee balanced integration. However, these home loans were also made available to Blacks who wished to move out of Shaker Heights entirely, as was revealed in a special report by the *New York Times* in 1991. In reality the system was a clever way to stem white flight and to carefully manage the percentage of African-American residents living in town at any one time.

The public schools are top-notch and well-funded by taxes, but the Shaker elite—those folks who own homes along South Woodland—also have the option to send their kids to some of the best private schools in the country. University School and Hathaway Brown are your best bet if you want to send your kid to Harvard one day (and if you have an extra $30,000 for tuition).

But in the early 1990s, when most of this story takes place, many of the doctors and lawyers who lived there still sent their kids to public school. Integration was *de rigueur*. Middle-school students were required to enlist in racial-sensitivity training. There was optimism that whatever made Shaker Heights so special could be maintained through inclusion, that maybe it might still be a grand utopia, after all.

This is our stage. It is here that a boy named Dan Dreifort fell in love with a girl named Lisa Pruett. To say their first kiss sealed their fates is no exaggeration. From that moment on, the two of them were drawn inexorably toward tragedy. And Lisa's violent end, when it came, finally ended that utopian dream called Shaker Heights.

Chapter Two

THE BIKE IN THE BUSHES

During the evening hours of Thursday, September 13, 1990, Officer Edward Curtin patrolled Zone 4 in his cruiser. Zone 4 was a section of Shaker Heights that included the intersection of Lee Road and South Woodland, one of the busiest intersections in town. Curtin was a career cop. Hardscrabble. He had served and protected the residents of Shaker Heights for fifteen years. Before that, he'd done eight years as an officer for Warrensville Heights. When he was a kid, he'd swept the floors at Republic Steel. He was as Cleveland as Cleveland can be.

At 1:05 A.M., a call came over Curtin's radio. It was Sharon Mapp at dispatch, asking Curtin to report to a residence near Lee and South Woodland. A young man named Dan Dreifort had called police after his girlfriend skipped out on a late-night rendezvous. He was worried for her. A strange request. Not the normal domestic or disorderly that made up much of the job.

Two minutes later, Curtin pulled up to the Dreifort house. A teenage boy waited at the end of the drive. This, too, struck the officer as unusual. Most times he met the caller at their door.

Curtin stepped out of his cruiser. The boy immediately launched into his story.

"My girlfriend, Lisa, was supposed to be at my house at twelve-thirty," Dan said. "I haven't heard from her. And my dad heard screams. I didn't hear them, but he told me that he heard screams."

"Did your parents know that Lisa was supposed to come over?"

Dan said they did, which was a lie. "I think I found her bike," the boy said, leading Curtin south, down Lee, away from his house. About forty feet from the driveway, they came to a girl's bicycle propped against the bushes that lined the sidewalk.

"I touched it," said Dan. "So my fingerprints might be on the bike. I just wanted to straighten it. I think she was pulled off her bike and dragged away, pulled inside a car and driven away."

"Why don't you go back inside," the officer said. "I'll come over after we're done searching."

Curtin examined the bike after Dan walked away. He looked at the bushes, the ground. There were no signs of a struggle. No scuff marks on the sidewalk. The bike looked like it had been placed gently against the shrubs.

Another cruiser arrived. It was Officer Michael Matsik, with his German shepherd, Drill. Matsik was a sort of neighborhood celebrity, the cop everyone knows and likes, the one they put in the paper. Six years with the military police, nine with the Geauga County Sheriff's Department, three on the force in Shaker Heights. He and Drill received regular commendations for catching burglars and finding missing kids. His file at the Shaker Heights Police Department is full of awards and letters from people thanking him for saving their lives.

Earlier that night, Matsik had parked his car just a hundred yards from here to shoot the shit with another cop. He remembered that right about 12:30 A.M. someone had called to report a woman screaming. He'd had a look around, but he hadn't seen anything. And he hadn't heard the screams himself, even though he'd been talking through an open window just around the corner.

Matsik let Drill out of the car. Drill was good at scents. He could track a man running through backyards and jumping over fences. Matsik brought Drill over to the bicycle in the bushes. The dog picked up a scent around the back tire and then started walking south, down Lee, heading for the intersection. There Drill took a right, pulling Matsik west along South Woodland, and then right again at the next street, Sedgewick. The dog walked another fifty feet up Sedgewick and then sat down. He'd lost the scent.

The two policemen and the dog started back toward the Dreifort mansion. First they stopped at 16401 South Woodland. An older couple lived there, the Bushes, an African-American couple with grown kids. Curtin and Matsik turned down their driveway to check out the backyard, which abutted the Dreifort property. Curtin shone his flashlight on the ground in front of them, searching for footprints. Matsik got his flashlight out, too. Beams of light crisscrossed over the grass and then fell upon the body of a young woman. Her eyes were open, unfocused, staring into the dark of night.

The girl was wearing a pretty blue top, which had been pulled up around her neck, exposing her bra. Her jeans and underwear were down around her right leg. Her left tennis shoe lay beside her.

She'd been sliced all down her neck and chest, and her porcelain skin was covered in blood. Someone had stabbed this girl to death only moments ago. A rageful, violent murder.

Curtin went to the girl and touched the skin over her carotid artery. No pulse. He noted a large gash on the left side of her head was still bleeding a little.

At that moment the two men fell into their practiced routines. They called the rescue squad. Matsik got out the tape and secured the scene. Then they called their shift commander and reported a homicide.

Chapter Three

NIGHT VISITORS

IT WAS AROUND 1:30 A.M. when Gary Pruett was jolted awake by the sound of someone knocking loudly on his front door. The doorbell rang. The knocking continued, persistent. Gary got out of bed and walked downstairs in his pajamas and a blue bathrobe.

The Pruett residence was out on Norwood, east of Lee Road, on a curvy street behind the country club, a brick two-story shaded by tall trees. Gary worked as a chemist for British Petroleum at their lab in Warrensville Heights. His daughter, Lisa, was currently studying chemistry in high school, and he delighted in helping her with homework at the end of the day.

Gary opened the door to find a police officer standing on his stoop.

The policeman introduced himself as Corporal William Misencik. "Are you the father of Lisa Pruett?" he asked.

"Yes."

"Do you know if Lisa is home?"

"She's in bed, upstairs."

"Would you please check?"

Gary turned and hurried back up the stairs toward Lisa's bedroom. He opened the door. Turned on the light. His daughter's bed was empty.

Things became disjointed for Gary then, and later he would have trouble recalling specific details: what was said when and by whom. He came back downstairs; his wife, Lynette, was beside him now, and he told the cop at his door that Lisa was missing.

"Does she have a bicycle?" Misencik asked.

"Yes."

"Would you see if it's still here?"

Gary walked through the house to the door that led to their attached garage. Lisa's twelve-speed Miyata, which should be with the others, was missing.

"Are you familiar with a house at 2940 Lee Road?" the officer asked him.

"That's Dan's house," said Lynette. "Lisa's boyfriend."

"I think you should come with me."

Lisa was a good kid, and the idea that she would have snuck out to meet up with her boyfriend was out of character. She took honors classes. Wrote poetry. Played the flute in band. This was a girl who simply didn't get into trouble.

Dan Dreifort was a new part of her life. They'd started going steady after a band trip to Germany on spring break. They had a number of mutual friends who were always hanging out at Dan's house, and over the summer Lisa had been there a lot, until Dan had to go to the hospital. Lisa had come to Gary, then, to explain how Dan and his father had a tough relationship and she didn't think that Dan should have been put into a psychological facility. She thought his father was just being mean. For weeks Lisa put together care packages for Dan: boxes full of letters, chewing gum, a roll of quarters for the pay phone. Lisa called Dan at the hospital sometimes and pretended to be his sister so the nurse would put him on.

Earlier that day Lisa had passed her driver's exam. She'd also aced a big test in German class. Lynette had prepared a special dinner to celebrate, with all of Lisa's favorite foods. And then Dan had gotten out of the hospital. It had been a great day for his daughter. One of those days that stand apart from the others and live on forever in memory.

When Gary arrived at the Dreifort house, he found more police cars and a yellow ribbon draped along the hedges behind the sidewalk. He jumped out of the car. An officer approached him immediately.

"I'm Gary Pruett, Lisa's father," he said. "What's going on?"

"I have to keep you from getting any closer," the officer said.

"Where's Lisa? Is she all right?"

The officer wouldn't answer, so Gary moved closer to the tape. The cop blocked his way.

"There's a girl," the officer told him. "She received a blow to the head. She does not appear to be breathing."

Chapter Four

THE BOYFRIEND

DAN DREIFORT SAT AT A desk inside the Shaker Heights PD and continued his statement for Detective Tom Gray. In the beginning the detective wanted to learn about his subject. Who was this boy? Dan told him how his dad was an administrator at the Cleveland Clinic, the premier hospital in the region. Dan was popular at school, at least with the band geeks, he said. Kind of a goof, a prankster, a class clown. Sometimes, when Hans Bohnert, the band teacher, left the class alone, Dan would stand up and conduct an impromptu rendition of "Louie, Louie." He was in a rock-and-roll band that played the occasional, honest-to-goodness real gig. They called themselves Your Mother and Her Howling Commandoes, a reference to an elite squad of soldiers from Marvel comic books. Dan also fenced with a small group of friends, who referred to themselves as the "Black Glove Cult" because of the black gloves they had to wear when sparring. They'd gotten in trouble for posting flyers about their gang at school. Lately he and his father hadn't been getting along. There was a fight. A particularly bad one. And afterward, Dan's father had him committed at the hospital where he worked.

"I was discharged from the Cleveland Clinic yesterday at about two P.M.," said Dan. "I went home, put my stuff away, and rode my bike to school. I saw Lisa. I surprised her. She didn't know I was being discharged. I walked around the school with her and walked her to her mom's car. It must have been around two-thirty.

"Then I hung out with some friends until about five-thirty. Came home, ate dinner. My parents went out and my next-door neighbor cut my hair. Then Tex Workman came over. I don't know, around eight P.M. Then my parents came home. We spent some time with them, and then Lisa stopped by after her flute lesson at about nine P.M., with her father, who waited in the driveway. She asked if it was okay if she stopped by later. I don't think she gave me a time.

"Then I was with Tex till ten P.M. He left and I went inside and talked to my mom for a while. Then Lisa called and said that if she came over, it would be between twelve-thirty and one A.M. and that she would just, like, throw a rock at my window.

"At eleven o'clock I watched the news, and then went to my room at exactly eleven thirty-two P.M. I listened to music and put away some more of my stuff from the hospital. My sister called at midnight. I talked to her till almost twelve-thirty, said good night to my parents, and went to my room. Then I heard screaming coming from outside, and my father said that he looked at the clock and it was twelve-thirty, and we were concerned about the noise.

"My dad noticed that I had shoes on. He said to go check it out. I went out front to the edge of our property and saw nothing, heard nothing. Went inside and suggested to my father to call the police, but we both agreed that there was nobody out there, nothing that we could do.

"I went into my room and put some more stuff away. That's when I remembered that Lisa said she might come over. I don't know exactly when I suspected that might have been her screaming, and I went back outside."

The detective waited for Dan to continue.

"It must have been twelve forty-five A.M. and I waited for a little bit, and then I was gonna, like, walk to where I might see her coming.

First I went to the edge of the property, then I went a little further and saw her bike in the bushes. I touched it, to pull it out to see if it was hers. I saw that it was and ran back to my house and called Lisa's house. Nobody answered. I got the answering machine, didn't leave a message. Then I called 911."

Back at the Dreiforts' house, a small army of police officers were processing the scene. One officer operated a video camera, documenting every room. Others gathered evidence in plastic bags, carefully noting each new clue.

In the bushes near the body, someone discovered a hammer. They also found a rusty key, a glass bottle, and a paper bag with a bloody shoe print on it, left behind by someone wearing a shoe with a herringbone pattern on its sole. There was a *Sunday Magazine* from an old *Plain Dealer* newspaper. A Hawaiian Punch bottle. And in the driveway they found one condom, half out of its wrapper. On the front steps of Dan's house, they found two red berries: one smashed, one whole. Both matched the type of berries found on a bush beside Lisa's body.

In Dan's bedroom police discovered a pocketknife and another brown paper bag, this one filled with empty cough syrup bottles.

Someone collected Lisa's bike.

"Could you describe what you remember of the screams?" asked Detective Tom Gray.

"It sounded like someone being forced to do something that they didn't want to do," said Dan.

Tom Gray had not set out to become a detective. It wasn't some boyhood dream. He'd gone to Ohio University and gotten a degree in business administration, but then kind of puttered around for a bit. He worked as a line cook in Cleveland. Managed a Wendy's in New Orleans. Came home, tried working for an insurance company for a spell. When he applied for a position with the Shaker Heights police, they asked him why he wanted to be a cop. Gray told them he needed a change in career and being a cop paid better than a line cook. This was his first major case.

"When you heard the scream, where were you in the house?" asked Gray.

"I was in my room, which is facing Lee Road, on the second floor."

"What exactly were you doing?"

"Listening to a tape and putting something away. I had many, many bags of stuff from the hospital. I was neatening my room up."

"What tape was it you were listening to?" the detective asked. These small, seemingly insignificant details were actually quite important. Later, they would have to interview the boyfriend again, and if these details were different, that could mean the whole statement was an improvised fabrication. Hard to remember all the little lies when you have to repeat them.

"R.E.M.," the boy said. "*Document,* recorded live in Holland, October 12, 1987."

"While listening to the tape, were you wearing headphones?"

"No, I was not."

The detective shifted back to the crime. "After you heard the scream, what action did you take?"

"Went to my window, pulled up the shade, looked out, and my father said, 'Did you hear that?' I said, 'Yeah.'"

"Did you open the window?"

"Oh yeah, I opened the window. I closed it a couple minutes later, though."

"After opening the window, what did you hear outside?"

"The screaming continued."

"So that I understand you correctly, you heard the scream, your father yelled to you something to the effect, 'Did you hear that?' You opened the window, and you heard the screaming continue?"

"Yes," said Dan.

"After the screaming stopped, what action did you take?"

"While the screaming was going on, I went downstairs and out the front door, to see what I could see."

"How far out the front door did you go?" asked Gray.

"I walked to the edge of our property."

"When you reached the front door, and as you were walking out into the yard, could you still hear the screaming?"

"No."

"Was your father with you at this time, and if not, where was he?"

"My father was at the door."

"What did you do next?"

"I stayed for ten seconds, and then walked back to the house, told my father that I saw nothing."

"You stated you went outside a second time, is that correct?"

"Yes, it is."

"How long was that after you had returned to your room?"

"Maybe fifteen minutes."

"Did you advise either your father or your mother that you were going back outside?"

"No."

"So that I understand you correctly, you went back outside the second time because you realized that Lisa Pruett might be coming over to see you, is that correct?"

"Yes."

"At that point, did you think that the screams that you heard might possibly have been from Lisa Pruett?"

"No. I didn't think that for a couple of minutes, but then I thought it might have been her." Dan told the detective that when he got back inside, he tried calling Lisa, but hung up when the machine kicked on, before dialing 911.

"Why did you call Lisa's house?"

"I was hoping that maybe it wasn't her bicycle and that she had been home, and I felt that if it was her bicycle, her parents should know."

"Did you ever see this bike before?"

"Yes. It's Lisa's bike."

"So you knew when you saw the bike, right away, that it was Lisa Pruett's bike?"

"No," said Dan. "I thought it was, but I wasn't sure. I was scared that something had happened to Lisa, so I ran to the house and tried to call her on the phone."

"The answering machine was on, is that correct?"

"Yes."

"Did you listen to the whole message?"

"No. I immediately hung up the phone."

"Immediately after you hung up, you called 911, is that correct?"

"Yes."

"At that point, had you made your mother or father aware of your fears?"

"No."

"Why not?"

"I was too busy calling and running around. I wasn't thinking straight. I was in a rush."

"Are you right- or left-handed?"

"Right-handed."

"Could you describe any physical contact you have had with Lisa since your release from the hospital?"

"I hugged and kissed her when I arrived at school. I hugged her when I walked her to her mom's car at school. She touched my freshly cut hair while at my house, and I hugged and kissed her as she was leaving."

"To the best of your recollection," said Gray, "how many times in the past has Lisa come over to your house late at night?"

"Twice. Maybe once."

"Could you describe when this was, and how she got to your house?"

"This was four months ago and she rode her bike."

"At what time did you become aware of the fact that Lisa was no longer alive?"

"At four A.M., when I was informed that I was a suspect for aggravated murder."

"Do you know of anyone who had or might have had a serious disagreement with Lisa Pruett, which might have caused them to harm her?"

"No."

"Would you be willing, with your parents' consent, to submit to a polygraph examination in reference to the murder of Lisa Pruett?"

"Yes."

"Did you kill Lisa Pruett?"

"No, I did not."

Dan Dreifort finished his statement at 4:15 A.M. His father, Robert, signed as a witness.

Chapter Five

THE SAID LISA LEE

AT 5:16 A.M., THE BODY of a sixteen-year-old girl arrived at the Cuyahoga County Coroner's Office inside a large black bag. Two leichendieners attended to her body. Every morgue has these guys, assistants who clean the body and prepare it for autopsy—*leichendiener* is German for "corpse servant"—and they needn't be doctors. In fact, sometimes they're simply interns. These two men undressed the girl and laid her body on a stainless-steel table. The chief deputy coroner, Dr. Robert Challener, came in early to conduct the examination. Whatever coroners are supposed to look like, this guy doesn't. He was all ears and glasses, more like a beloved history teacher than a coroner you'd see on TV. The autopsy room resembled an operation suite, with the exception of sterile equipment—no need to worry about infection if the subject is already dead. Stainless-steel sinks, a drain in the floor, red tile, and chrome.

For the first time Dr. Challener observed the totality of the trauma that had been inflicted upon Lisa Pruett. It was impossible not to be moved by the violence. There was a routine for autopsies. A checklist of observations. Dr. Challener understood that if the routine is followed closely, there might still be justice in the end.

And while everything about this autopsy was routine, that does not mean it was without artistry. Dr. Challener was a conductor stepping onto a stage. He was a poker player sitting down at his first table of the night. He was the carpenter, measuring twice.

"External examination," Dr. Challener reported. "The body is that of a well-developed, well-nourished white female appearing somewhat older than her stated age of sixteen years, measuring sixty-seven inches in height and weighing one hundred thirty-two pounds. Rigor mortis is fully developed in all areas."

Dr. Challener examined the girl's eyes, her pierced ears, her teeth. A friendship bracelet was still tied around the girl's wrist.

"The injuries are numbered for purposes of identification only and not to imply the sequence in which they were sustained. Both those produced by blunt force and an edged pointed instrument are observed."

The coroner found a large bruise on the girl's neck, near her jawline. He noted scrape marks along the left side of the girl's chest and down her back. There was a two-inch stab wound on the girl's scalp, coming from above and downward, and another stab wound on the left side of her neck that went three quarters of an inch deep. There were four more stab wounds on her upper back, as if she'd been stabbed from behind and the weapon had cut upward. More stab wounds to her left breast. The weapon had cut deep there, sinking into her lung and perforating her carotid artery. She died fast, probably before she knew it was possible. In total, Dr. Challener counted twenty-two stab wounds.

Dr. Challener then opened up Lisa's body and removed her vital organs so that he could weigh them, one by one. The organs were catalogued, transposed from the organic into stark numbers on a page. Lisa's heart weighed 220 grams. Lisa's liver, 1,138 grams. Lisa's brain, 1,481 grams.

Her body showed no signs of rape and no sperm was found.

"Upon full inquiry based on all the known facts, I find that the said Lisa Lee Pruett, came to her death officially on the 14th day of September, 1990, on ground, rear yard of 16401 South Woodland Road, and was officially pronounced dead at 5:16 A.M. Death in this case was the end result of injuries sustained when stabbed by person or persons unknown and was homicidal in nature."

DR. CHALLENER DID his best to document Lisa's body, an exit interview of the corporeal. But he could not document her spirit. Let us know something about Lisa's soul.

Lisa Pruett was a poet. A writer. In fact, a girl who never took much of a break from writing.

Lisa submitted a poem for the spring 1990 edition of the Shaker Heights High School literary magazine, *Semanteme.* That edition was dedicated to a seventeen-year-old student, Brian Hutton, who had perished in a car crash. A semanteme, by the way, is the smallest unit of meaning within a language, the pixel of linguistics, if you will. A semanteme is any word that conjures an image all by itself. Boy. Girl. Kiss. Haunt.

This is what Lisa wrote in her poem "Crystal Dreams."

Flitting, floating, falling on the ground,
I freeze on children's eyelashes, and blur
Their altered vision of the world.
They see a different earth than I,
Of candy and playgrounds and eternal smiles.
I see the truth
Cold bare trees, stripped of life and
Hard ground...

When Dan was committed to the hospital, Lisa sent him a cassette tape titled "The Long, Boring Side" and "The Shorter but Still Boring Side." On the tape was a recording of Lisa's voice, reading from her "happy book," a collection of news articles she'd gathered into a binder, random stories that made her laugh. Later in the tape she sang along to "True Colors" by Cyndi Lauper. She started crying toward the end.

Lisa played field hockey. She was a member of the student group on race relations. She listened to Cat Stevens and James Taylor.

Sometimes Lisa sent Dan secret, coded messages by marking letters in a copy of *Adam's Daughter* by Gertrude Samuels, which they passed to each other in school under teachers' watchful eyes.

Chapter Six

THE OLD MAN

BY THE TIME THE STENOGRAPHER arrived at the station, it was 10 A.M. and Robert Dreifort had been sitting in a small room with Detective Richard Mullaney for quite some time. Bob was the administrator for the Department of Pediatrics at the Cleveland Clinic, so he was used to a certain amount of bureaucracy. He was used to waiting.

When the stenographer was finally set up, Bob gave his statement, which began as a summary of events from the day before. He'd had dinner with his wife, Jean, at home. His son, Dan, had helped him load logs into the back of his van. Then he'd driven to the pet store for dog food. When he returned home, Dan was outside with Tex Workman. Tex was dating Debbie, Bob's daughter, and was friends with Dan. Debbie was going to school at Ohio University in Athens, Ohio, about three hours away.

At midnight Debbie called home, looking for Tex, but he'd already left. Bob spoke to his daughter on the phone in the master bedroom. Then Dan spoke to Debbie, alone, and hung up around 12:15 A.M. After the call Dan went to his room, which was on the other side of a Jack-and-Jill bathroom from the master. Bob read a book. Jean turned over and fell asleep.

"At approximately twelve-thirty A.M.," said Bob, "I heard a shrill and lengthy scream coming from an area in front of the house." The screams were so loud, he said, that he could hear them through the closed window.

"I immediately called out to Daniel, who was in his bedroom. I said, 'Dan, did you hear that?' To which he responded, yes. I then hear him move to his window facing Lee Road and heard that window being opened. I myself immediately turned off the table lamp and lifted a panel on the venetian blind and looked out to Lee Road. I saw nothing unusual. While I was looking out the window, Dan came into my bedroom. My first inclination was to run outside and see what happened. Realizing I was stark naked, I looked at Dan. Seeing that he had on essentially the same clothes that he had been wearing, I noted and even questioned him about whether he had anything on his feet. I then noticed he was wearing a pair of brown moccasins. This was important to me because I knew that he could get out quicker than me."

Bob continued, "By the time I was on the first floor, Dan had opened the front door, which we keep locked and bolted, and was proceeding down the steps and across the lawn. I myself only went as far as our front steps. Dan told me that he saw nothing unusual."

Bob said that after Dan came back to the house, he locked up again and they talked about calling the police. He decided it wasn't necessary and everyone went back to their bedrooms. Bob said he fell asleep after reading another page of the book he was working on. A short time later, Dan woke him up again.

"He was telling me something about Lisa and a bicycle and the police," said Bob. "I still had on the clothes that I had put on to go and investigate the scream, so I immediately went downstairs with Dan to see what was happening." When Bob got outside, he found two police cruisers parked at the curb. That's when his son told him that Lisa had planned to sneak out of her house and come see him and he now thought the scream they'd heard could have been Lisa.

A short time later, Bob saw two people standing on his tree lawn. It took him a moment to recognize Lisa's parents. He went outside to talk to them. Gary Pruett said he thought there was a dead girl in the bushes.

"To your knowledge, how long has your son known Lisa Pruett?" asked Detective Mullaney.

"They have been classmates for at least a year," said Bob. "I am only recently aware of her becoming a special friend among the many friends that Dan has, and I have heard him refer to her as his girlfriend a few times over the past six months. She's been a guest in our home on a couple of occasions."

"Was there any friction between yourself and your son over his relationship with Lisa?"

"Absolutely not," said Bob. "Unfortunately, I never got to know Lisa very well, but she seemed like a nice girl."

"Were you aware that Lisa Pruett was to visit your son between twelve-thirty and one A.M.?"

"No," he said.

"While you were going outside, did you feel any apprehension about him going out there alone?"

"Any apprehension I may have had was lessened by the fact that I myself was hot on his heels."

IN CLEVELAND, IN 1990, there was only one major daily newspaper—the *Plain Dealer*—and just about everybody had a subscription. In 1990, reporters were still respected, and the reporters of the *Plain Dealer* always got the goods.

When the sun came up, the phones at the Pruetts' began ringing, but the Pruetts did not answer. A man named Isaac Schulz did. He was the school board president, and father of one of Lisa's closest friends. He had assumed the role of gatekeeper for the family, holding the press at bay, refusing to even relay questions to the grieving parents. The intrepid journos, brave enough to drive out to the residence, were turned away by a policeman. A cruiser remained stationed out front for ten days. Crime beat reporters were bewildered by this cold shoulder. If the murder had occurred just a half mile closer to the city, in that ruined wasteland between East 55th and 93rd, there would be no spokesman to answer the phone, no cruiser parked on the curb.

And there was something else that made crime in Shaker Heights personal for *Plain Dealer* reporters. They had lost one of their own to shocking violence there, not long ago. A beloved editor, Philip Porter, and his wife, Dorothy, had been stabbed to death in their Shaker Heights home in 1985. They had lived just eight houses north of the Dreiforts. That case was still unsolved and it was unclear what, if anything, the detectives were actually doing to find their killer.

Some wondered if the Shaker Heights Police Department was adequately equipped to investigate one high-profile homicide. Let alone three.

Chapter Seven

THEY CALL HIM "TEX"

THE NEXT PERSON THE POLICE interviewed was Ken Workman, better known as "Tex." The cops knew Tex well. He was a burnout, a troublemaker; he liked to get into fights. More importantly, Tex was not from Shaker Heights. He'd moved into town recently, a bit of the city grit blown in from the west. And now this kid was one of the last people to see Lisa Pruett alive.

"I know Lisa through Dan," Tex explained. "I met Dan at school and I met Deb at Arabica coffee shop. Deb is my girlfriend."

The detective asked Tex to walk him through his memory of the day of the murder. "I was sittin' at Arabica most of the day," said Tex. "And Ken Mitsumoto told me that Dan was out of the psych ward. I went home and called Dan and asked him if I'd be allowed over.

"I took the Rapid and I forget what time I got to Dan's house. It was somewhere around, like, nine P.M. Then we just went outside and started talkin' and he played his guitar a little bit. Between nine and ten P.M., Lisa came over to talk to Dan. She stayed ten or fifteen minutes. Dan and Lisa went around the corner of his house. I don't know what they were talking about. Dan told me that she was supposed to sneak out and come over about twelve or twelve-thirty

A.M., and then some other kid was supposed to come over. I think his name is Chris Jones."

The detective jotted down the name. Dan hadn't said anything about a friend named Chris Jones.

"After Dan told me that, I didn't really want to be around, 'cause I don't know Chris Jones, and when Dan and his girlfriend get together, they, like, kiss all the time and I don't like watching that. At ten P.M., I took Dan's bike over to the gas station and bought him a pack of cigarettes, and I was sittin' in Arabica for, like, forty-five minutes talking to Kevin Young."

The cops knew Kevin Young, too. He was an odd young man with a history of antisocial behavior. He'd called 911 not long ago after a suicide attempt; he'd taken some pills, got scared, chickened out. Not an uncommon event.

"I left Arabica, like a quarter to eleven P.M., and I rode back to Dan's house on his bike, and I gave him his bike back and his cigarettes and told him I was just gonna go home. So it was like eleven-fifteen or something and I went to the Rapid stop at the corner of Lee and Shaker Boulevard and stood there for a whole forty-five minutes waiting for that damn Rapid to show up." Shaker Boulevard was one block north of Lee and South Woodland.

"How did you first learn about Lisa Pruett's death?" the detective asked.

Tex said that when he got to school that day, he went to see Mr. Vlah, the assistant principal, to pick up a work permit. He was going to drop out and get a job. "The secretary said Mr. Vlah wasn't going to be in for a while, so I went over to Dan's house and I seen all these cops and stuff and these two officers, and I walked over and they told me that Dan wasn't home. I asked them what happened and they said to watch the news, and so I ran back to school, and I went to Mr. Annandale's office, and he told me that a girl had been killed over there by Dan's house. I asked some girl in the hallway and she said it was Lisa Pruett. Then I just went to Kevin's house and told him."

"Have you ever known Dan Dreifort to take any kind of medication?" the detective asked.

"He was doin' Robitussin a lot," said Tex.

"Why was he taking that?"

"To get some kind of high off of it."

"Did you ever know Dan Dreifort to take any other kind of drugs or to abuse alcohol?"

"He drank and he did pot, and when he came back on leave from the psych ward, he tried to commit suicide with nine antihistamines."

"He did this when he was at the Clinic?" the detective asked.

"He did this at home, when he was on a pass," said Tex. "The only people that know about that is me and his sister. She called the Poison Control, and they said, like, he would fall asleep, and we went back to his house and he was up running around, so it didn't seem like anything was wrong with him."

"Did Dan tell you why he tried to commit suicide?"

"No."

"Did Dan ever tell you about his relationship with his father?"

"Yes. He hated his father."

Chapter Eight

THE ECHO OF A SCREAM

JEAN DREIFORT WORKED AS A medical librarian at Brentwood Hospital. She was a short woman, with curly hair and a round face. If you saw her on the street, you'd smile at her because you couldn't help it. She had this friendly look. She looked like a mom. Like a suburban mom from central casting.

"I was at work until almost five P.M., so when I got home, Dan was not there," Jean told the detective. "I didn't see him until he came home, I'd say about five-thirty P.M. We were in the process of unloading the car, Dan and Tex helping us carry the bags in, when Lisa walked in the door. It was about nine P.M. I spoke to her and asked if her father wanted to come in, and she said he was listening to something on the radio and would be happy to stay out in the driveway. She could only stay for five minutes.

"A few minutes later, I looked out the door and heard that they were still there, and again said something to them, because I did not like it that Lisa's father was sitting there all that time." That's when Lisa left with her dad.

"Before we left to go shopping," said Jean, "Daniel asked if it was all right if he cut his hair. He wanted to spread some papers out in front of the hall mirror, and we said sure, and he also found the clipper set we have and was using those, as best he could."

The rest of the evening was uneventful, she said.

"Somewhere in there my husband went to bed. And Daniel and I talked for a long while about the hospital experience and who he had seen up at the high school that afternoon. At about midnight the phone rang, and we don't believe in answering the phone that late, but we heard on the answering machine that it was my daughter, so we answered it.

"Bob stayed on the bedroom phone and I went into the adjoining office and talked on that phone. We spoke for about ten or fifteen minutes, and Dan came in and took the extension in the office and I went back in the bedroom and closed the door.

"I can't remember if I read, but I usually do. I turned off the light and started to go to sleep. I heard my husband shout, something like, 'What was that?' And I could hear in my mind, the echo of a long scream. I put it that way because I was mostly asleep, but I heard a long scream.

"Through all the rest of this, I remained in bed with my eyes closed," she said. "I heard a vehicle pull away, out in front of our house. It was like two sounds, like changing gears, with a pause. I was very aware of it because we had just heard the scream. It's the kind of thing I listen for when I hear something out of the ordinary. I heard no other traffic. The next thing I remember is Bob coming back in the room, and I think he asked me if I should call the police, and I said something like, 'We're always calling them, let somebody else call them.'"

Jean fell asleep again for a bit. "The next thing I know, Dan is waking us up, and I had a real hard time waking up, so that I only heard little pieces like, 'The police are here,' 'Lisa's bicycle,' and I'm lying in bed with my eyes closed, didn't want to wake up. Bob went downstairs. Somewhere in there I realized that all this wasn't going to go away, so I got up and threw on some clothes and went downstairs.

"The rest is really muddled. From this point on I just remember snatches, like snapshots. Sometimes we were downstairs, sometimes we were upstairs. Dan at that point had already gone to his room and closed the door. Then I saw Mrs. Hall in her nightgown in front of her house, and she called on the telephone. She asked what was happening, who had been killed, and I said to her, 'What do you mean "killed"? Did the police tell you that?' and she said something like, 'No, but there is a body,' or 'they found a body,' or something like that. I know she's the neighborhood gossip and so she might have been leaping to conclusions. I told her we didn't know anything.

"I told her that a girlfriend was going to visit Dan. And I told her to please not say anything to anybody. I told her that much because she had gone on at great length about hearing someone breaking branches, and her dog barking and she seemed quite upset. She had heard the scream also."

"Do you recall what type of shoes your son was wearing?" the detective asked.

"Tennis shoes," said Jean. "I can't pin it down any closer than that, except that I know they weren't the holey ones."

"Could you describe Kim Rathbone, the girl who cut your son's hair? Where does she live and what is her relationship with Dan and your family?"

"The Rathbone property adjoins ours at the rear line," Jean explained. "She is a classmate of Dan's and is also in the band. They have had many fence talks. Last year she was his wake-up service. She called every morning at seven so that he would have to come to the phone and would help wake him up. She is going with one of Dan's very good friends, Brian Keating."

"To your knowledge, does or did Kim Rathbone ever have any type of romantic relationship with your son?"

"Definitely not, they're just friends."

AT THE CHURCH of Christ, over on Taylor Road, the good Christian children were writing letters to the departed. Lisa was an important member of their youth group, the one who pulled everyone else together. When a new kid joined, the counselors could count on Lisa to make them feel welcome. She'd participated in Bible study there and had gone with the group on trips to Cedar Point Amusement Park and South Bass Island. The church elders knew that Lisa was destined for some big college, for some bigger life away from Shaker Heights.

After her murder the youth group leaders asked the children to write letters to Lisa as a way of dealing with their grief. It was a way for them to tell Lisa the things they'd say to her directly if they had one more chance:

Dear Lisa, I love you. I enjoyed the time we spent together. I will comfort your parents. I will always keep you in my mind.

Dear Lisa, The Lord wanted you in his presence and that says a lot. Oh goodness, what pain!

Dear Lisa, As I write this, all I can really think about is the campout last year. I learned that you were warm and sensitive. I don't think of you as dead, but alive in God's kingdom.

Dear Lisa, Thank you for being my friend. You have comforted me in times of trouble.

Bright, warm, cheery and always loving Lisa, I love you. I pray that you did not suffer.

ON SATURDAY, THE sun came up over Elsmere Road and women in long dresses set up buffet tables for the annual block party. Kids tossed a football on a lawn nearby. Preparations were made for a six-year-old's birthday party over on Daleford. And as everyone went about their day, it all appeared quite normal on the surface, another day in suburbia. But if you listened closely, you could hear the adults speaking in low voices about murder.

The front page of the *Plain Dealer* that day read: KILLER CUTS DOWN SHAKER GIRL, 16. It was the kind of article filled with all the private details of a family in the midst of an incalculable loss. "Tragedy struck Lisa's family, before," the reporter wrote. "The couple's first child, Brian, died at 1½ of a heart defect."

Chapter Nine

HAVE YOU TALKED TO KEVIN?

AT A QUARTER TO FIVE that Saturday, a handsome young man named Johnathan George arrived at the Shaker Heights police station. He was one of Lisa's friends and knew Dan from band. Word was, the police were looking for suspects and he was anxious to tell them what he knew about Kevin Young.

"Dan and Lisa have been going out for a couple months now," John told the detective. "But Kevin supposedly has liked Lisa for a long time. One day we were at Arabica, me and Shane McGee. We were standing by Shane's car, talking with Kevin, and we were talking about Dan, and Kevin said something like, 'I'd hate to be Dan because he doesn't get any play,' and me and Shane both laughed."

The detective waited for the boy to continue. What the hell did that have to do with anything?

"Kevin was like, 'Why are you guys laughing?' and we were both, like, because Dan gets a lot of play from girls. And Kevin said, 'Well, he's not getting any from Lisa.' And I said, 'Yes, he is. He's sleeping with her.' And then Kevin just freaked. He was like, 'That asshole! I hate him. I'm going to kill him. I want her dead.'" That got the detective's attention.

"Could you describe Kevin Young physically and where he lives?" he asked.

"He's about six feet tall," said John. "About one hundred sixty pounds. Listens to heavy metal, Metallica, Anthrax. He basically doesn't like the world. Doesn't like Blacks, Jews, Polish people..." Johnathan was an African American. "In ninth grade," he said, "Kevin was infatuated with a girl named Marisa. She was going out with a friend of mine and we were in Canada on a school trip and Kevin was threatening that he would commit suicide unless Marisa broke up with my friend and went out with him. The band director took Kevin's sleeping pills away," said John. "Kevin's a heavy drinker. He drinks by himself. He likes to get drunk and wander off. He lives across the street from the high school in a white house with a swimming pool."

"Do you think that Kevin would be capable of killing someone?"

"Yes," said John.

"Why?"

"Just basically because of how he talks. And he can become very aggressive."

"Is there anyone else you think could be capable of killing Lisa Pruett?"

"Yes," said John. "Dan's father."

"Why Dan's father?" the detective asked.

"Dan and Dan's father don't get along at all. Dan's father is known as a very crazy man. This is also from his sister, Debbie, and most of her friends."

"Why would you think Dan's father would be capable of killing Lisa?"

"As soon as I heard she was dead, I was thinking of who would have done it and I thought Dan wouldn't have done it, but Dan's father would have, but I ruled that out last night when I found out that Dan's father sent him outside to find out who was screaming."

JOHNATHAN'S BUDDY SHANE McGee sat for the detective next. Shane did not live in Shaker Heights. He was from Bay Village, a Waspy neighborhood on the west side of Cleveland, half an hour away. Shane relayed for the detective the same story that Johnathan had just told, about how Kevin became upset after finding out that Dan and Lisa were having sex. "Kevin seemed more set on killing Dan than Lisa," said Shane. "I told Kevin that Dan had a gun so that he would leave Dan alone, and it seemed to scare him. Dan did not have a gun."

"Has Kevin Young ever become violent with you?" the detective asked.

"Last year Kevin was becoming extremely mad that I was going out with a girl who would have nothing to do with him. He didn't like the idea of other people having girlfriends. He came by a party I was at and made threats of violence, which almost came to a fight, but I backed down. Later he played it off as if nothing had happened."

"Do you think that Kevin Young would become violent enough to be able to commit murder?"

"Yes."

"Is there anything else you wish to add to this statement?"

"The people that know Kevin think of him as a walking time bomb."

SEVENTEEN-YEAR-OLD Becca Boatright came in to the station that day, too. Becca was a senior at Shaker High, with straight, shoulder-length hair and bangs in that early-nineties style made popular by DJ on *Full House.* Becca knew Kevin well. She'd been his date for prom, before he canceled on her (or before she canceled on him, depending on whom you believed).

The detective asked Becca what she remembered about the day of the murder.

"Dan called me at about eight-twenty P.M.," she said. "He asked if I wanted to come over and told me a bunch of people were coming over, and I said, 'Like who?' and he said Chris Jones, Lisa Pruett, and maybe Dan Messinger." That was another new name for the detective. Just how many people were planning to go to Dan's the night of the murder? "I told him I didn't think I could get out. I was tired and wanted to go to bed.

"The next day, during first period, our principal, Dr. Rumbaugh, said that Lisa had been involved in a homicide, and since nobody really knew how it had happened, the basic rumor was that she had been hit on the head with a blunt object and her body had been found on the sidewalk at the corner of South Woodland and Lee.

"Later, I went up to Arabica, and since Kevin was the only one I knew up there, I sat down and talked to him. Basically, he said, 'Has your day been as bad as everybody else's?' and I said, 'Well, it was pretty depressing.' I said, it doesn't seem like the type of thing that would happen in Shaker, and I was really worried for Dan, since no doubt he is probably a suspect. Somehow or other we got onto the topic of rape. I said, 'Well, if she was raped, isn't there a possibility that they will find a semen sample on her body?' and Kevin said, 'I don't think she was raped.'"

This detail surely interested the detective; they had not released to the press the fact that Lisa had not been raped. Most people still assumed she had been. It was information only the killer should know.

"Then I told him that I had heard she had been pulled from her bike and that she had been hit on the head with a blunt object. He said, 'No, I think she was stabbed.' I said, 'Well, that's not what I heard.' He said, 'I'm pretty sure she was stabbed.' Then I went to get a pink lemonade, and when I came back, I said, 'Some extremely psychotic person had to have done this.' He said, 'What makes you think that?' and I said, 'Well, it's not the type of thing a perfectly sane person does.' Then he sort of, like, sat up and said really loudly, 'Well, I would only kill in self-defense.'"

Chapter Ten

THE NIGHT SEASON

AT 8 O'CLOCK THAT EVENING, two police officers arrived at Kevin Young's house. His mother, Maryanne Young, answered the door. One of the men introduced himself as Detective Mullaney. He asked if he could speak with Kevin.

"Why?" she asked.

"It's routine," said Mullaney. "We're talking to all the kids who knew Dan and Lisa."

Maryanne told Mullaney that Kevin was out, and she didn't know where he was, but that he was supposed to call home to check in at 11 P.M. "It will be late," she said, "but do you still want to see him?"

"Yes, please."

"Is everything okay?"

"It's just routine," the detective assured her.

Kevin called at 11 P.M., like clockwork. He told his mom he was hanging out at Arabica. She drove to the coffee shop and picked him up and took him to the station.

"Do you think this is unusual?" she asked Kevin.

Kevin told her not to worry. "All the kids are talking to them," he said.

Mullaney met them in the parking lot.

"Should I come in?" asked Maryanne.

"There's no need for that," said Mullaney.

"Should I wait?"

"You don't need to. It'll be about an hour."

Since they were interviewing all of Dan's friends, Maryanne could think of no reason not to trust the detective. She returned home and went to bed. Her husband, Tal, would pick Kevin up when he was done. Maryanne needed a good night's rest; she planned to drive Kevin to Columbus in the morning. He was starting college on Monday. His bags were already packed, waiting by the door.

Mullaney led Kevin into the station.

Kevin was a strikingly handsome young man. Young-Republicans haircut. Broad shoulders. Chiseled chin. He could have played Clark Kent in a high-school production of *Superman.* But he was also a messy kid. He left a trail of candy bar wrappers and old homework in his wake. His shirts were always untucked. And he'd been in some trouble over the years: He'd once planted a tree in the middle of the high-school football field as a prank, for example. And he'd called in a bomb threat one day so he could stay home and play with his friends.

Kevin sat with Mullaney, and the boy explained how he'd gotten to know Dan and Lisa. Earlier that year Kevin had, indeed, asked Becca Boatright to go to prom. But that didn't work out and he needed a date at the last minute, so Dan Dreifort had introduced him to a girl named Ellen Donald, a freshman. Kevin gave Ellen a ride home after school one day and asked her if she'd go with him. At first, Ellen's parents balked at the idea—Kevin was much older. But after some convincing they relented. He could take her, as long as he had her home by 11:30 P.M.

On prom night Kevin picked Ellen up at her house and then the two of them went to the Dreiforts and picked up Dan and Lisa. The four of them had dinner at the Samurai restaurant in Beachwood.

Afterward, Kevin and Ellen continued to the prom, which was held that year at the Crawford Auto-Aviation Museum.

They had a decent night. And, as promised, Kevin got her home by 11:30 P.M.

When the small talk was over, Detective Mullaney advised Kevin of his constitutional rights—"You have the right to remain silent," etc.—and then asked him to explain his whereabouts on the night of the murder.

"I remember hanging out at Arabica until about four P.M.," Kevin said. "It might have been later than that. I went back to Shaker Square, around seven or eight o'clock, and waited until Tex got off work. Tex mentioned a potential 'Robitussin party' at the Dreiforts' house."

The police were quickly learning that Robitussin was a cheap and available drug for the kids in town. The popular cough syrup could be purchased over the counter at the drugstore, no questions asked. Robitussin contained dextromethorphan, a powerful hallucinogen when taken in large doses.

"At a quarter to eleven, we headed our separate ways," said Kevin. "I went home. I got there a few minutes after eleven P.M. I tried to go to bed at around quarter to midnight and did not sleep well that night.

"Now we're at Friday, eight-thirty in the morning. My mom woke me up and told me that Tex was at the door, wanting to talk to me. Tex told me that Lisa had been murdered and raped that night. He also mentioned stab wounds. I met up with Tex again before noon at Arabica. Tex got hysterical. He was worried about people thinking that he did it, because he had left his knife at Dan's house.

"He was accusing Dan of Lisa's murder," said Kevin. "He was threatening to kill Dan if he found out that Dan killed Lisa. He asked me to tell the police that I was with him Thursday night. I told him I would tell the police we left Shaker Square at a quarter to eleven, as happened. He told me he was worried because he had no alibi. He said he left Dan's at eleven-fifteen that evening. He told me the bus ran an hour late that night and he didn't catch one until twelve-fifteen. Tex was a wreck. He was smoking like a fiend, very scared, and, like I said, accusing Dan.

"I'm really worried that Tex did this," said Kevin. "I hope it's not true. But if he did this for me, because of a crush I had on Lisa, back around the time of the Germany trip, this will be on my conscience forever."

"So that I understand you correctly," said Mullaney, "Tex advised you to make sure you told the police that you were with him until ten forty-five the previous evening, is that correct?"

"That's true."

"Did anybody see you when you arrived home?"

"My mother and father saw me," said Kevin. "They were watching the news in our living room."

"Did you ever threaten to harm or to kill Lisa or Dan?"

"I threatened nothing to Lisa," said Kevin. "I may have threatened Dan back in July, before he went into the hospital. But if I threatened to kill him, I certainly wasn't serious about it. If I said that, I meant only that I'd give him a few good licks, which I didn't even plan on doing. I felt it was better to just leave him alone."

"Were you jealous of Dan for having Lisa as his girlfriend?"

"For a few weeks I was, although it was not an overriding issue. I was interested in several other girls."

"Did you ever have sexual intercourse with Lisa Pruett?"

"I did not."

"To your knowledge, do you know anyone who did?"

"Dan told me that he did. I'm pretty sure that Dan was her first. That's the way he described it to me."

"Is there anything you wish to add to your statement?"

"I feel like crap and I really need some sleep."

That ended the formal interview. Off the record now, Mullaney's countenance changed. "Do you know you're eighteen years old?" he said.

"Yeah," said Kevin. "So?"

"Do you realize the penalty for murder in Ohio is death?"

"Oh yeah? Good.'"

"What if I told you that someone is placing you at the scene of the crime?" said Mullaney.

"Well, if you told me that, I'd tell you they were full of shit."

Mullaney got up and walked out of the room. A few minutes passed. Then another cop poked his head in. "Hey, Kevin," he said, "don't worry. If you didn't do anything, you have nothing to worry about."

After a couple minutes Mullaney came back. He took Kevin's hand and held it in his own. "Kevin," said Mullaney, "I've been a cop for twenty years and I've seen a lot of shit."

It felt like an apology to Kevin. Or the closest Mullaney could muster. Then Mullaney told Kevin that the whole time he was being interviewed, another detective had been searching through Kevin's bedroom for the murder weapon. But they didn't find it.

THE SOUND OF car doors woke Maryanne from her slumber at 3 A.M. She went downstairs to find her husband just returning with Kevin. And Tal had more bad news for her: The police had executed a search warrant and had searched their house while she was sleeping. And now Kevin might be in some kind of trouble.

Here's what the warrant said:

> Kevin Young, son of J. Talbot Young, Jr., does reside at ***** Onaway Road, Shaker Heights, Ohio. That Kevin Young knew Lisa Pruett, and her boyfriend, Daniel Dreifort; That in June 1990, at Arabica Coffee House at Shaker Square, Cleveland, Ohio, Kevin Young stated in the presence of several Shaker Heights High School students that he desired to kill Lisa Pruett and Daniel Dreifort; That Kevin Young was seen at Arabica Coffee

> House, Cleveland, Ohio, on the evening of 09/13/90, and learned from Kenny James Workman that Daniel Dreifort was home from medical treatment; That at that time and in the presence of witnesses, Kevin Young became emotionally distraught, crying uncontrollably, and appeared angry intermittently; That Kevin Young was observed walking in the Shaker Heights area toward South Woodland Road at approximately 11 p.m., that evening; That on 09/14/90, Kevin Young argued with friends about the homicide indicating facts known at this time only to investigative authorities including preliminary findings from the Cuyahoga County Coroner's Office that the victim was not raped; And further that Kevin Young, through reliable information, was found to be an unstable individual, inordinately jealous of male/female relationships and is known to carry a switchblade or lock knife; That it is necessary to conduct this search in the night season because this request is made at 11:45 p.m., on 09/15/90; That Kevin Young is known to be leaving for Ohio State University on 09/16/90 and that the evidence sought is subject to destruction if not retrieved at once.

Though the police did not find the murder weapon in Kevin's bedroom, they did find a diary and some old homework. Kevin had scribbled some things in the margins of his assignments that alarmed them.

For instance, Kevin liked to draw swastikas. And he doodled upside-down crosses and left himself little messages, such as *Can we use Satan to our advantage? Man says, Hell yes.*

On another assignment, Kevin wrote, *Do you want Britannia to rule the Western Hemisphere? To put our colored cousins in their place?*

Do you want the SS to prove the theory of uncle Adolf's Teutonic master race? Later, they would learn that these questions were inspired by lyrics from a Pink Floyd song, but in the moment they seemed very incriminating.

Police flagged some more of Kevin's writing as "occult," but later learned those passages were backstories that Kevin used for creating a Dungeons & Dragons campaign. They confiscated a flyer for a band called The Circle Jerks, who were on a double bill with The Weirdos at the Phantasy.

They also found information about a nonprofit that Kevin was planning to create, The Adam Smith Foundation, named for the English free-market economist.

Here are the bylaws of the Adam Smith Foundation:

End all unnecessary government intervention in economic affairs and private business.

End censorship of materials deemed "harmful" or "sinful."

Force the military to act like a real business and abolish mandatory service.

Repeal moronic drug laws; use drug money to educate, repair roads, etc.

Kevin was a radical. No doubt. But was he also a murderer?

On a crumpled piece of paper, police discovered this little ditty: *The real enemy is the mutant and the Jews, dad, not your own son.*

And there was this typed letter to the high-school newspaper:

> Dear Shakerite,
>
> I am very tired of all the attention paid to problems of a racial nature. Aside from the fact that the Blacks have invaded the school, both sides choose voluntarily to segregate themselves. Attempts by the administration to cancel segregated clubs, dances, and other events are only a lame attempt on their part to uphold this community's image.

> I am tired of the special treatment Blacks want in college admissions and other related areas and the whites who offer it make me even more sick. Somewhere, somehow, this madness has got to stop. American Blacks have already made this nation a far worse place for all of us. Slavery really was a horrible idea.
>
> Sincerely,
> *Kevin Young*

Beneath this, written in Kevin's messy script, is a warning: *I will kill all the undesirables! I must!!!*

Police also confiscated a petition that Kevin had passed around school after getting mad at a girl:

> Dear Mr. Stokes,
>
> I am a student at Shaker. We have long sought a law that would make Debbie Rosner shut up. Her voice gnaws at our minds and we need action taken immediately.

Only one other student had signed it.

And then there was his diary, which Kevin referred to as "Ron Lafter," and he often began new entries with "Dear Ron."

> 8/5/89 (vacation)
>
> First day at Stone Harbor. I really feel pissed. I got here and now I want to leave. It really pisses me off when I see all these couples paired up. I just want to take over the world. Make the Blacks and Jews and the Slavs and Latins and the yellows and the Semites subordinate to us. I'd also ship all the defense cutters up the river. I am worth absolutely nothing. I'm sick of these Jew-bastards and Arab slime that's on the news right now.

> 8/8/89
>
> I hate God. He kills members of my family while letting these Jews live. He should send another Hitler to kill them. My grandmother is very sad because Jack is dead.

They also found what they believed to be a suicidal note that Kevin had written before another failed attempt to kill himself.

Chapter Eleven

THE DARK HALLWAY

On Sunday, Dan Dreifort returned to the police station for follow-up questions. The boy began his interview by amending his initial statement. He had left out some important details. Like the fact that on the night of Lisa's murder, he'd planned a little party to celebrate his release from the psychiatric ward.

"I'll start off with various phone calls," said Dan. "Becca Boatright called at around eight-thirty P.M. I invited her over and she told me she was tired and was going to go to sleep. I also spoke to Chris Jones and invited him over, and he called back and told me he was tired and sleeping."

The detective asked about Tex, whom Dan had sent to Shaker Square to pick up a pack of cigarettes. On his errand Tex had bumped into Kevin Young, but then Tex's story became murky. He claimed to have waited for a bus for forty-five minutes at the north end of Dan's block.

"Did you see Tex leave your residence after he gave you the cigarettes? And if so, which direction did he go?"

"I saw him exit via the driveway."

"To your knowledge, what is the relationship between Tex and Kevin Young, such as, are they close friends or not?"

"They are not close friends."

FOLLOWING DAN'S INTERVIEW, police brought Tex Workman in again. Tex was the conduit by which Kevin had found out about Dan and Lisa's late-night rendezvous, and was becoming an important subject in the developing case.

"Have you stayed at the Dreiforts' house before, when Debbie was not home?" the detective asked.

"Not when Deb wasn't home," Tex replied.

"How many nights have you stayed at the Dreiforts' house when Deb was home?"

"A lot," said Tex. "The last month before she went to college, I stayed there almost every night."

"Were Debbie's parents aware that you were staying there?"

"No."

"Have you ever attended a Robitussin party at Dan's?"

"Yes."

"What was, in your opinion, the result of the people who drank Robitussin at this party? That is, what was the effect of the Robitussin on them, and how did it affect their actions?"

"They just went crazy," said Tex. "Dan told me that it makes him feel strong and said something about some kind of trance they go into. When they get into this trance, whoever they see at the end of this hallway, they do whatever they can to get them out of the hallway. They kill if they have to. That's what he said."

"Would you explain what 'this hallway' means?"

"Dan said that everybody's got a hallway," Tex explained. "And when you take Robitussin, it brings you back to your hallway. And it's like if you take it, you see a hallway. It's like a mild form of acid."

"Have you ever done Robitussin?"

"Yes," he said. "I fell asleep."

"Have you ever seen Dan under the influence of Robitussin?"

"The only time I seen him, he was just comin' down from it."

"How did he act?"

"He just sat there and stared. Like he was asleep, but he had his eyes open."

"When was this Robitussin party, and who all was there?"

"It was after I got out of rehab, and before he went into the psych ward. Becca Boatright, me, Dan, and Deb was there. Dan Messinger was there, too."

"On Thursday evening," the detective continued, "you stated you stopped in a vacant lot, a few doors down, is that correct?"

"Yes."

"Was that to urinate?"

"Yes."

"Approximately, how far into that lot did you go?"

"I put Dan's bike down where the entrance is and I walked a couple steps in."

"When you arrived home, who was there?"

"My mom and her fiancé."

"Did you have conversation with them?"

"I just told my mom I didn't want to stay at Dan's tonight."

"Approximately, what time did you call Debbie from your apartment?"

"Probably around twelve-thirty A.M."

"How long did you talk to Debbie?"

"About thirty minutes."

"On the morning of September 14, when you first learned of the death of Lisa Pruett, did somebody tell you how she was murdered?"

"Somebody told me she was hit with something."

"Did anyone tell you that she had been stabbed?"

"No."

"Did anyone tell you that she had been raped?"

"No. I heard that on the news."

"At that time, when you advised Kevin of the death of Lisa Pruett, did you tell him that she had been stabbed and raped?"

"No."

"You are absolutely sure of that?" the detective asked. Just the day before, Kevin had been adamant that Tex had told him Lisa was stabbed and raped. That meant somebody was telling stories.

"Yes," said Tex.

"Did you make a statement to Kevin that on the evening of September 13, Dan told Lisa Pruett that he wanted to cut her hair, and he wanted you to hold her down while he did it?"

"He was just playin' around when he said it."

"Did he make that statement?"

"Yes," said Tex.

"Since the murder of Lisa Pruett, have you threatened to kill anyone?"

"Yes."

"Who?"

"When I thought it was Dan, I was gonna do the same thing to them as whoever did that to Lisa."

"How would you describe your relationship with Kevin?"

"We're friends until he, like, starts goin' nuts."

"Would you consider him to be your best friend?"

"Sometimes."

Chapter Twelve

WE'RE BOTH CRAZY

At 4 p.m., on Monday, September 17, the Pruett family held a funeral service at the Euclid Avenue Congregational Church for their departed daughter because their home church didn't have the capacity to handle all of the bereaved. They asked that donations in Lisa's name be given to the Girl Scouts or the high-school band. The receiving line trailed through the aisle and out the door and down the sidewalk, and by the time they'd shaken everyone's hands, Gary and Lynette were very tired.

During the service a girl named Jenny Margulies held Dan's hand. The rest of Lisa's friends huddled together, close by. These were the elite students of Shaker Heights High School's junior class, a tight-knit group of smart, well-heeled white kids who referred to themselves as the "AP Posse," because they shared the same Advanced Placement classes that were meant to prepare them for universities like Harvard, Yale, Columbia.

At 8:29 p.m., that day, a young man named Stanley Kramer sat for his interview at the Shaker Heights Police Department. Stan worked at Arabica, which police now realized was an important nexus of information for this mystery, given that whoever killed

Lisa must have known she was sneaking out of her house that night and the coffee shop was where Tex told Kevin about it. It was possible others had overheard that detail, too. Stan was interviewed by both Detective Gray and Detective Mullaney.

"Stan," Mullaney began, "could you state the approximate time you went to work at Arabica the night of the murder?"

"Okay," said Stan, thinking. "Scoops closes about ten o'clock, and after we close, I usually do the mopping." Scoops was an ice-cream shop that shared space with Arabica in an old storefront on Shaker Square. "At about ten-fifteen P.M., I noticed Kevin Young was sitting at a table. It looked like he was crying. I continued mopping and I saw Tex come in and sit with Kevin. I clocked out and decided to join them. Kevin was upset because a friend of his was in Iraq. I don't know if he is living or dead, but Kevin was like hallucinating, wanting his friend to walk through the door so Kevin could give him a hug, say hello, how've you been, and so forth.

"My dad got to Arabica at about ten forty-five, which is when I said goodbye to Kevin and Tex. My dad asked me to go in and get him a Coke. Came back and Kevin and Tex were walking out the front door to go home. Tex was riding Dan Dreifort's bike. When me and my father pulled out, I saw Kevin walking up the street, alone, and it looked like he was heading home."

"When you were at Arabica with Tex and Kevin, did you hear any conversation about a possible party at Dan Dreifort's that night?" the detective asked.

"No, I did not."

"How well do you know Kevin Young?" asked Detective Gray.

"I know him pretty well. I used to play Little League baseball with him."

"What do you know about him?"

"From what I remember, he did quite well in school," said Stan. "He wasn't one of the types to slack off. He was really concerned with his life when he got out of school. Lately what I've been hearing is that Kevin is having somewhat of an alcohol problem."

"How well do you know Tex?"

"Ever since Tex came to Shaker Heights High School as a freshman, which was last year, I've known him quite well. We're both pretty much the same. We're crazy, we're both crazy."

"Crazy, how?"

"Well . . . I mean the usual things: drink, and every once in a while, just party, go down to Coventry, look for fights. We were crazy one evening and we became blood brothers, so I'd say Tex and I are darn close. This summer I was on vacation, so I didn't really see Tex that much. Him and Debbie Dreifort have a weird relationship. They've broken up three times and now they're engaged, which really confuses me.

"Tex and I were both caught smoking outside of the school," Stan continued. "And we were both suspended for three days, which my parents didn't know about, so hopefully they won't hear from this. After that, Tex dropped out of school. He got a full-time job. He started dressing nice. He was, like, really getting his life back in order."

"Do you have any knowledge about how Mr. Dreifort felt about Dan going out with Lisa?" asked Detective Mullaney.

"I'm really wondering about Mr. Dreifort," Stan admitted. "He supposedly had a crush on Lisa. I don't know how long it's been, but he supposedly really liked her. I mean it's a rumor. I didn't hear it from Dan, but he has had a crush on her and she has been going over to the Dreifort house to see if Dan was home yet from the hospital."

"Can you tell me who you heard this from, about Mr. Dreifort having a crush on Lisa?"

Stan gave the detective the name of a girl from his class.

"Is this a rumor that you heard prior to Lisa's death or after?"

"After," said Stan. "I heard it this afternoon on my way to the funeral."

Detective Gray asked one more question. "Is there anything else you can think of that you've heard, thought, saw, or otherwise, in the last few days, that might be of value or interest to us in trying to figure out what happened to Lisa?"

"Dan and Dan's father were supposedly out the evening Lisa's incident happened," said Stan. "They were both in the same room and they both heard a scream. I don't know if Dan's father and him were actually in the same room. Dan's father might have told Dan, 'Look, you're gonna be looked at as a suspect in this, because Lisa was heading over here. I'll say that me and you were in the same room, talking or whatever, and that's when we heard it.' Dan's father might have heard Dan talking on the phone to Lisa and met her outside before she actually got to the house. That's really off the top of my head. But I could picture Mr. Dreifort doing something like this."

Chapter Thirteen

DON'T KILL THE MESSINGER

DETECTIVE RICHARD MULLANEY PULLED UP to an apartment building just beyond the border of Shaker Heights. These were multifamily units, beehives for people, but still better than the city projects. This one was marble and brick, with embellishments that made it appear like a castle.

Mullaney went inside and knocked on the door to the apartment Tex Workman shared with his mother, Linda Meadwell. Linda answered and let him in. Debbie Dreifort was there with Tex. Mullaney explained that he needed Tex to come with him to the station to clarify his prior statement. Nobody had been ruled out as a suspect, he said. And that included Tex.

Before they left, Linda told the detective what she remembered about the night Lisa was murdered.

"Tex was planning to stay at Dan's, so I was surprised when he called at eleven-fifty to say he was coming home," said Linda. "He was calling from the Rapid stop at Shaker Boulevard and Lee. He gave me the number of the phone booth and asked me to find out when the next bus would be by and then to call him back."

Linda called the Rapid Transit Authority's service line and was told that the last bus had already left. Then she called the pay phone, but Tex didn't answer. She waited a bit. Around 12:15 A.M., she and her boyfriend were heading out the door to go look for Tex when he arrived. He told his mother that he'd caught the last bus.

AT THE STATION Mullaney pulled Debbie Dreifort into his office to speak privately before interviewing her boyfriend. He wanted to know how Tex's version of events stacked up against what she knew.

Debbie told the detective that she'd called Tex after she spoke to her parents, using a calling card from her room at Ohio University. She and Tex talked until one A.M. She said Tex had told her that Lisa and Chris Jones were going to meet up at her house and they were going to hang out in Deb's old room with Dan, and he just didn't feel like being a part of that.

"What do you know about the cough syrup?" Mullaney asked her.

"Dan went to this youth conference retreat over the summer and learned about it there," she said. "If you take four ounces of Robitussin, you can trip very hard. It's like LSD. I've done Robitussin twice and had very hard trips."

She told the detective that "Robo" parties, the nickname for Robitussin, were popular in Shaker Heights. "A lot of the kids are doing it. Dan did it a lot. That was part of the problems he had with our parents over the summer."

Finally Mullaney brought Tex into his office and they went over his statement one more time. But Tex's story didn't change.

DAN DREIFORT'S BEST friend was a boy named Daniel Messinger. They'd met in seventh grade, when they were introduced on the school bus. Since then, whenever they met new people, they would put an arm around the other and they'd both say, "I'm Dan," in stereo. The day of the murder, Daniel told police, he skipped German class to hang out with Dan and the two of them rode their bikes to Chris Jones's apartment. They ate Snickers bars while Dan read to them the letters that Lisa had sent to him in the hospital.

Then Chris left for fencing practice, and Daniel and Dan rode their bikes to another classmate's house, Leslie Ruch's place. This was another detail that Dan had left out of his timeline of events.

"At Leslie's house I was walking around a lot, just being nervous for some reason, and Dan sat and talked to Leslie," said Daniel. "Then I went home and Dan went home. This was around six P.M., I believe. I called my Voice Tell mailbox to see if I had any messages and Lisa had called me. It was five twenty-three that she called. She was very excited. She said how she had had a great day and that she wanted me to call her back. I was going to save the message, but for some reason I deleted it. Then I called Lisa back and she said she would be our chauffeur, Dan, Chris, and I. She said that she had to go to her flute lesson soon, but she would call me later that night. Then we said goodbye.

"The next day I got a call around five A.M. The call was from Lynda Mayer, who is my German teacher, and she told my parents what had happened to Lisa. My parents told me that Lisa had been murdered.

"Between six and six-thirty A.M., I called Chris Jones and told him. I was afraid he wouldn't find out until later. He was also a very good friend of Lisa's. Chris told me that he didn't believe me and that I should stop joking around. He hung up the phone. About twenty minutes later, Chris called me back and he asked me, 'Is it really true?'"

Daniel and several of Dan's friends gathered at Kathryn Schulz's house later that morning to talk about what had happened. That would be the daughter of the man who kept the press from contacting Lisa's family after the murder. Daniel's father drove him to Kathryn's, and on the way they listened to the news breaking on the radio, on 1100 AM. "They said that a Shaker Heights girl had been murdered and that she was raped and bludgeoned to death," Daniel told the detective. "At Kathryn's we all talked and cried. Kim Cole was on the phone with Kim Rathbone. When she got off the phone, she told us that Kim Rathbone had heard screams the night before." Rathbone's house was situated behind the Dreiforts', on Sedgewick Road.

More and more classmates gathered at Kathryn's throughout the day to discuss the crime. "We all shared what information we knew at the time," he said. Around eight-thirty A.M., several of them decided to go to school and to gather in the band room, to share memories. Someone suggested they should buy flowers and deliver them to the Pruetts' house.

"Once I got home, I told my parents that I was going over to the murder scene," said Daniel. "I walked over and I saw the tape. I asked a few policemen if anything had been discovered that they could tell me about. No one had anything to say."

A news reporter from Channel 5 was on-site getting B-roll. The journalist told Daniel that people were gathering at City Hall for a press conference. So the boy and a couple of his friends decided to go see what that was all about.

"We sat in the second row, but because we were behind the cameras, I moved to the other side so I could see the chief clearly. A few people from the press came over to talk to me, but I had no comment, except to say how great Dan and Lisa were. I also talked to the chief and said that if he wanted to talk to me, I'd be willing to talk."

After the presser Daniel returned to Dan's house. "Stanley Kramer was there," Daniel recalled. "And Dan talked to Chris Jones alone a few times. We sat out on his back porch and talked about everything that had happened."

At some point Dan walked over to the boundary of the property and showed them where Lisa's body had been found.

"He showed us where he saw the bicycle from the night before," said Daniel. "A police car came over and took down all of our names and asked us not to come by there again, because we could either get contaminated with evidence or we could mess up what was there."

"How much have you seen of Dan this summer?" the detective asked.

They'd seen each other a lot, until one night in July. Daniel told the detective that he'd planned to secretly meet up with Dan after everyone's parents had gone to bed. When he got to the Dreifort home, hidden in the shadows, he was surprised to find the house lights still on. Through a window he could see Dan's father yelling at Dan. After the argument was over, Dan came outside. Then he brought Daniel into the basement, where there was a kind of playroom that Dan called his "Howling Commando Room." The two boys talked until 3 A.M. Dan talked about Lisa, mostly. How much he loved her. He talked about his father and how upset he was with him. The next day Dan's dad had Dan committed to the psychiatric unit at the hospital where he worked.

During Dan's committal Daniel called Dan regularly. The staff mistakenly assumed that he was Dan's father when he called. "I spent almost every day with Lisa," said Daniel. "We would talk a lot about Dan and she would come over, or I would go there almost every day. She jumped in our pool with her clothes on and we had a great time."

"Could you describe what you know about the late-night meeting between Dan and Lisa, and how you found out about the meeting?" the detective asked.

"When I was over at Chris's apartment, on September 13, I realized that Dan and Lisa would probably be meeting each other," he said. "It was a normal thing for Dan and Lisa to meet each other late at night."

"Did Dan invite you over to his house on the evening of Thursday, September 13?"

"He did not invite me over."

"Have you ever heard, or have you ever attended, a party at Dan's where Robitussin was consumed?"

"Yes," he said. "I did not have any Robitussin, but one night Becca Boatright and another girl, Andy Conrad, were at Dan's. I called Dan up that night and he said I could stop by. He told me he had four ounces. Dan and Becca and Andy ran around in circles in the backyard."

"Did Dan ever tell you any strange effects he got from consuming Robitussin?"

"Yes. He told me many times. He said that there were stages to Robitussin. There was one main thing that he said it did for you. It made you feel like everything was out there. It was not a big change in what you could think, he would say, it was the added things you saw."

Chapter Fourteen

SCHOOL TIES

HOLLIE BUSH AND HER HUSBAND owned the property next door to the Dreiforts', where Lisa's body was found. They were one of the few African-American families in that area. The Bushes had lived there for eighteen years and they knew their neighbors well. The night of Lisa's murder, Hollie's eighty-seven-year-old brother was staying with them, visiting from Atlanta. Hollie recalled the events of that evening for detectives.

Hollie said she had watched the 11 o'clock news, then stood in the kitchen for a bit, polishing her nails. That's when she heard a noise.

"My first thought was that someone was tampering with a rented car we had in the driveway," she said. "I turned out the kitchen light and looked out the window. I saw nothing. I turned on the yard light and looked out the door and I saw nothing."

She thought at first that maybe it was her brother. But she could hear him in the guest room upstairs, making noises. So she dismissed the sounds and went to bed.

"I went to sleep soundly and was awakened by screams," she said. What she heard sounded like a child screaming. Three screams. "There was a scream, a pause, a scream, a pause, and another scream," she said. "I asked my husband, 'Did you hear the screams?' He said, 'Look out the window.' And I said, 'I'm going to call the police.'" She went to the kitchen, where the number for the Shaker Heights Police Department was written down near the house phone. She was told the police were on their way.

"Can you tell me the normal use of your property by the neighborhood kids?" the detective asked.

"When we first moved, the children who lived on Lee Road frequently came through, until we got the police to help us stop it. Months ago my husband asked the Dreiforts to not come through anymore. But recently I saw a young woman come through from the Sedgewick side. She walked through our yard and went through the shrubbery between our property and the Dreiforts'. I did not speak to her."

Detectives canvassed the block, knocking on doors up and down Sedgewick and Lee. Detective Robert Schippling interviewed Ann Sethness, who lived halfway up Sedgewick. She told him that sometime after midnight, the night of the murder, she had taken her dog out for a walk. She was still in her driveway when she heard voices. "She heard a commotion that sounded like kids having some sort of party," Schippling noted in his report.

ON TUESDAY, SEPTEMBER 18, police visited Shaker Heights High School to interview Lisa's friends. A tape recorder captured their words, thus freezing them as teens forever.

"Hi, Kim," said Detective Mike Klima, "would you please explain to me anything you can about Lisa Pruett, and if you would be so kind, describe Lisa to the best of your knowledge."

"I guess, you know, there's a lot of words to say," Kimberly Cole began. "She's an extremely happy person who spent a lot of her time trying to cheer other people up and not worrying about herself." Kimberly was only too familiar with tragedy. Earlier that year she'd been involved in the car accident in which another student, Brian

Hutton, was killed. In the hard weeks that followed, Lisa was always there for her. "She has a really close family," Kimberly explained. "At the funeral I could only say how intelligent she was."

Kimberly walked the detective through her last memories of her friend. On the day that Lisa died, Lisa had called her after school. "Dan got out of the hospital, but that's not important," Lisa said to her.

Kimberly didn't know what could possibly be more important to Lisa, who'd been anxiously awaiting Dan's release for over a month.

"Guess what I got?" said Lisa.

Suddenly she knew. "Your driver's license?"

"Yeah."

Lisa wanted to call Dan right away to share the news, so they ended the conversation. Kimberly called Lisa back, about 8 o'clock that night. She'd left a textbook at school that she needed for homework and thought Lisa might have a copy.

"Hey, when's your flute lesson?" she asked.

"Right now," said Lisa. "I'm walking out the door."

"Do me a favor and put your science book outside your screen door and I'll get it back to you." Lisa said she could do that.

But when she arrived at Lisa's, there was no book by the door. So she rang the bell, knowing that Lisa had left for flute practice and that probably meant she'd have to find someone else to lend her the book. Luckily, Lisa's mother was still home.

"What are you doing here?" asked Lynette when she answered the door.

Kimberly explained about the textbook and Lisa's mother said she could come in and check Lisa's room. The girl ran upstairs, found the book, and returned home to finish her assignment.

Then, about 9:20 P.M., she went back to Lisa's to return the book. Lisa invited her in. They were having a home-cooked dinner and cake to celebrate Lisa's victory at the DMV.

"My mom never makes me cake," said Kimberly.

"Then stay and have some," said Lynette.

So she did. And afterward, she and Lisa sat on the porch and discussed topics for Lisa's English paper, which she'd been avoiding. By then, it was getting late. At 9:45 P.M., Cole went home.

"Did Lisa ever mention that she was going to see Dan later that evening?" the detective asked.

"No," she said. "But I know he had come to her house a few times. She would tell me afterward, 'cause she'd be exhausted and I'd say, 'What's wrong?' And she'd say, 'Dan was over last night.'"

"When Dan would come over, would this be without her parents' knowledge?"

"I don't think either parent knew," said Cole. "He would come to her house and sit in her basement family room. He used to bring a guitar. I'd be willing to stake just about anything that it wasn't Dan. I used to go and punch him in the stomach all the time, kidding around, and he would throw me over his shoulder and spin me in circles, but he'd never get angry. I get that it doesn't look good, but I've known Dan since seventh grade, and I could never see him doing anything of the sort." Then she added, "I have heard Kevin Young's name thrown around a lot."

"By who?"

"I don't know who said it. It's kind of just, I think, you know, it's just something that's been said. I mean, you know, a lot of it could be hearsay, but I figure, you know, I should tell you everything I know. You're the one that's gonna decide what's right and what's not."

"That's what I want to know," said Klima. "I want to know everything that you know."

"I had heard Kevin left Arabica upset, at about ten-thirty that night, on foot."

"Is there anything that you think is important that we should know?"

"Yeah . . . I think Kim Rathbone, who lives behind the Dreiforts', I think she said that on September 2, her screen doors were cut. Nobody came into her house, but they were slashed or caught or ripped or something. I don't know if there's any connection, but Dan's backyard is there, and many times I've walked between the two, using the hole in the fence. I talked to Kim and told her if I talk to you, I was going to say something to the police, and here I am telling you."

LATER THAT DAY Klima spoke with Kathryn Schulz.

"Lisa is someone you can depend on to be there for you when you need her," she said. Kathryn spent a lot of time with Lisa. They both worked on the school paper and they talked on the phone almost every day. "We were really, really close friends. When I say we were close, I mean we were, in essence, best friends. She told me, you know, what was going on in her mind and we talked a lot."

Klima also spoke with several of Lisa's teachers. The band director, Hans Bohnert, told Klima that Lisa had designed the T-shirts for their school trip. Klima asked Mr. Bohnert what he remembered about Kevin Young. Bohnert said that the school had to remove Kevin from eighth-grade band for behavioral issues. But Kevin was allowed to return in tenth grade and things were better after that. Bohnert made special accommodations for Kevin because he was such an exceptional musician. But the boy had zero confidence. Bohnert told the detective about the band trip to Toronto where Kevin threatened to commit suicide when a girl wouldn't go out with him. After that, Kevin had been hospitalized at Hanna Pavilion and Bohnert visited him there. When the band went to Germany the next year, he only allowed Kevin to go because his father, Tal, volunteered to chaperone.

"The best word I can use to describe Kevin is 'scary,'" Bohnert told the cop.

Lynda Mayer, the German teacher, gave Klima a list of Lisa's male friends who, she suspected, could be involved in drugs or alcohol. She said that Dan Dreifort had flunked out of German as a freshman and was "not stable enough" to go on the trip to Germany that first year. She felt he was deliberately failing her class. On one test he simply wrote *Billy* for every answer. But after a conference with his parents, Dan's behavior had improved. "He might hurt himself," said Mayer, "but he doesn't strike me as someone who would hurt others."

When asked about Lisa's relationship with Dan, Mayer stated, "I have trouble believing that Lisa was deeply in love with Dan, but kids' emotions are not easily understood."

ENGLISH TEACHER CHRISTIE BOTT relayed a story about Stan Kramer, the kid who'd worked at Arabica the night of the murder. Stan had come to class the next day and had bragged that he was a suspect. Robert Annandale, the guidance counselor, said that he had confronted Stan about his alcohol abuse and chemical dependency at the end of the previous school year. But being eighteen, Stan chose to withdraw from school instead of getting help.

Klima asked each of Lisa's teachers who would have wanted to kill the girl. Their answer was unanimous: "No one."

Klima summed up his findings of Lisa Pruett in a report for the detectives: "They all spoke of a young woman with great leadership ability, an independent thinker, and extremely outgoing, with an upbeat personality."

LATER THAT WEEK the principal of Shaker Heights High School, Dr. Jack Rumbaugh, called the station. Something weird had happened with the marching band. Maybe it wasn't important, but it was odd. On the day of Lisa's murder, Rumbaugh had called over to Parma High School to let their principal know that the marching band would not be performing at that night's game because of the tragedy. He was surprised when the principal from Parma told him that someone had called *a week before the murder*, and had introduced himself as the principal, before telling her that the band would not be playing for them that night. To this day the identity of that caller remains unknown.

Chapter Fifteen

THEORIES

FROM AN INTERNAL MEMO, CIRCULATED among Shaker Heights detectives, titled *Theories*:

> In order to prove a criminal case based solely on circumstantial evidence, we must be able to disprove every other theory that presents itself during the course of the investigation. The following theories exist:
>
> - That Lisa Pruett homicide was a random killing, a crime of opportunity.
> - Dan Dreifort (Lisa's boyfriend) killed Lisa Pruett.
> - Tex Workman killed Lisa Pruett.
> - Kevin Young killed Lisa Pruett.
> - Robert Dreifort (Dan's father) killed Lisa Pruett.
>
> Theory A: The possibility that the murder of Lisa Pruett was a random killing perpetrated by a stranger is possible, but highly improbable. The statistical odds against a chance, violent encounter vs. a planned one are astronomical, considering the circumstances surrounding the incident. The predator would have had to

> have known that Lisa was going to be at 2940 Lee Road at or about 12:30 A.M.
>
> The "rendezvous" was not discussed or planned prior to September 13th. Several people were aware that Lisa Pruett was going to meet with Dan Dreifort sometime in the evening of September 13th or between the hours of 12:30 and 1 A.M. Those persons include Chris Jones, Jennifer Margulies, Becca Boatright, Tex Workman, Kevin Young, and Dan Dreifort. A limited number of people were invited by Dan to attend. Those persons were Chris Jones, Becca Boatright, and Tex Workman.

Shaker Heights is a small town inside a big city, and the rumor mill is well-established and can spread news through landline phones faster than any disease. After Lisa's murder the town succumbed to a bout of old-fashioned fear and superstition. A killer was on the loose and anyone might be the next target. Katrina Messina, a senior at Shaker Heights, brought her seventh-grade sister, Kari, to the police station. Kari had heard at school that a gang called the Zodiaks, which trolled Cleveland roads at night, searching for victims, had killed Lisa. The Zodiaks, she said, were influenced by the sign of the current zodiac symbol; and however many letters that symbol had, that's how many people they would kill that month.

A palpable gloom was settling over Shaker Heights and its residents were seeing monsters in the fog.

It was a full week after the murder before Christopher Jones sat for his formal interview with police. Chris was one of Dan's best friends and had been invited to the Dreifort house the night of Lisa's murder. According to Dan, Chris had decided to stay home that night. In his statement Chris told police that after school that day, Dan had come to his apartment with Daniel Messinger and stayed until he had to leave for fencing practice. When Chris got back, there was a note waiting for him, saying that Lisa had called. When he tried to call back, her line was busy.

Then, around 8 P.M., Dan called Chris and asked him to sneak out and come over.

"We talked for a while and he said he was going to have some people over and that I should give him a call later if I wanted to come," Chris told the detective. "I called him back, about quarter to eleven P.M., and said that I wasn't going to come over. Then I finished the paper I was working on and went to bed.

"I got a call at six-thirty A.M. the next day from Messinger, saying that Lisa had been murdered. I didn't really believe him and tried to go back to sleep. Got a call about five minutes later from Kathryn Schulz, saying the same thing. I asked her if I could go over to her house because some other people were over there at that time. I called Messinger back and asked him if he wanted to go over to Kathryn Schulz's house, too.

"He picked me up about five minutes later. We got to Kathryn's house and Shelby Hyvonen was there, and Kirsten from Germany, and Regina, who was Lisa's foreign exchange student, and Kim Cole. We talked for about half an hour. Then I went to school.

"We went to talk to certain teachers, and we got back together and got rides to Kathryn Schulz's house. There were about twenty people at Kathryn's house by then. We ate lunch and talked about things.

"At about three P.M., myself, Jenny Margulies, Judy Miller, and Rachel Lowenthal went to Dan Dreifort's house. Dan wasn't home and the police were searching all around the house. About fifteen minutes later, Mrs. Dreifort came back in the car with Mr. Dreifort, Dan, and Debbie. We went inside, into Dan's TV room, and we talked about what Dan had heard, and we watched the news. Dan was pretty angry about being a suspect."

After that, Chris Jones and Dan Messinger got a ride from Scott Fiero to the Pruetts' house. They asked Lisa's dad if they could spend some time, alone, in Lisa's bedroom. This was a bit of new information to the police. Messinger hadn't mentioned that trip to Lisa's house or how they'd spent time alone, in Lisa's room. Why had he skipped that detail? "Then me and Messinger got a ride about halfway to Dan's house from Randy Stokes. We got back to Dan's house and I spent the night there."

Later that night he, Dan Dreifort, and Debbie discussed the possibility that Kevin Young might have murdered Lisa.

"Could you briefly describe Dan Dreifort?" the detective asked.

"He's had a rough family life," said Chris. "Because of that, he's been kind of extroverted. He's pretty much always joking around. He'll always put on a show of being in a good mood. But under that, he's afraid to trust people. He's intelligent and he has a sense of what he should do. Lisa was one of the only persons he really trusted. He hasn't had that many people that he can trust. He loved her very much."

"Could you briefly describe Kevin Young?"

"Extremely touchy, very powerful, very angry," said Chris. "He likes to joke around, but you never really know if he's serious or not. He's always on edge, like wired."

"Can you describe Kevin's relationship with girls?"

Chris remembered one particular incident. "Andy Conrad and I were at a party. She was one of the girls he felt he was in love with, because he knew her from band. I was kind of going out with her at the time. Whenever she would come over and talk to me, or come and sit by me, Kevin would give me really dark glances. He simmered down after I talked to him. He just made me feel really uncomfortable."

AROUND 2 P.M. that day, Deputy Chief James Brosius interviewed Jenny Margulies and Rachel Lowenthal, who were good friends of Lisa's and part of the popular crowd at school. Their parents came with them.

Jenny explained that she had talked to Lisa on the phone the day of the murder, and that Lisa was all bubbly and excited, bragging about what a great day she'd had. Lisa was debating whether or not she should sneak out and go to Dan's house that night. Jenny encouraged her to do so.

But the real reason Jenny wanted to come in and speak to the police was to tell them about Kevin Young. Jenny stated that when she first heard her friends were suspects, she eliminated most of them in her mind. However, when she heard the rumor about Kevin Young, it made sense to her. She believed that Kevin was capable of murder.

Before coming to the station, Jenny had written down some recollections. She recalled one night when she and Rachel had gone to see *The Hunt for Red October*. After the movie they'd gone to Arabica, where they ran into Kevin.

He was talking about some "super prep" girl that he used to like in middle school who had invited him to a private party at a hotel. He was upset because when he met her there, the girl's boyfriend had shown up, and they had kicked Kevin out of the party.

"He went into his standard dissertation about women being bitches and whores," said Jenny. "Kevin said, 'Guys like Dan always get girls like Lisa to suck their cock, and I don't get anything.'"

Jenny told the detectives about another incident that occurred a couple weeks before Lisa's murder, again at Arabica. Kevin had said what an asshole Dan was and how it was too bad that he was in the hospital because he had "business to take care of with him and the slut."

"He said, 'I was going to fuck with them real good before I leave.'"

Chapter Sixteen

THE GIRL NEXT DOOR

On September 22, Kim Rathbone came to the Shaker Heights Police Department to speak with Detective Mullaney. Kim lived behind the Dreiforts', on Sedgewick, in a sprawling mansion with a mansard roof and a cavernous portico. She was the young woman Dan's mother referred to as her son's "alarm clock."

"Kim," Mullaney began, "could you explain how you know Dan Dreifort?"

"I knew Dan since sixth grade," she said. "He lives right behind me, so we've always been people who if you can't find anything else to do, you just go over to their house. He's one of my very best friends, and umm . . . Oh! I went out with him in sixth grade, which is nothing. It was like for a month or something, and we walked to school together and stuff like that. Is that all you want to know?"

It was not all the detective wanted to know. "What contact did you have with either Lisa or Dan on Thursday, September 13?"

"Okay," Kim said, thinking back. "Well, first I'll tell you about Dan. That was the first day that he came back from the hospital and Lisa and I were sitting together in school. I was helping her with her chemistry, which is funny, because she's the smart one, and umm, we were sitting down and he came around the corner, like he'd been there the entire time. So I saw him then, got hugs and everything 'cause I hadn't seen him for a while. After school I went over and I was cutting his hair. That was my special treat. He never let anybody cut his hair. And then my boyfriend came and he picked me up, and said hi to Dan, and then we left.

"That's all I'd seen. Except I heard her scream that night, not knowing that it was her. There are screams all the time around Lee Road and South Woodland, and I was up doing my history, and I put it off, and when I heard the scream, I woke up and looked, and walked through the house, and it happened toward the back of the house. My little brother leaves his window open and our rooms are connected. We're through a bathroom, and the bathroom doors were open, and his window was open, and I heard her scream and I went and I looked in my windows to see if there were any bicycles or cars or anything. There wasn't anybody. I thought it was weird, but I still didn't do anything about it. And I found out Friday, at, like, seven o'clock."

"Seven in the morning?"

"Yeah," said Kim. "And we didn't even know it was Lisa, it was like tapes and dogs and everything. And so my parents were all in front of the house. My grandmother lives with us, and my brother sleeps like a log, and he didn't notice anything, and I guess my grandmother's windows were shut. I don't know why she didn't hear."

"Do you remember about what time that was that you heard those screams?"

"Around twelve-thirty," said Kim. "I was hoping that it wasn't her, but just from what I heard from other people and everything, putting everything together, it seems to be . . . so I'm not even absolutely sure that it was her."

"How do you know about what time it was?" the detective asked. "Were you aware then what time it was, or did you just kind of hear what time it happened later, and then . . ."

"No, no. I glanced at the clock when I heard it. I don't know why, because I was just, like, working really hard, and it distracted me out of my work, so I just glanced to see what time it was."

"So you were awake at the time?"

"Yeah. I was up."

"Doing your homework?"

"Studying my history."

"Did Lisa tell you what her plans were for the evening?"

"No," said Kim. "I didn't even know that she had been over at Dan's house before. Sometimes you can hear from Dan's backyard, you can all the time hear . . . If our screen doors are open, you can hear what goes on in his house . . . so I guess I just wasn't really concentrating on what was going on over there."

"Describe for me, as best as you can, what the screams sounded like."

"Like somebody was scared. I was just . . . It didn't sound like a play scream, like you hear like when people are driving by and stuff . . . but it still didn't actually occur to me that it might be somebody really getting hurt, 'cause I don't know why . . . It was somebody being scared."

"Did it sound like a male or a female?"

"Oh, a female."

"Definitely?" asked Mullaney.

"Yeah."

"What time did you go over to Dan's house that day?"

"Uh . . . it had to be after four P.M."

"So you went over there between four-fifteen and four-thirty P.M., and you were over there for about forty-five minutes?"

"Yeah, I guess so."

"Who else was at Dan's at that time?"

"Outside with us? No one."

"Just you and Dan?"

"Umm, yeah."

"And you cut Dan's hair then, right?"

"Yeah."

"In general, what did you and Dan talk about that day?"

"Oh, well, he had just gotten back . . . He was tellin' me about the people, what he had seen, and just . . . I had sent Dan a care package, it was just mementos and stuff when he was in the hospital. But I wanted some of it back, because it was the only things that I had of him, and he had stuff about me, so I still needed those things. And we were talking about how short he wanted his hair, and whether he wanted me to put it in a point in the back or not, and he said that he trusted me and I could just do whatever I wanted to. He had complete faith in me."

"Do you know anybody that might want to hurt either Dan or Lisa, that you're aware of?" asked Mullaney.

"That would actually do it? Or that I think that might do it?"

"You know, saying that somebody would actually do something is . . . you don't know, we don't know . . ."

"Yeah, I have a hard time believing that anybody's capable of it," said Kim. "But my guess is Kevin Young."

"Kevin Young?"

"Well, he used to threaten 'em all the time. He used to say weird stuff."

"Like what?"

"He said he wanted to . . . Well, he was in a mental or psych ward or something when he was a sophomore, and he said that he wanted . . . Generally, he said he wanted to get back at the rest of the world for putting him through what he'd been through, and he was going to do something to make everybody remember him, and he said that he was gonna get Lisa. He said that how come Dan could get any good girl he wants, getting any girl that he wants to suck his dick, but he can't get anybody. Stuff like that."

"Have you ever heard any of these threats from Kevin directly, or do you just hear about them?"

"Umm, he sat next to me in biology his sophomore year, when he was in the institution . . . whatever it's called . . . He must have said something like that every now and then."

"But do you remember any specific instances that he actually made threats when you were present?"

"I don't remember a day. It was in biology he did that one."

He'd asked the question twice already, and Kim had cleverly dodged the answer. So Mullaney pressed harder. "But you heard it," he said. "Do you remember what it was exactly, or as close to exact as you can remember?"

"He was saying he was just so happy to be out of there, and he just wanted to hurry up and get out, and he was gonna make everybody remember him."

"But what I was talking about specifically, did he threaten Dan or Lisa directly in your presence?"

"No, just the world."

In the span of a minute, Kim had gone from "He said that he was going to get Lisa," to saying she'd never heard Kevin directly threaten anyone. It was clear that she'd already heard Jenny Margulies's version of events through the grapevine. Or, perhaps more likely, directly from Jenny herself. The children of Shaker Heights were writing a narrative, and they wanted Lisa's killer to be Kevin Young.

"Now I'm going to ask you a question, and the answer, I don't care about who's involved in what, but did you ever hear anything about any kind of parties at Dan's involving Robitussin? Drinking Robitussin to get high?"

"Do you mean did I ever hear of a party where we did that, or did I ever hear about them doing that, period?"

"Did you ever hear about them doing that, period?" said Mullaney.

"Yeah."

"Okay. What do you know about that?"

"I know it doesn't show up on your drug test," Kim explained. "Uh . . . you want me to tell you who did it, or how they did it, or . . ."

"Yes."

"Both?"

"Yes."

"I don't really know how they did it. I could never figure it out really. I guess they drank a lot of it, maybe they like the taste."

"Were you ever present when anybody ever did this?"

"No. I just . . . I saw the bottles, but I was never present when they ever did it."

"Okay. So, how did you know, just by seeing the bottles, that somebody didn't just have a bad cold?"

"Dan had told me about it."

"What did he tell you about it?"

"He told me that . . . that it . . . that I . . ." Kim laughed nervously. "He told me that he got high off of those because that way he wouldn't ever be really using any real drugs, and he could still feel good, I guess. And that was just . . . uh . . . I can't remember who the people he said he'd done it with."

"Did he ever tell you what he felt like when he took Robitussin?"

"He said the first time that he did it . . . I'm trying to remember the words he used, what he used to describe being high."

"Did he mention, other than being high, any kind of unusual reaction or effect that it had on him?"

"Well, I remember him talking about his friend was just totally out of it, talking about like going in a forest, or something, 'Like there are the trees right there,' hallucinating or something."

"Do you remember who the friend was that he talked to?"

"No," said Kim. "Why are you asking me about the Robitussin, anyway?"

"It's just something that's come up in other statements."

"Well, Dan doesn't drink anymore because he was ill with Robitussin."

"What do you know of Kevin's feelings toward Lisa, if he had any feelings toward her?"

"Umm, you mean out of his mouth? I don't really know. But recalling from just everything that I've heard . . . Umm . . . that, uh . . . it seemed like he might have been jealous of Lisa spending time with Dan, not really jealous of Dan because he has Lisa. Seemed like it was the other way around, just from what I've heard. It sounds kind of weird."

"Okay, so this is what you've heard from other people?"

"Yeah."

"Who has been talking to you about it?"

"Jenny Margulies."

"Did Dan mention anything to you about the relationship between Mr. and Mrs. Dreifort and Dan? How did they get along?"

"Well, Dan and his father have always had this thing going," she said. "I mean it's a lot less worse now. I mean, I haven't . . . Because I told you, when the screen doors are open, you can hear everything? You could hear Dan's father screaming at him for whatever reason, just 'Clean your room!' and 'Shave!' and 'Why don't you help me with this?' and stuff like that. I've always heard stories about what happened when they were younger."

"Like what?" Mullaney asked.

"Like what? Well, they're kind of far-fetched. I never knew whether to believe them or not, uh . . . but I had heard that his father had gotten violent with Dan and Deborah, and I think his mom. And that's why Dan started lifting weights in, like, sixth grade. He wanted to stand up to his father, and uh . . . I had heard once . . . and this sounds really far-fetched, but I remember it, and I don't remember whether I heard it from Debbie or Dan, but when Dan was little, he had to use the bathroom, and his father said, 'No, hold it as long as you can,' and then he couldn't hold it any longer. So he ended up wetting his pants, and his father got mad because he wet his pants, and, like, pushed his head into the toilet or something."

"Who would you say would be Dan's best friends?"

"Dan's best friends? Well . . . Lisa. We spent a lot of time together, used to share a lot of hidden thoughts . . . Uh, I don't know if he would actually call me one, but I would like to think that I was one."

AS THE INVESTIGATION progressed, two things became clear to the detectives working the case: Lisa was likely murdered by someone who lived close to the crime scene, and that person was almost certainly a classmate. Whoever had stabbed Lisa to death had been waiting behind the bushes for her to come through to meet with Dan, which suggested they had to be one of the handful of kids who knew Lisa was sneaking out of her house that night. Lisa's screams had prompted Mrs. Bush, Dan, Dan's father, and Kim Rathbone to look out their windows. Nobody had seen a car at the corner. Nobody had seen anyone run from the scene down the sidewalk. All of this suggested the killer had come on foot and had used the patch of trees and bushes between Lee and Sedgewick to remain unseen until they were far enough to slip back onto the streets in their escape. Or they lived so close to the scene that they could simply return home through a back door.

But a kid killing a kid was a rare tragedy. What teenager could possibly have the capacity for such unchecked violence? Who would want this girl dead?

In these sorts of cases, the boyfriend is usually the best suspect. But Dan had impressed the cops with his openness: He came into the station that night for a statement, and submitted to lie detector tests. He showed proper shock and sadness when he was told Lisa was dead. He sure didn't act guilty.

Maybe his friends were right. Maybe it was that weird kid from school, Kevin Young. There was little doubt that he was a disturbed young man. And he'd heard about Dan and Lisa's rendezvous from Tex. He admitted to taking late-night walks, and if Dan's friends were telling the truth, he'd threatened the young lovers in public. He had the means and motive. As far as opportunity Kevin claimed he was playing video games with his father at the time Lisa was killed. But what father wouldn't cover for his son? And his dad was a lawyer, after all.

Detective Gray soon eliminated each of the teens in his mind and came to believe that the only one who could have committed the murder was Kevin Young. And from that moment on, there was nothing anyone could say to change his mind.

Chapter Seventeen

BREAKING KEVIN YOUNG

On Wednesday, September 26, a caravan of "the finest" from Shaker Heights traveled to Ohio State University, in Columbus, in hopes of eliciting a murder confession out of their favorite suspect, Kevin Young. They sent their big guns: Deputy Chief James Brosius, Detective Tom Gray, Detective Sergeant Dan Velardo, Detective Tom Kohanski, Detective Sergeant Tim Reed, and Detective Tim Ward. This was the moment Shaker Heights cast its lot, the moment of no return. By sending that many officers, it assured the story would inevitably leak; even without a confession, Kevin Young's name would forever after be attached to the murder of Lisa Pruett. But they were confident that morning. And everyone understood that the reputation of the police department was on the line with a move this big. It was important that everything go as planned and they return with Kevin Young in handcuffs.

Before they left, these policemen received a personal letter from Prosecutor K. J. Montgomery that read like the speech a platoon leader gives to the grunts before commanding them to take the next hill:

> You leave the Department today with a lot of adrenaline, apprehension, and expectation. You are demanding a

> great deal of yourselves. I first want to wish you well and, of course, share your desires for an ultimate result.
>
> As you proceed through the tasks you've programmed for yourselves, proceed as you always do: be efficient, be careful, be thorough, be confident. You all possess the ability to do the job. Don't worry about the ultimate result. If you rely on your training and trust your instincts, the desired result will follow naturally. And if the ultimate result does not materialize today or tonight, it will materialize tomorrow or the next day or the day after that. Of that, I am confident.

When they arrived on campus, the Shaker Heights regiment met with two detectives from the university's police department. Campus police had already placed an undercover officer in Kevin's dorm, dressed as a maintenance worker, so they would know exactly when Kevin returned to his room. While they waited, the Shaker Heights cops booked accommodations at the Ramada Inn and grabbed some dinner.

Around 9 P.M., the undercover officer at the dorm reported that Kevin was currently in his room, drinking a can of soda. Detective Gray and Jim Younger, of the OSU police, drove out to the school and entered Kevin's dorm. They identified themselves to the security guard posted by the door and took the elevator to the fifth floor. Kevin's room was part of a pod that shared a common living space with three other units. Kevin's door was closed, but the doors to the other rooms were open, and several students milled about, curious about the visitors. Younger knocked on Kevin's door, Room 554. Gray remained a few feet behind him.

When Kevin answered the door, Younger showed him his badge and asked him to step into the hall so they could talk in private. Once Kevin was in the hall, Detective Gray introduced himself. "I'm from the—"

"Shaker Heights Police Department," Kevin finished for him.

"I need your help," said Gray.

Kevin invited the detective into his room, but Gray suggested they go to the campus police station instead. That made Kevin nervous, so Gray said that they could go to his room at the Ramada if that suited him better. That sounded fine to Kevin.

After Kevin pulled on his shoes, he picked up the room phone and dialed his parents. But he put the phone down before it connected.

"Can I call home later?" he asked.

"You can call home whenever you want," the detective said. Did the tone in Detective Gray's voice just then remind Kevin of Honest John from *Pinocchio*? Maybe not. Kevin went with him, after all. But the impersonation was spot-on.

Kevin rode with Gray to the hotel in an unmarked police cruiser. On the way Gray made small talk. They chatted about college life and the classes Kevin was enrolled in. The detective was building trust. Kevin said that he was interested in studying economics and that he'd started another conservative nonprofit. Its mission: to bust the teachers' union back at Shaker High.

They arrived at the Ramada Inn at 9:45 P.M. Gray brought Kevin to his room. Kevin again asked about calling home. Gray assured him that not only could he call his parents at any time, but that he'd pay for the call.

"Have a seat," said Gray.

Kevin took the couch by the window.

"I've spent the last two weeks talking to people, gathering information so I can find out what happened to Lisa," said Gray. "I need you to give me some insight."

"I'll help any way I can," said Kevin.

"We're under pressure from the media," said Gray. "There are some loose ends and I have questions about your involvement with the case."

"How long is this going to take?" asked Kevin.

"I'm not sure. Since I came to you for help, you can decide when you're ready to stop talking and then I'll take you back to your dorm."

"I'm a night person," said Kevin.

"Can I get you a pop?"

"Coke," said Kevin. "From the can."

Gray got Kevin a soda. "I want to remind you that I'm a police officer," said Gray. "I'm investigating a crime in which you are still a suspect. You have the right to remain silent. You don't have to talk to me."

"I want to help," Kevin said.

"We can stop anytime you want."

"I know."

"You can talk to an attorney . . ."

"I know my rights."

Gray began his questions. "Tell me what you think about the incident."

"I'm afraid that Tex did it," said Kevin. "And what scares me even more is that Tex might have done it for me. I don't think I could live with the guilt of it if Tex killed Lisa for me."

On the night of the murder, Kevin was worried about bigger problems than girls, he explained. He was thinking about the war in Iraq. "I have a January birthday," said Kevin. "I would be one of the first kids drafted."

"I remember worrying about the draft," said Gray. "They stopped the draft the year I graduated, though."

Kevin told the detective that the war in the Middle East should be fought through economic means and not ground warfare. He rambled on about free markets.

"Do you enjoy thinking about things in theoretical terms?" Gray asked.

"Yes."

"Well, that's what I need help with. It would be a great help in figuring out what happened to Lisa Pruett. Could you put yourself in the place of the person who did this?"

Kevin got quiet for a beat. "Just between us?" he said.

"Yeah," said Gray, knowing that this conversation would be recorded for posterity.

"Okay."

"Do you think Lisa was riding her bike, or was she walking when this happened?"

"I think she was riding her bike," said Kevin. "I think the person grabbed her off the bike and then the bike rolled into the bushes."

"Go on."

"Whoever did this didn't really plan on it to happen, and he didn't really think about it ahead of time. He was just walking around that night, kind of wandering, and he saw Lisa, and when these two people got close, something snapped. Something snapped and this anger came out that he couldn't control. He knocked Lisa off her bike and she was stabbed with a knife, and she died so fast that he got scared. He did not want that to happen. He started acting frantic, running around doing things really quick."

"What happened next?"

"He ran." Kevin thought for a moment, then added, "I'm sure that he will never kill again. I'm sure he's sorry that Lisa died."

"Kevin, I'm afraid that he might snap again and hurt someone," said Detective Gray.

"I don't think he would. I think he's gone on to another life and this could never happen again."

"How do you think she died?"

"I think she was stabbed from the front. He stabbed her once or twice, maybe more."

At that time Kevin asked if he could use the bathroom. He was in there for a couple minutes, and when he tried to open the door, it stuck. Gray had to pry it open. Then the detective went to fetch another soda with caffeine for Kevin. It was getting late.

When Gray returned, he picked up his line of questioning. "How familiar are you with the area where the murder happened?" he asked.

"I take walks at night sometimes, but I don't usually go down Lee Road. I usually just walk across the street and sit in the stadium at the high school. I don't sleep well."

"Where do you think the person who stabbed Lisa went to wash the blood off his hands?"

"I think the way Lisa was stabbed, this person didn't get any blood on him."

"How do you think the killer felt after it was done?"

"Guilty," said Kevin. "I think he felt guilty, because I always feel guilty when I do things I can't control. I feel guilt about Lisa's death because I should have been there to stop this person. Logically, I know I shouldn't feel that way."

"How did Lisa feel?" asked Gray.

"I think she felt surprised because she knew the person and was scared when she realized what was happening."

"Do you think he heard her scream?"

"Of course. He would have been so close the screams would be like yelling in your ear."

"Strange things happen to people under stress," said Gray. "Sometimes, when a police officer is involved in a shooting, they don't remember hearing the shots."

"I don't believe it."

"What do you think should happen to the person who did this to Lisa?"

Kevin sat up and looked the detective in the eyes. "The person that did this should be electrocuted," he said. "He should hang. Or at least spend the rest of his life in prison." Then Kevin looked away, to the open space in the center of the room. "But if he's under twenty-one, he should be treated like a juvenile, because you don't have any real rights until you're twenty-one, anyway. And I think this person needed help and didn't really mean to do it."

"That's exactly why I came to Columbus," said Gray. "I think I've spoken to Lisa's killer already. And in order to help him, I need to get through to him. The reason I'm involved in all the interviews is that I convinced my boss that this kid needed help. The kid who did this is not a criminal. But time is running out."

Kevin listened.

"I need your advice on how to convince this person that he needs help, and that the only chance I have of convincing others is for this person to trust me. Someone has to present this case to the prosecutor, and how the case is presented determines what the person is charged with."

After a moment the detective continued. "I view myself as a neutral outsider in the judicial process," he mused. "It's my duty to gather facts and put pieces together and then present it to a prosecutor. If the facts showed evidence of a cold-blooded killing, I would be forced to present those facts. But if the facts showed someone that needed help, then I would present those facts. My fear is that this person needs help and I might not be able to get through to him."

"I think you can get through to him," said Kevin. "But I think it would be very difficult for him to admit what he's done."

"How can I get through to him?" asked Gray.

"You'll have to meet with him again and again and again. You'll have to push him real hard and get them emotional and force them to want to talk about what happened."

"This interview is very important to me," said Gray. "I interviewed people all day, and after speaking to them, I decided I had to talk to you. That it couldn't wait. There's a lot of people, my boss included, who believe you were involved with what happened to Lisa. I need your help to explain this all to my boss."

"I didn't do it."

"Who do you think did it?"

"Tex."

"Do you think he's capable of murder?"

"He threatened to kill Dan Dreifort when he heard about it."

"I have a lot of unanswered questions," Gray continued. "What would you say if I told you that someone saw you out of your house that night?"

"No one saw me out of my house," said Kevin. "It was too dark out there for anyone to see me. I went to bed. I couldn't sleep. So I just walked around the house. I got this sharp pain while lying in bed, around twelve-thirty A.M. I should have realized something was going on, I should have gone out to do something about it, but I stayed inside. I spoke to my neighbor and they got the same pain I did, at the same time that night. I think that's eerie."

"Is there any reason we might find your fingerprints on Lisa's jeans?"

"My fingerprints aren't on Lisa's jeans. Take my prints. Compare them with any fingerprints you find."

After a few minutes Detective Gray tried again. "I need you to be honest with me."

"I am being honest," said Kevin. "I didn't do anything to Lisa."

"I need your help to resolve this either way. Detective Mullaney told me that during your first interview, you offered to take a polygraph."

"I'm still ready."

"I can arrange that," said Gray. "Next week. Tomorrow. Whenever you want."

"How quickly can you do it?" Kevin asked. "I'm ready now."

"Do you want to go back to your dorm and get some sleep?"

"If we can do it early, I can just stay here at the hotel," he said. "I have classes at eight A.M. I don't want it to interfere with classes."

"Well, I brought our polygraph operator with me," said Gray. "If you want to do it tonight, I can make arrangements."

Kevin became emotional, thinking about it. He lit another cigarette and then said, "I'd rather do it now so that I can prove once and for all that I didn't do anything to Lisa."

Detective Gray left to tell his polygraph operator to get ready and then he returned to the room. "You want another pop?"

"I'm out of cigarettes."

"I'll get you a fresh pack."

"I'd like a few minutes to smoke before the test," Kevin said.

Detective Gray got Kevin some smokes and left him alone. Then he went to Room 516 and spoke to his polygraph operator, Shaker Heights detective Tom Kohanski.

"Is Kevin rested enough to take the polygraph?" Kohanski asked. It was after midnight.

Gray returned to the room where Kevin was. "Have you ever taken a polygraph before?"

"No," said Kevin.

"Well, you need to be rested and calm and prepared," said Gray. "It's late. You can sleep here or in your dorm."

"I feel good," said Kevin. "I'd like to get it over with."

While they waited for Kohanski, Kevin talked to Gray about how excited he was to be at Ohio State. "Whoever picks roommates does a really good job," he said. "Me and my roommate clicked right away. He has a nice girlfriend. Things are going better here. Just today a girl walked up to me and talked to me in class."

There was a knock at the door. It was Kohanski. Gray introduced him and then Kohanski began to set up his equipment on a table.

"Is there anything else I can do for you?" Gray asked.

"No," said Kevin.

"If you have any problems, I'll be in the other room."

Gray left them alone. It was now 2 o'clock in the morning. Entering Room 516, Gray discussed the ongoing interview with the other detectives waiting there. They decided to call Jim Wright for guidance. Wright was a special agent at the FBI's Behavioral Analysis Unit. Wright got on the phone even though it was late. He cautioned Gray that both he and Kevin might be getting tired. Maybe it should wait. But Gray didn't want to wait. He wanted his confession.

At 2:45 A.M., Kohanski came to the room to discuss the results of the first polygraph he'd just given to Kevin.

"There's slight deception on all but two of my questions," he said. "But Kevin has an extremely high heart rate. Maybe because he's tired. I have not confronted Kevin with the results."

Gray returned to Room 520, where Kevin was waiting. He pulled a chair in front of Kevin and sat down. "I'm concerned," he said. "You did not do as well on the interview as I'd hoped."

Kevin listened.

"There were a number of questions where you showed deception. It's late. Do you think it's because you're tired?"

"That must be it," said Kevin. "I'm telling the truth."

"Did you kill Lisa Pruett?"

"I didn't do it."

"I'm down here to learn the truth," said Gray. "I'll do whatever you want to do. I can take you back to your dorm and I can come back next week. I can take you back and we can meet again after your classes. Or we could continue to talk."

"I want to keep talking."

They took a short break. Kevin took a piss. Gray got him another pop. When Gray returned, he told Kevin how important it was to get through to the person who killed Lisa so Gray could get him the help he needed. "Most of the police have kids and they're only out to solve a crime."

Kevin said nothing.

Gray tried a different approach. "How did you find out about what happened to Lisa?"

"I only know what Tex told me."

"And what did Tex tell you?"

"That Lisa was knocked off her bicycle, bludgeoned, and raped."

"I have information that you told people Lisa had been stabbed and not beaten and that she had not been raped."

"I never said that."

"I'm scared," said Gray. "I think you were involved. And I'd hate to see you go to prison for the rest of your life. I need you to tell me the truth."

Kevin leaned back in his seat and looked around the room. "I'm tired," he said at last. "I need a break."

Gray offered to take Kevin back to his dorm, but Kevin said he'd prefer to stay at the hotel. So Gray packed up his stuff and gave his room to Kevin so the boy could have the bed. It was 4:45 A.M. Gray slept until 8 o'clock. At 8:30 A.M., Kevin called his room and said he was ready to try again. Gray offered to take him to breakfast before they started the polygraph. Kevin suggested Bob Evans. So that's where they went—Gray, Kevin, and Kohanski, the polygraph examiner. Kevin ordered French toast and orange juice. While they ate, the boy talked about video games. He'd recently mastered *Super Mario Bros. 3*.

Kevin mentioned calling home. But again he thought better of it and decided it could wait until they were done.

At noon Gray led Kevin back to the hotel room. Then he stepped away with Kohanski to go over the new plan. If Kevin showed deception this time, Kohanski was to confront him with the results. If at that time the boy seemed ready to confess, Kohanski was supposed to leave the room and have Gray come in to close.

But the polygraph had to be put on hold because they'd only booked Gray's room until 2 P.M. So they went out for pizza while the polygraph machine was set up in a new room. More soda and cigarettes for Kevin. After lunch Kevin sat down for another test.

Just before 3 P.M., Kohanski returned to Gray with the results. "I ran two tests," he said. "Kevin showed deception on most of the questions about Lisa. I confronted Kevin. He got tears in his eyes. He said he didn't do it."

Gray returned to the room where Kevin was seated by the polygraph machine. This time he brought Deputy Chief Brosius with him. Gray sat beside the boy.

"I know the machine can't lie," said Kevin. "I don't understand."

"If you really weren't involved with what happened to Lisa, then everything will work out," said Gray. "Whoever did this to Lisa needs me as a friend. They need me to present to the prosecutor what happened, objectively. I think the person who did this needs help. They don't deserve to spend the rest of their life in prison... or to be executed."

When Kevin didn't answer, Gray continued.

"I think the affection between Dan and Lisa bothered you." Gray held up some of Kevin's personal writing that they'd taken from his bedroom back home. He read a passage aloud. "'It really pisses me off when I see couples paired off... I am worth absolutely nothing.' Some of your thoughts bother me, Kevin." He read more: "'I will kill all the undesirables! I must!!! I am hated by virtually all my classmates. Males think I am a loser and a psychotic, a scar on the school's mere existence; females despise me as if I was the ugliest person on this planet, which of course I am.'"

The detective read a final passage. "'If I ever lose control of myself, withdraw into an alternative world and let animal instincts take over...'" He handed the paper to Kevin so he could see his own handwriting. "You can't stay in this alternative world," said Gray. "The truth must come out."

Kevin said nothing.

"If you were involved in any way in what happened to Lisa, you will never escape it," the detective warned him. "Until this is resolved you can't go back to Shaker because everyone in Shaker will think of you as a suspect. And you can't go back to college now because everything there will remind you of Lisa. You can't go back until you tell the truth."

Kevin leaned forward and looked into Gray's eyes. "I could have told you I did it and spent a couple years in a hospital, then got on with my life," he said. "But I've got to tell you the truth, and this is the truth." For a couple minutes Kevin didn't say anything more. Then he said, "I'm scared. I feel suicidal."

"Then I think you should call your parents and talk to them about getting into a hospital."

"No," he said. "I can't call home. My mom wouldn't believe me. Can I call my doctor?"

Gray agreed to let him make the call. But Kevin got an answering machine. A few minutes later, he tried again. Finally his doctor called back and said he could arrange for Kevin to be admitted into a hospital right away, but he had to call his parents first because of insurance issues.

"Will you visit me?" Kevin asked the detective.

"I promise," said Gray.

Gray left the room so Kevin could finally call his mom. Kevin came out a couple minutes later and said his mother wanted him to call a lawyer.

"Does this mean you can't visit me in the hospital?"

"You need to make those arrangements with your parents and your attorney."

Gray walked Kevin out. At the elevator Kevin hugged the detective and said goodbye.

Chapter Eighteen

RETURN TO SHAKER

As Kevin was sitting down to speak with Detective Gray at the Ramada Inn, a team of Shaker Heights detectives executed a search warrant at his dorm room. Detective Sergeant Reed, Detective Ward, and Officer Herr were joined by Captain Younger. The assistant director of Morrill Hall used a duplicate key to let them inside. The policemen bagged up Kevin's shoes. They took a pair of Kevin's jeans they found in his closet—the jeans had red stains near the cuffs that looked like blood.

At 7 A.M., Detective Richard Mullaney received a call at his house. It was Jim Brosius. He wanted to fill Mullaney in on Gray's interrogation. The kid knew information about the crime that only the killer could know, he told Mullaney. They were confident they had the right man. "Call his father," said Deputy Chief Brosius. "Set up an interview."

At the time Kevin's father, J. Talbot Young, worked as an attorney practicing estate law with Squire, Sanders & Dempsey. Squire, Sanders & Dempsey was arguably the most prestigious firm in Cleveland, connected to the biggest politicians and businessmen in Northeast Ohio. In fact, Stephen Alfred, the mayor of Shaker Heights, was also a lawyer at Squire, Sanders & Dempsey, a fact that would never not be mentioned in forthcoming newspaper articles.

Speaking to Tal Young was part of the strategy the police were developing to coerce a confession from Kevin. They wanted Kevin's father to believe that his son was the most likely person to have committed the murder. If they couldn't break Kevin, perhaps they could break Tal.

MULLANEY CONTACTED TAL at his office and asked him to come to the station. Tal took a cab and arrived at 9:45 A.M. He was escorted to the conference room to meet with Mullaney and another detective.

Mullaney was direct. He told Tal that they believed his son had killed Lisa Pruett. He explained how Kevin had become their prime suspect after classmates reported his strange behavior. Mullaney told Tal they'd found alarming messages in Kevin's diary.

"We conducted a search of Kevin's dorm room," Mullaney told him. "We located some more writing that is concerning. He's fixating on some females at school that he doesn't know and we're afraid his emotions might take over again."

Mullaney told Tal that he'd sent samples of Kevin's writing to the Behavioral Analysis Unit at the FBI. In fact, detectives from Shaker Heights had flown to D.C. just days before to speak directly with the BAU agents. The expert profilers believed Kevin was capable of murder.

"We're not looking to hang someone for this," Mullaney said. "But we want to see that your son gets the help he needs."

"Kevin has had problems in the past," Tal admitted. "But he seems so much better now, happier. I'm sure the personnel at the FBI is very capable, but I'm sure my son is in no way involved or capable of doing what happened to Lisa Pruett. The night of the murder, I was home, watching TV. Around eleven o'clock Kevin came into the room and talked to me and my wife. After the news ended, around midnight, Kevin and I played Nintendo together. I was awake, doing paperwork upstairs, until about one A.M. If Kevin had left the house, I would have heard him."

"Has he ever left the house at night to walk around?"

"Sometimes he walks over to the high school and walks around the track for a while, but he always lets us know. He has no reason to sneak out of the house, anyway—he's eighteen."

"Is Kevin taking any medication?" the detective asked.

"Not now," said Tal. "But he has been on a generic form of lithium."

"Our concerns for Kevin's well-being are very real," said Mullaney. "The FBI profiler tells us that if Kevin is, in fact, the person who killed Lisa, and both the FBI and the Shaker Heights police are convinced he is, he will kill again."

Chapter Nineteen

HISTORY REPEATS

THIS ALL GOES BACK TO Watergate, because of course it does.

Flashback to Saturday, October 20, 1973: An orange Volkswagen Bug makes its way through the milled sandstone skyscraper caverns of downtown Cleveland. It's raining. It's late. A young man sits behind the wheel, listening to news on the radio. He's a third-year student at the Cleveland-Marshall College of Law, with a job clerking at the federal public defender's office. These are stepping-stones to his real goal: elected office. Big ambitions for a kid from Parma, the son of a union contractor who built trestles for the railroad. Meet Mark DeVan.

At school his professors were focused on the developing Watergate scandal. Every day there were new revelations and DeVan studied the details through the lens of the Constitution. When he was clerking for the federal defender, he liked to stop in courtrooms to watch the lawyers battle, studying their moves like a rookie chess player watching the grand masters. He had begun to ask himself if politics was really why he went to law school or if he was more attracted to trial work. He was a young man searching for a sign.

The car turned onto West 25th Street as the radio started talking about the massacre.

They were calling it the "Saturday Night Massacre." And while nobody was really killed, it's the night Mark DeVan's aspirations for political office died.

Richard Nixon was president. He was a Republican and the world was at war, and at home the liberals were protesting. There had been an election in 1972, the year before, and Nixon had done some underhanded things to win. Some of his foot soldiers had broken into the goddamn Democratic headquarters inside the Watergate Hotel. They had hoped to bug the office, to figure out the Dems' game plan. Well, long story short, they got caught. And it was a big deal. The top lawman in the land at that time was Attorney General Elliot Richardson, who pledged to hire a special prosecutor to investigate any role Nixon may have played in the crime. So, to this end, Richardson hired Archibald Cox—the James Comey of his day.

On Friday, October 19, 1973, Cox issued a subpoena for audiotapes recorded in the Oval Office. Nixon went ballistic. And the following day, Saturday, Nixon demanded that AG Richardson fire Cox. Richardson refused and resigned. So then Nixon went to Deputy Attorney General William Ruckelshaus and told *him* to fire Cox. Ruckelshaus told Nixon to get bent and then also resigned. Nixon finally got Solicitor General Robert Bork to fire Cox in exchange for a quiet promise to nominate Bork for the U.S. Supreme Court when a seat opened up.

Back in Cleveland, Mark DeVan pulled to the side of the road by the West Side Market and listened to the news as it broke, piece by piece. By the time Cox was fired, DeVan no longer wanted to be a politician.

After graduation DeVan took a job at the public defender's office, and wrote briefs for Elmer Giuliani on the side. Giuliani was a legendary defense lawyer who represented some of Cleveland's most notorious mobsters, men like Danny Greene, who was later assassinated outside his dentist's office (car bomb, so it goes). Later, DeVan left the public defender's office and Elmer took young DeVan under his wing. Together they worked many of the organized-crime cases as the Irish went to war with the Italians, and capos died by car bombs every other week. The 1980s saw the downfall of La Cosa Nostra in Cleveland and their leaders were replaced with politicians.

By 1990, the biggest goons were in prison and DeVan was thinking of moving and starting over in a new city. He'd served on numerous bar committees and had successfully defended several high-profile cases, but Cleveland was awash with legal talent and the competition was fierce. Truth be told, DeVan was burned out. Perhaps a new locale would inspire him. It was nearly a done deal. And then he got the call.

It was Charlie Clarke, a senior partner at Squire, Sanders & Dempsey. "I have a matter you might be interested in," said Clarke. It seemed that another lawyer in his office was in need of a defense attorney to represent his son. Clarke didn't mention a charge, except to say the story had been in the news.

"I'm dressed casual," DeVan said. "Is that all right?" He'd come in late that day, in just a sport coat and shirt, no suit—typically, a major faux pas when meeting a new client.

"Don't worry, just come over."

So DeVan hurried over to the Squire, Sanders & Dempsey office, and there, waiting in a side room, was a well-dressed young man. Kevin Young looked nervous. As he should have. They talked. And by the end of the conversation, DeVan came to believe that Kevin was innocent, and that disturbed him greatly. He believed that when you represent a defendant who you know is innocent and lose, it leaves a scar on your soul for the rest of your life.

By the time DeVan left the Squire, Sanders & Dempsey office, he had a new client and Kevin had a lawyer. And DeVan never did leave Cleveland.

Chapter Twenty

BIG FISH

THAT FRIDAY, AFTER KEVIN YOUNG had lawyered up and there was little hope for further interrogations, Police Chief Walter Ugrinic held a press conference. He told the gathered members of Cleveland media that there was no cause for alarm in Shaker Heights. They knew who had killed Lisa Pruett and they planned to file charges in a matter of days. Justice would be done. Until that time the killer was being kept away from the town's vulnerable young women. "We have identified a suspect who is presently under a doctor's care," the Shaker Heights chief of police said.

At the same time as the press conference, Dan Dreifort was invited to attend a separate, private meeting with police. They explained to Dan all the reasons why they believed Kevin had killed his girlfriend. Dan was no longer a suspect.

The next day the headline POLICE SAY ARREST NEAR IN SLAYING appeared in the *Plain Dealer*. And while the suspect's name was not published, everyone in Shaker Heights knew that they were talking about Kevin Young. And that's what the detectives wanted. That press conference was what journalists term a fishing expedition. Now that they were so close to an arrest, the police hoped someone who had more information about their prime suspect would contact them. They didn't have to wait long.

On that very day sixteen-year-old Judy Miller walked into the Shaker Heights police station. For a time she had been one of Kevin's closest friends.

Kevin used to visit with Judy at her house after school. She recalled one day that Kevin talked to her about Dan and Becca Boatright. "I guess that Dan and Becca had been fooling around," Judy told the detective. "From what Kevin told me, Kevin and Becca had been fooling around, too. Kevin said he and Dan had talked about it and they'd both decided to end it with Becca." That was the real reason that Kevin had not taken Becca to the prom last year, she said. He had believed that Becca was cheating with Dan, behind Lisa's back.

The Friday after Lisa was murdered, Judy saw Kevin walking down the street. She was in a car with friends, but they stopped to talk to him. Judy asked Kevin if he'd heard that Dan was being questioned. "Kevin got really angry and yelled at me. He said, 'Dan didn't do it. Why is everyone saying Dan did it?' And he got really upset about it. He was acting weird," she told the detective. "It wasn't normal. When I saw him, he was really disheveled, his shirt untucked. He didn't act like himself. He didn't act like it never happened, but he wasn't sensitive about it, either."

"Are you afraid?" the detective asked her.

"Yes," said Judy. "I'm afraid, but I know that I really shouldn't be. I'm sure that it's Kevin and he's somewhere where he can't hurt me, but I never thought until now that he could do anything like this. I don't really know who to trust anymore."

The detective asked Judy if she knew anything more about Kevin and his interactions with other girls.

"He always managed to make things cheaper than it really was," she said. "And most girls resented that. That's the way he always talked about past relationships. It was purely sexual, even if there was emotion involved. A lot of girls were really intimidated by him, and I think he's not really mature enough to handle a relationship with anybody."

Judy had come to the station with her boyfriend, Jeffrey Stear. Shaker Heights will always be a small world. And so it was no big surprise to the detective that Jeffrey had been Lisa's boyfriend before she'd gotten together with Dan.

"When I first heard that Lisa was murdered," said Jeff, "I really thought Dan would be the prime suspect, but I know that Dan couldn't do that to Lisa. He loved her too much and wouldn't be capable of doing it. But when I heard that Kevin Young was a suspect, I started thinking that it was possible, because Kevin was always unpredictable and a crazy sort of guy. You never knew what he was going to do."

Jeff told the detective that Kevin was jealous of Dan and that he thought Lisa hated him.

"Can you think of anyone else that Kevin threatened?"

"He was upset with Kathryn Schulz," said Jeff. "He thought that she spread around that he was going to ask a girl to the prom and he thought this turned the girl off to him. I discussed this with Kathryn and she attests that she never told anyone about Kevin and this girl. But thinking about it now, I realized that the weekend Lisa was murdered, Kathryn's front door was broken in the middle of the night, and that there may be some connection."

The detective made no note about this statement in his report, and maybe he didn't make the connection, but that made two girls whose doors were slashed in the days surrounding the murder: Kathryn and also Kim Rathbone, who lived behind the Dreifort house. Was there a connection or were they separate crimes?

"Is there anything else you would like to add to this statement?"

Jeff thought for a moment. "I had this letter from Lisa asking me to describe what really happened on the Unitarian rafting trip last summer," said Jeff. "She had heard rumors that Dan and this girl,

Lehna, had had an encounter, and she wanted to know what really happened. Dan had told her his side of the story, but she was asking me what really happened, because she thought that Dan may be lying to her. She wanted to remain naïve and trusting, but she couldn't if people lied to her. So I told her that on the rafting trip, Dan and Lehna did have a fling, and that despite what Dan said, it was premeditated on Dan's part. I'm not sure what came out of this. I don't know what Lisa told Dan. I also know that people were saying that Dan was leading Lisa on and that he didn't really like her."

THAT FRIDAY WAS a big day for the Shaker Heights police. They had successfully assured their residents that the Lisa Pruett case was solved and now it looked like the old Porter murders were about to be closed, too.

A man named Donny Soke (pronounced Sokie) arrived in their municipal jail after being transferred up from Lucasville, Ohio's maximum-security prison. Soke was a twenty-two-year-old punk with a rap sheet longer than Van Aken Boulevard. He was serving a life sentence for the murder of Karen LaSpina, a stay-at-home mom who had been stabbed to death in her Eastlake home, in 1985. He'd told police that he had information about the stabbing murders of Philip and Dorothy Porter that he wanted to share in exchange for better accommodations. Mayor Alfred confirmed to reporters that Soke was being questioned in the Porter homicides, which appeared to have been a burglary gone wrong.

But Mayor Alfred's luck was short-lived. On the following evening his business connections to Tal Young, Kevin's father, were made public in a special report by Carl Monday, an on-air investigative reporter at Channel 8. For those not from Northeast Ohio, Carl Monday is a goddamn legend, our very own Keith Morrison. Monday embraced the trope of the legendary gumshoe reporter—he wore the fedora and trench coat, with a magnificent mustache—and never treated himself too seriously. He was such an icon in the region, he lost his anonymity, and when he'd show up to shame some guy skimming money in an auto parts yard, the perp would take one look at him and run away, screaming, "Stay away from me, Carl Monday!" Anyway, Monday knew how to get attention.

In his Saturday night report, Monday talked about how Mayor Alfred and Tal Young worked together at Squire, Sanders & Dempsey, the implication being that the main suspect in Lisa's murder was getting preferential treatment from his dad's friend—the mayor. In order to report on this, Monday had to make Kevin's name public. He was the first in Cleveland to do so. And at that moment Kevin lost his anonymity, forever.

ON OCTOBER 4, Kevin and DeVan met Sergeant Gray at the police department in Willoughby, neutral ground in nearby Lake County. Gray obtained Kevin's fingerprints and a nurse took samples of his blood—type O—as well as some samples of his hair. Then the physical evidence was taken back to Shaker Heights.

Later that same week, in response to additional news reports, Shaker Heights police officially acknowledged that Kevin Young was their lead suspect in Lisa's murder. Now all they needed was an indictment.

On Friday, October 19, Detectives Ward and Reed traveled to the Justice Center, downtown, where they met with Jack Hudson, a Cuyahoga County prosecutor. They brought with them a typed warrant for yet another search of the Young residence. Hudson arranged for the detectives to meet with Judge Patricia Cleary right away. The cops explained the situation to the judge in her chambers and she signed off on it.

Detective Reed took the warrant back to the station, then immediately left for the Young residence, with Detective Gray. Kevin's mother, Maryanne, answered the door. The detectives introduced themselves.

"We have a warrant to search the premises," they told her.

They were looking for the murder weapon, a knife that the coroner told them would have a blade length between 2½ and 2¾ inches. They were also looking for shoes with herringbone-pattern soles, to match to the bloody print at the scene, as well as items belonging to Lisa Pruett—specifically, her pink wallet, which was missing.

"Come in," she replied.

The detectives stepped inside.

"I'd like to call my attorney, if that's okay," Maryanne said.

They waited patiently while she dialed the number. When she connected, she explained the situation as well as she could.

"Who signed the warrant?" she asked the detectives.

"Judge Cleary."

She listened for a moment, then hung up.

"Thank you," she said. "My attorney said I should make sure to get an inventory of items."

They showed her the form she needed to fill out. "You're welcome to follow us around," said Detective Reed.

As they walked through the house, Maryanne wrote down each of the detectives' names. Her daughter, Maureen, followed close behind.

The detectives photographed every room. In a first-floor office they found a Macintosh SE computer and lots of floppy disks. They confiscated these to review at the station. From Kevin's room they took an Adidas sweatshirt that had some promising stains on it. But no weapon was found.

As they were finishing up, Tal Young returned home. They gave him a copy of the warrant. "I'd like to ask that you return the computer as quickly as possible," said Tal. "I have business records on it."

"We'll get it back to you," they assured him.

At the police station Officer Herr plugged in Tal Young's computer. Once it booted up, he discovered that Tal had created a spreadsheet to keep track of the names and events related to the investigation of his son. They found nothing incriminating.

Chapter Twenty-One

SHOE LEATHER

IT WAS CLEAR TO KEVIN'S lawyer that Shaker Heights police detectives had made up their minds about the Lisa Pruett homicide. They were no longer actively investigating other suspects. They believed they had identified their killer, and they were diligently building their case against him. The only way for Mark DeVan to assure that Kevin was never arrested was to find out who really did kill Lisa before a grand jury could issue an indictment.

So DeVan began his own investigation. He hired one of the best private investigators in town, Terence Sheridan. Sheridan was a wild card of a man, who dressed like a Manhattan dandy, but talked like a steelworker. Terry Sheridan had worked as a reporter at the *Plain Dealer* back in the 1960s, when the *click-clack* of typewriters and the smoke of a hundred thin cigarettes filled the newsroom. His editor was the legendary Philip Porter, who had been stabbed to death in Shaker Heights some years later, in 1985. Sheridan recalled riding an elevator with Philip Porter one day and cringing at his editor's taste in music. Philip asked him what he thought of the weird names the new bands were using: The Animals, Lovin' Spoonful.

"I like it," Sheridan said. "What do you like?"

To which, Philip replied, "I think 'Four Freshmen' has dash."

Sheridan was a character from a time before the age of political correctness. He was prone to direct questions and double entendres. His idea of breaking the ice with one of the young women just hired by the paper was to roll up to her desk and ask her if she was a virgin. He wrote the cover story (with that forgiving woman's help) for the very first edition of *Cleveland Magazine,* which hit stands in April 1972.

Later, Sheridan recalled with fondness the long hours and thankless copy he'd written for Porter, in his essay for the book *Plain Dealing.* He was assigned to the crime beat at the time. "This was the place for me," wrote Sheridan. "Good guys and bad guys, though you sometimes needed a program to tell them apart."

Sheridan was still interested in crime when DeVan tracked him down. But now he helped to solve them instead of just writing about them, conducting investigations for lawyers. The first person he interviewed for DeVan was a boy named Andrew Katona, a friend of Debbie Dreifort's, who thought they should know about her father's straight-edge razor collection. It bothered him. Why would someone display hundreds of razors, let alone collect them?

SHERIDAN REACHED OUT to Alita Hall, the woman who lived in the house across the street from the Dreifort family. Alita was worked up about the announcement the police had just made in the papers, about their suspect in the murders of Philip Porter and his wife. She didn't believe a word of it. She'd known the Porters—their home was just eight doors north of the Dreiforts' house.

"This guy they have talking to the police, this Donny Soke, he told the police he picked that house for two reasons. One, the bushes were real high, and second, there was mail piled up on the porch. It could not have been the Porters' porch they were talking about," she said. For one, the bushes at the Porters' place were not high. Also, the Porters had hosted a cocktail party the night before their murder. They wouldn't have left their mail sitting out on the porch when company was over. "I think the police, they brought this guy in and said you're going to be in jail, anyway, and if you admit this, we'll give you a nice cell." She asked Sheridan if he thought the murders of Philip and Dorothy Porter might be related to what happened to Lisa Pruett.

"No, I don't think so," said Sheridan.

As Sheridan continued to canvass the neighborhood, he discovered that the families who lived on Lee and Sedgewick had been the victims of a persistent burglar in the months leading up to Lisa's murder. Someone had used a knife to cut through the screen on a door at the Rathbones', just behind the Dreiforts' house. And directly across Sedgewick from the Rathbone mansion were the Mesters, whose alarm had gone off when someone had tried to get into their home just a week before the murder. The Mesters figured whoever had tried to get in that night had been the same person who'd shimmied up their gutters and opened up their skylight some weeks before.

Sheridan knew that the night Lisa was murdered, Hollie Bush had heard someone messing around with the rental car in her driveway shortly before the screams started. Could it possibly have been the same prowler?

Next, Sheridan interviewed the people who had worked at Arabica the night of the murder. The one thing the defense and the police agreed about was the fact that Arabica was an important piece of the puzzle. It was where Kevin had met with Tex and learned about Lisa's plan to sneak out of her house to visit Dan that night. Sheridan interviewed a young man named Stefan Ravello, who was one of the baristas on duty that day. Stefan remembered that night well. He remembered Kevin sitting with Tex. And there were two other people there at the same time: a young couple, David Branagan and Holly Robinson.

"David Branagan and Holly Robinson, you don't know how to get ahold of them?" Sheridan asked.

"I don't think I could."

"I'd very much like to talk to them," he said. "So if you find out how I can get ahold of them, I'd appreciate that telephone call. And don't forget my name if the time ever comes that I can do something for you."

"Okay."

But Stefan never did follow up with Sheridan. If he had, it's possible that all the bad things that are about to happen never would have.

BY THE END of October, DeVan was growing increasingly upset that Walter Ugrinic's detectives were telling some witnesses not to cooperate with his investigator, and the mutual animosity was reaching a crescendo. On October 26, the Shaker Heights chief of police sent a letter to Mark DeVan.

"In response to your request that I review with my detectives the 'proper admonition to witnesses,' I consider your request to be unwarranted and unnecessary," wrote Ugrinic. "My detectives are well aware of the proper admonition to witnesses.

"Your attempt to excuse the ineptness of your investigation by asserting that my detectives are enfeebling his work is invidious.

"Several witnesses in this case have told my detectives that your investigator, Terry Sheridan, has subtly implied that he is an official from the Shaker Heights Police Department. I suggest you counsel Mr. Sheridan on the implications of his tactics."

Slowly Lisa's murder began to grow cold.

Chapter Twenty-Two

GODS DON'T LIKE TO BE IGNORED

By the summer of 1991, as the Soviet Union broke apart, piece by piece, on the evening news, a new cold war was being waged in Shaker Heights. On one side the detectives (led by Gray and Mullaney) searched for a way to build a case against Kevin Young. On the other side Kevin's defense team worked night and day to keep that from ever happening. Their battlefield was the pages of the *Plain Dealer,* where each side launched pithy rejoinders aimed at the enemy in an effort to weaken their spirit. It was a stalemate, with no resolution in sight.

Detective Gray believed that Kevin had come close to confessing during his marathon interrogation the year before, and he was anxious to try again. But if he was going to come at Kevin, hard, he needed to make sure he got the confession this time.

That's why, on June 11, 1991, Deputy Chief Brosius got on the phone with Dr. Murray Miron, a psycholinguist from Syracuse University. Dr. Miron believed that he could predict future behavior based on a subject's choice of words during questioning. He had already consulted with the FBI on some of the most high-profile cases of the twentieth century, including the Patty Hearst kidnapping and the Son of Sam serial killer. He coauthored a seminal paper on the use of psycholinguistics in criminal investigations, with famed FBI profiler John Douglas, titled *Threat Analysis: The Psycholinguistic Approach.*

During the standoff between the FBI and the Branch Davidians cult, which would occur two years later, Dr. Miron analyzed letters from the Davidians' leader, David Koresh. It was Dr. Miron's opinion that Koresh had no intention of surrendering peacefully. The Feds believed him. On April 19, 1993, the FBI engaged the Branch Davidians, launching tear gas into their compound. Fire erupted inside, and by the time it was all over, seventy-six people had died, including twenty-five children.

Shaker Heights police wanted Dr. Miron to analyze Kevin Young's writings and the statements he made to Detective Gray during his interrogation and to tell them two things: One, would Kevin kill again? Two, how could they get him to confess?

"Lisa and the affection that Kevin seeks may have very well have become the surrogate for [his] mother," Dr. Miron explained to Brosius. "It's anger that's producing his depression. The ideologies of depressions . . . one of them is anger, and these are barely controllable impulses that leave the person in the state of depressed ideation. If he can't be good, he can be bad. And so he pulls out every kind of negative image he can think of—Nazism, anti-Semitism, racism, everything he can think of that will find disfavor among others. He's a bright fellow. He's able to manipulate the feelings of others. I think Kevin was manipulating the interviewer, extending, spinning out this interview far longer than any reasonable person would have spun this thing out.

"You know, at some point the kid should have said, 'Hey, listen, I've answered all your questions. I can't go anymore. Stop this nonsense.'"

"We couldn't get him out of there," said Brosius, laughing. "He just wouldn't leave."

"So I think that he's vulnerable on that point," Miron continued. "I might have been tempted at some point to say to this kid, 'You fucking bore me. Just go away. I don't wanna sit here and masturbate. When we want you, we'll come fetch you.' And then let him stew in his own juices. Our problem now, of course, is he's represented by attorneys, but I think this guy will come back again. Is that your impression?"

"Yeah, I think so."

"So we just reinforce the dissociative reactions this guy has," the doctor said. "Let me explain what I mean by that. All of us have the capacity to isolate and compartmentalize thoughts or incidents or situations that are anxiety producing. In terms of all the adaption strategies, it is considered to be regressive, infantile, and destructive in form because, essentially, it's a denial of reality.

"Notice Kevin's diary continually explores this notion of the fantasy of reality . . . There is no real cause and effect . . . He believes that reality is a dream. He has this rich fantasy life and he is able to move between his fantasies and reality in a fashion that blurs the margins between them, and to compartmentalize acts that are alien to him. So every time he succeeds, every time he gets our attention, it achieves significance. And he leaves this, not having to pay for his sins. We have built another successive layer of scar tissue, a wall that protects this deep, scarred secret of his having done it."

Brosius asked Dr. Miron what they should do next.

"What we need to do is call him up," said Dr. Miron. "See if we can arrange an appointment, then fail to make the appointment." Dr. Miron laughed as he imagined the scenario playing out. "Uh-oh! You just got busy. Or, we'll reschedule another time. Do that a couple times. Don't show up. Have him come and sit there, just sit, and nobody pay any attention to him whatsoever. Now at some point the lawyer's going to get on to you and he's gonna figure out that you're harassing Kevin, but, you know, so what?"

At this point the chief of security at Syracuse University, who was listening in, spoke up. "Where are you with him now?" he asked Brosius.

"Well, we think he's probably going to be going back to Ohio State University," said Brosius. "Right now, we're hung up with zero physical evidence. We haven't been able to put this kid on the scene."

"Was he known to carry a knife?"

"No," said Brosius. "This kid was kind of part of the group, but outside of the group. He was never really accepted. Everybody thinks he's kind of weird. Well, we talked to the rest of the kids in this group. They're all weird. Even the girl's boyfriend was described by Jim Wright as sort of a paranoid schizophrenic, and he just got out of a mental institution the day of the murder..."

"The boyfriend did?" asked the security chief.

"Yeah."

"I think Kevin has trouble masturbating," said Dr. Miron, in one of this case's most absurd non sequiturs. "I think he's probably so guilt ridden with respect to any kind of sexuality. He's a prude... an absolute, dyed-in-the-wool prude, sexually extraordinarily naïve... and it would frighten him, what he calls public displays of affection. They arouse in him these erotic impulses that he just can't deal with. They cause him enormous anxieties."

"What are you going to do now?" the security chief asked.

"Well, we're just kind of waiting," said Brosius. "We're pretty much cut off by the lawyer. The family is very well off. The mother is from a blue-collar family and they moved into this wealthy area. She's very blue collar, from Indiana, but she was complaining to me that her kid didn't fit in here and that he had problems with these elitist kids, and she told me that she felt that she was blessed by God because she knows that her son was in the house the night of the killing, which there's no way she could have known. I mean she even slept through the search. There's no way. As a matter of fact, I didn't respond to any of her questions. She told me that one of the kids that talked on the TV station about the case was a queer and that he was saying bad things about her son because he wouldn't respond to his homosexual approaches. Kevin was identified as a suspect mainly by the kids in the neighborhood."

Brosius then told Dr. Miron about how Detective Gray had shown Kevin pictures of the crime scene during the interrogation at Ohio State.

"That was the scary part," said Brosius. "When he started describing what took place there."

"The initial officers seemed to think the boyfriend may have done it?" asked the security chief.

"Yeah, that was our first thought," said Brosius. "I mean, she was only thirty-some feet from his front door, and the boyfriend had just gotten out of a hospital. His father says he was there with him and they went outside together and, uh, I don't know. That family's screwed up, too."

Brosius steered the conversation back to Kevin. "I'm curious, what do you think is going to happen down at Ohio State?" he asked. "I don't know what he's planning on doing for attention next time around."

"Hard to predict," said Dr. Miron. "I've seen kids like this involved in nuclear bomb hoaxes. But murder? I'm reluctant to predict. The problem with this homicide is, it seems to me that it's an impulsive act. It would have produced enormous anxieties in an attempt to deny the act itself. I would think that another homicide is not a likely prospect. Understand, I've got a spread of one. You've given me no other suspects. I would appreciate if you send this other stuff about the boyfriend, anything you have. Please send that along, just for the sake of completeness. Until a better suspect drops out of the sky, I'd say Kevin is a logical suspect."

"I can tell you right now, the attorney for this kid is making a case on the boyfriend, Dreifort," said Brosius. "That's exactly what he's doing. He's saying this kid has got the same problems and he could have done it, and he's a more likely candidate, so we're doing just as much investigation on Dreifort as we did on Young. The parents could have fashioned this whole story about him coming and their hearing the screams and grabbing him and going outside and all this kind of stuff, but I don't know . . ."

If Brosius really thought that his department was looking into Dan Dreifort with the same intensity as Kevin Young, he really had no clue what was going on. After all, on the day they held the press conference targeting Kevin, his detectives had told Dan he wasn't a suspect anymore.

A couple weeks later, Dr. Miron followed up with Brosius after he'd had time to review the evidence against Dan Dreifort. "The father indicates that Dan was, in fact, in his room and that they both heard the screams together. Yes, that's very powerful," said Dr. Miron. "I must say that we had difficulty still with Dan's subsequent behavior. Apparently, Dan re-exits the house to find the bicycle and then, without telling the parents, uh, called 911 on his own to report what he believes to be now-suspicious circumstances, but then when the parents hear the Pruetts outside on the lawn, you know, they're distraught, and here are all these police vehicles and the crime scene being established, and Dan goes to bed."

"Right," said Brosius.

"I found that unusual and somewhat disconcerting," said Dr. Miron. "But what we decided here was that, well, that's academic, because it's not Dan that we're going to be interrogating, it's Kevin, and whether he is the guy or not, we want to use the best psychological coercion we can."

"Right," Brosius agreed.

"Here's what I was thinking. We need to shape up Kevin's behavior the same way you would try to shape a behavior in a laboratory mouse. You take a mouse, a rat . . . a laboratory rat, and you want him to, let's say, twirl around three times clockwise in a sort of ballet-like pirouette. So what you do to control it is you control the reinforcements. You don't need to punish, but you can withhold reinforcements. It takes an enormous amount of patience because you have to wait for this behavior to appear.

"We need to operant condition Kevin," said Dr. Miron. "'*Clockwork Orange*' on Kevin, if you've seen that film. And the way we do that is when he takes the Fifth, and he almost certainly will take the Fifth, you turn your back on him. You ignore him. In fact, even better, you should talk to someone else so that Kevin understands that there is a reward out there to be given, because Kevin loves attention. Gods expect people to worship them. It's their due. But if you ignore them, gods don't like that. Gods don't like to be ignored. So the next time he asks for water, you don't give it to him. We just need to manipulate the reinforcements."

Chapter Twenty-Three

PROPER PROTECTION

ON JULY 17, 1991, NOT long after the conference call with Dr. Miron, Cuyahoga County prosecutors invited members of the Cleveland media to the Shaker Heights police station for an official update on their investigation. The meeting was closed to anyone without proper press credentials. Reporters were escorted into a conference room, one by one. Mark DeVan was turned away at the door. Inside the conference room Police Chief Ugrinic, Shaker Heights prosecutor K. J. Montgomery, and Assistant County Prosecutor Carmen Marino were seated at a table.

Channel 5 reporter Bill Younkin remarked that the setup reminded him of the military briefings he'd attended in the Persian Gulf.

When everyone was situated, the investigators announced that they were no closer to charging someone with the murder than they were the day it happened. However, the FBI was still testing hair and blood taken from the scene and they were anxiously awaiting the results. The reporters were told that County Prosecutor Stephanie Tubbs Jones had recently reviewed the case and had decided not to bring it in front of a grand jury yet, as there was not a good chance of conviction at this time.

But that didn't mean that the police hadn't solved the case, Montgomery assured them. "We believe that we have focused on the correct suspect," she said, meaning Kevin Young. "Based upon the evidence to date, though, we believe that we have insufficient evidence at this time to seek a grand jury indictment."

"A source very close to the investigation says there is little doubt police are focusing on the right person," said Tom Sweeney, on Channel 3, later that night. "But rather than indict now on probable cause and face the possibility of losing a murder case, the investigators say they will wait and search for the physical evidence that will give them a case that is winnable."

DeVan was livid. The prosecutor knew they didn't have enough evidence to indict Kevin, so the politicians of Shaker Heights were convicting him in the court of public opinion. "We are considering civil action," DeVan warned the *Plain Dealer*. He said that the Shaker Heights officials were too embarrassed to admit they'd been chasing down the wrong leads. "They bungled this investigation from the beginning, and it's their own fault that the true killer has slipped away."

DEVAN AND SHERIDAN continued to run down leads as the Shaker Heights police made their case for Kevin Young in the press. One boy told them that Dan had threatened to give Lisa a coat hanger abortion if she ever got pregnant. A rumor circulated that several girls had attacked Lisa, stabbing her with their own knives, an ending fitting for Agatha Christie.

Tal Young told DeVan that he'd learned a criminal justice teacher at Shaker Heights had asked the students to discuss Lisa Pruett's murder in class. One of Lisa's close friends spoke about the odd activities of Detective Tom Gray. She said that Tom Gray had met with the teens shortly after the murder and was leading everyone to conclude that Kevin was guilty. Since then, Principal Jack Rumbaugh had removed two police officers from the high school after he discovered they had been peeping at kids through holes in a door.

One day, Sheridan uncovered a new lead from a young man named Jerry Eisenberg. Jerry claimed he'd been with Dan Dreifort the day of the murder, and had bought condoms for him in preparation for meeting Lisa that night. He recalled the specific brand—Trojan—which matched the brand of the single condom and wrapper the police had found in the Dreiforts' driveway. Jerry said Dan had given him the leftover change so he could buy some cigarettes.

Chapter Twenty-Four

WE LOST FEAGLER

On August 2, a common pleas judge unsealed a search warrant that had been served at Kevin's home early in the investigation. Carl Monday was on it, like ham on rye. It became his exposé for that night's news.

"According to the document, Young was seen near the murder scene just ninety minutes before Lisa's death," said Monday. "What's more, the affidavit says Young had threatened to harm Lisa. Several Shaker students had reportedly overheard Young say that he had a desire to kill Lisa and her boyfriend."

Anchor Leon Bibb said, "And in August of the same year, Kevin told fellow band members and acquaintances he was going to 'expletive' Daniel Dreifort and his slut, referring to the victim, Lisa Pruett."

Shaker Heights leaders had done the impossible; they'd found a way to get good press without having to actually solve their case. Everyone now knew who was guilty, even without a conviction. Only later did reporters discover they'd been played. Shaker Heights had quietly hired a pricey PR firm, Wyse-Landau, to help them win back community support regarding Lisa's unsolved murder.

Their media strategy was developed by Howard Landau, who outlined it in a memo to Rosemary Herpel, the city's press liaison.

Landau recommended that each public official who might be called by reporters have a copy of his prepared answers on hand.

"The same questions that the media will be asking are the questions that are on the minds of the community," he warned. "These questions are being asked at holiday parties all over Shaker this week and will continue until the case is resolved."

They should communicate directly to the social influencers of Shaker Heights, Landau wrote. And he pointed out how the recent resolution to the Porters' murders helped them immensely. He suggested that the mayor should write a letter to everyone in Shaker Heights, praising the police for their work on the Porter case, and include positive stats on community safety.

But there was still at least one journalist in town that nobody could spin.

In Northeast Ohio, Dick Feagler was a living relic, a curmudgeon of a journalist who'd made his name writing copy for the *Cleveland Press*, that famous daily newspaper built by Louis B. Seltzer. Feagler's column in the *Press* was some of the best culture writing in the country. He received offers from prestigious publications on the East Coast, but always turned them down, on advice from other reporters. Michael Roberts, a legendary journo in his own right, once told Feagler, "Why leave? You own the place."

Feagler understood Cleveland in a way few others ever could. He got down into the grit and grime to speak to the common man, and he did it with the same decency he showed to the city's grandest politicians. He once summed up Cleveland as "the one town in the universe where pain is unavoidable."

It likely came as a surprise to those fancy PR folks when Dick Feagler put Tal and Maryanne Young on TV. On August 4, Feagler's exclusive interview went out over the airwaves. Feagler was in rare form, full of his trademark gusto and hyperbole. He looked like a stern grandfather rearing up for a good strapping.

"The Youngs felt they had no choice but to publicly protest what they see as an injustice in the way their son has been treated by the Shaker authorities," said Feagler. "Tonight they answered some of the things that have been said about their son."

"He's never carried a knife," said Maryanne. "But it's easy for people, unidentified people, to say things like that."

Feagler asked about the lie detector tests. Had Maryanne taken one? Maryanne said she'd volunteered to sit for a polygraph, to prove she wasn't lying about Kevin's alibi, but the police were not interested.

At the end of the interview, Feagler told Kevin's father that he didn't know if his son was innocent or guilty. Tal said that was the real key to the matter.

"You're not supposed to know," Tal said. "You're not supposed to decide whether somebody is guilty of a horrible crime because of press conferences and stories in the media. These things are supposed to be decided in the courtroom."

Three days later, Feagler wrote a new column for the *Morning Journal.*

"I've never seen anything quite like it before," he wrote. "They convicted Kevin Young in a press conference. I guess they figured they wouldn't have to worry about whether he got a fair trial, since they have no plans to try him."

And then another embarrassing detail slipped out about how the police were using underhanded tactics to sway the court of public opinion. Detective Tom Kohanski, the same man who had given Kevin Young three lie detector tests, had visited the homes of forty "key communicators," presidents of neighborhood associations, and PTA members. Kohanski and Rosemary Herpel, the director of public affairs, had presented their case against Kevin directly to these professional gossips to make their truth spread faster, just like their PR firm had recommended. They told these citizens that Kevin had refused polygraph tests and was uncooperative with police, both lies.

Whatever goodwill the prosecutor and police had built with the media crumbled under Feagler's pen and the revelation of this latest bit of tomfoolery. Shaker Heights officials responded by going silent. They dropped the publicity campaign. And, for about a year, things in Shaker Heights settled down again.

Lisa's friends graduated high school and moved to colleges across the country. Kevin went searching for his own purpose, enrolling in classes at Case Western, closer to home. Dan Dreifort moved to Athens to attend OU, like his sister. DeVan took on other cases. Sheridan disappeared. It was rumored he'd gone to Bosnia to cover the war, or maybe to chase a lady.

And while nobody could ever really forget the murder of poor Lisa Pruett, people did begin to forget about the urgency they'd once had to solve it. The palpable fear that had covered Shaker Heights since 1990 lifted like a fog under the afternoon sun.

Then, in September 1992, Bill Younkin, the reporter from Channel 5 who'd once compared the tactics of the Shaker Heights PD to war zone press conferences, got one hell of a scoop: Kevin Young had confessed to a fellow patient while inside the psychiatric facility.

"The woman who asks that we protect her identity was a patient at Laurelwood Hospital, in November of 1990," said Younkin. "The woman says she could never forget a late-night talk she had with a young man, a nineteen-year-old at the time, who said he did it, but that his father, a well-known attorney, had him hospitalized to keep police away."

A woman was shown on-screen, obscured by shadow. "He said that he did it," she said.

Chapter Twenty-Five

NEW BLOOD

AROUND THIS TIME A NEW reporter began to cover Kevin's case for the *Plain Dealer.* His name was James McCarty. On the surface he seemed harmless. Most great journalists do. But his affable countenance belied an unrelenting nature. This was an old-school journalist, the type who'd sink his hooks into a story and not let go for dinner. He kept a notebook by his bed because he ran his articles through his mind at night, and sometimes he was inspired at 3 A.M. He couldn't stop thinking story. And he was a local boy, raised in Akron, a onetime groupie of the James Gang. As the old saying goes, he knew where all the bodies were buried.

At that time the *Plain Dealer* kept a small office at the Justice Center, staffed by a couple court reporters who were granted behind-the-scenes access to judges and prosecutors. That's where McCarty set up shop. Not long into the job, Carmen Marino called McCarty into his office. He had news for the rookie reporter: They were finally going to seek an indictment against Kevin Young.

In the October 6, 1992, edition of the *Plain Dealer*, McCarty revealed that there were now two witnesses from Laurelwood claiming that Kevin had confessed to them during his treatment.

"This is one of the benefits of waiting," Marino told McCarty. "When people see other witnesses coming forward, they become less intimidated. They feel they're not alone and it's not a forgotten matter. The facts are going to be presented that something is really wrong with this kid."

In his article McCarty referred to Kevin as "the son of a prominent Cleveland lawyer." That was a detail that had no bearing on the case at hand. But it sure told a story.

IN 1992, THANKSGIVING fell on November 26, and there was a rumor going around that Kevin's indictment would come before the long holiday weekend. Reporters from every TV station in Cleveland were hounding their best sources at the courthouse to get the scoop. While they waited, they searched for any new angle they could find.

Reporter Michael Drexler went to Arabica and interviewed Kevin's friends. A young man named Tim Calhoun said, "I suspend my judgment. And if he did it or didn't, he has still become my friend."

And then, on Tuesday, November 24, it happened. The indictment was issued. The charge: aggravated murder. The Shaker Heights cold war had ended; the age of assured mutual destruction had arrived. The Youngs retreated into the safety of their home. The Pruetts had no comment. But the media made up for that. In fact, for a while, it was all they wanted to talk about.

"Well, typically, indictments are short and to the point, and this one's no exception," reported Carl Monday, who then read from the document that had just become public record. "'Kevin Young purposefully caused the death of another: to wit: Lisa Lee Pruett.' Just after the indictment was rendered, we tried talking with Kevin Young's attorney, Mark DeVan."

On-screen Monday did his thing and chased after the defense attorney, microphone in hand. "Mark, we just got the word that Kevin has been indicted," he said. "Is there anything you'd like to say?"

"Not to you, there isn't," DeVan quipped.

"It was a day that would be like no other for the Young family," Paul Orlousky reported for Channel 3. "It began normally, the family cat was let out and returned at just about the time the indictment was issued, charging Kevin Young with murder..."

"The die is cast," said Lorna Barrett on Channel 5. "Kevin Young is now charged with the murder of sixteen-year-old Lisa Pruett."

"At last we're back in an arena with rules," Tal Young said to Dick Feagler, in another exclusive interview. The indictment came as a relief for Tal, who was a lawyer himself and had more faith in the judicial process than he did in any investigation by Shaker Heights.

The headline in the *Plain Dealer* the next day, above Jim McCarty's byline, was EX-CLASSMATE IS INDICTED IN PRUETT SLAYING. "A crime that had hung like a shroud over a community for more than two years produced a murder indictment yesterday against a former classmate of the victim, sixteen-year-old Lisa Lee Pruett of Shaker Heights.

"A Cuyahoga County grand jury charged Kevin M. Young, 20, with a single count of aggravated murder in the stabbing death of Lisa on September 14, 1990."

Kevin was arraigned in the Cuyahoga County Court of Common Pleas on December 2. He arrived at court in a navy blazer, carrying a copy of the book *The Game of Chess*. His bond was set at $50,000. Tal and Maryanne put their home up as collateral.

The death penalty was off the table, but if Kevin was found guilty, he would face life in prison.

"Kevin Young, the preppy house painter charged with stabbing to death a former high school classmate, pleaded not guilty to the crime yesterday and was released from jail," wrote McCarty.

The next day Maryanne found a strange letter in her mailbox:

> Dear Mr. and Mrs. Young,
>
> Instead of hiring a lawyer for Kevin, you should have done the decent thing and told him to kill himself. You've raised a monster. How can you live with yourselves?

It was signed, in an immature scrawl: *Shaker Neighbor.*

Part Two

TRIAL

Chapter Twenty-Six

TO SPEAK THE TRUTH

On March 11, 1992, Shaker Heights mayor Stephen Alfred announced that he would not seek reelection, citing "psychological, philosophical, and economic reasons." He'd been put in a no-win situation with the Lisa Pruett murder: One side looked at him with contempt, believing he'd called in favors for his law partner's son. Meanwhile, Kevin's team was forced to distance themselves from him at every opportunity for the optics of it all.

The trial was set for summer and DeVan made the most of the time left. He wondered, given all the media attention, if a fair trial was even possible. To find out, he hired a company to conduct a phone survey.

Their callers polled a random sample of 308 residents of Cuyahoga County. The questions started out innocently enough: "How many days in the last week did you watch the local news?" Then the callers would read this script: "'On September 14, 1990, sixteen-year-old Lisa Lee Pruett was found stabbed to death in the backyard of a Shaker Heights home. Over two years passed before anyone was charged with this murder.'" Then the caller would ask: "'The young man charged with Lisa Lee Pruett's murder was her classmate at Shaker Heights High School. The boy's father is also a prominent citizen in Cuyahoga County. Are you aware of the occupation of Kevin Young's father?'"

Then they would say, "'The state claims to have testimony from two mental patients that Kevin Young confessed to Lisa Pruett's murder while being treated at Laurelwood Hospital. Young insists he was home with his parents at the time of the murder. Which of these two accounts are you more inclined to believe?'"

And finally, "'Do you personally think Kevin Young, charged with aggravated murder, is definitely guilty, probably guilty, probably not guilty, or definitely not guilty of this offense?'"

The results were disturbing. Ninety-six percent of the people they'd polled believed that Kevin was guilty of killing Lisa Pruett. The Shaker Heights PD and county prosecutor had accomplished the unthinkable: They had tainted the jury pool before it could be called to service.

ON JUNE 20, the eve of the trial, the *Plain Dealer* checked in with both sides as they prepared for battle.

"There's no scientific evidence," Carmen Marino admitted. "But that's not unusual in circumstantial cases. If we get twelve decent jurors, we're going to get a conviction."

"What the state needs is not just a decent jury," DeVan countered, "but some decent evidence, which does not exist."

THE FIRST THING that happens during a murder trial is the process of voir dire, which, in its original French, translates roughly as "to speak the truth." This is where a pool of potential jury members is whittled down to twelve (with a couple alternates, in case another jury member is removed halfway through).

The prosecution and the defense both get to question the potential jury members, and each side picks a few to reject out of hand. For a murder trial, for instance, the prosecution might reject a person who has a relative serving time in prison, as they might have trouble sending someone else there. Or maybe there's a guy whose cousin was one of the detectives in the case.

The defense had their work cut out for them. Because of the polling they'd done, they knew that the majority of people seated likely knew about the case from the paper and already suspected that Kevin was guilty. A well-conducted voir dire was extremely important to securing a fair trial. The defense was looking for twelve "law and order" types, the kind of citizen who would be capable of condemning the state after they heard what the police had done to Kevin.

On the morning of June 21, 1993, a few dozen people, who otherwise would never have met, gathered inside the courtroom of Judge James J. Sweeney and waited for their turn to be questioned. Things started off weird. As everyone was being introduced, Kevin Young stood and addressed the potential jurors—not something that defendants usually do.

"Good morning, ladies and gentlemen," he said with a smile. He sure didn't look like a cold-blooded murderer. He looked like an Eagle Scout.

DeVan had hired an expert to advise him during jury selection, a man named Robert Hirschhorn. A Hirschhorn jury had recently acquitted William Kennedy Smith, the nephew of JFK, who'd been accused of rape, in Florida. On Hirschhorn's advice DeVan asked each potential juror to look into Kevin's eyes and pledge to judge him fairly. Two refused. They were dismissed.

Voir dire lasted four entire days. Toward the end DeVan asked the remaining potential jurors if they'd think poorly of Kevin if he refused to testify on his own behalf. One juror said, "The first person who came to mind for me was Jesus Christ. He was innocent and he didn't testify, either."

Hirschhorn passed DeVan a note. *Sit down,* it read.

Chapter Twenty-Seven

OPENINGS

On Monday, June 28, a jury consisting of ten men and two women, along with two alternates, arrived at the Justice Center, downtown. They were then driven to the scene of the crime, the corner of Lee and South Woodland, in Shaker Heights, and given a tour of the Dreifort property and the Bushes' backyard, where Lisa's body was found. "Observe this," the bailiff would say, pointing to a shrub or a patch of yard that everyone was supposed to remember. Kevin, dressed like he'd just come from the country club, watched quietly from afar with his legal team.

After lunch everyone returned to Judge Sweeney's courtroom, a large, square room with wood paneling and fuzzy, midcentury modern chairs. Sweeney was a strict, older fellow, a former prosecutor with years of trials behind him. Kevin sat with DeVan and his other lawyer, J. Michael Murray. DeVan had recently joined Berkman, Gordon, Murray & Palda as partner. The firm was founded by Bernard Berkman, a pioneer in constitutional rights; and before he'd passed, Berkman had told his partners that J. Michael Murray was just about the best lawyer he'd ever trained. Murray was a graduate of Notre Dame and the Cleveland-Marshall College of Law, where he'd placed second in his class. Every day during the trial, Murray could be seen scribbling in his notepad. He was prepping for closing arguments. Murray's mind was always on the closing.

Prosecutor Carmen Marino got up and gave his opening statement to the jury. Marino is an imposing man. Broad shoulders. Barrel-chested. Deep voice. He has a way of talking that makes you lean in. He's a storyteller, not far removed from that distant shared ancestor who spoke of dreams before a crackling fire. That area between the jury box and the judge was his stage, the only place he ever seemed to really fit.

"In a criminal case," Marino began, "the state has two serious issues to resolve with you. One is that a crime was committed, in this case aggravated murder, and we must prove that to you beyond a reasonable doubt. And, secondly, that the defendant committed that crime beyond a reasonable doubt.

"Numerous witnesses will testify to the facts, and these facts are designed to enable you to follow the sequence of events from Dan Dreifort getting out of the Clinic, making arrangements to see his girlfriend, the murder at the scene, and then the investigation into those people who could have been involved and how they narrow it down to the person who did, in fact, commit this crime. And we feel at the end of the state's case, that beyond a reasonable doubt, you will find that Kevin Young murdered Lisa Pruett."

When Marino had finished, DeVan stood. He had structured his opening based on something he termed "The Four C's," which stood for candor, contrast, clarity, and consistency. He believed that in order to write an argument that would convince a jury, a lawyer had to be open and honest, had to make it clear what the difference was between his story and the opposition's, and he should be clear and consistent with his message.

"Lisa Pruett is dead," he said. "She is the victim of a violent murder. We all feel her loss. The Young family and Kevin knew her, too. We mourned her loss, but we will save our sorrow for our private moments. We are here to challenge the state's claim that it can prove Kevin Young, in the middle of the night, murdered poor Lisa."

DeVan continued, "The evidence will show that Kevin Young has stood as strong as he could in the face of this investigation, being publicly targeted by the city of Shaker Heights. He and his family have withstood the tremendous pressures of a murder investigation and they have steadfastly denied Kevin's guilt.

"The evidence will show that the State of Ohio has brought the wrong person to trial. The defense does not have to prove anything, but we will. On behalf of Kevin Young, we will prove a case beyond a reasonable doubt of innocence. And I ask you, every time the defense raises a point of doubt, to make a mental note of that, because when it comes time to deliberate, you will be asked to total up those points of doubt and acquit Kevin.

"We believe that when this case comes to its end, you will agree with us that the State of Ohio has brought the wrong person into this courtroom and that the real killer of Lisa Pruett is still at large." There was no doubt that DeVan was talking about Dan Dreifort. And reporter Jim McCarty knew it.

The headline in the *Plain Dealer* the next morning read: DEFENSE AIMS TO PIN KILLING ON LISA PRUETT'S BOYFRIEND.

"The attack on Dreifort, a classic defense tactic, was not unexpected," wrote McCarty. "But how far it will carry the defense is a gamble because authorities cleared Dreifort of wrongdoing 2½ years ago. Dreifort and Young each plan to offer as alibi witnesses their parents who have said their sons were home with them when Lisa was killed."

A CLASSMATE OF Lisa Pruett's, a young man named Pete Mannen, contacted DeVan's office that day. He wanted the lawyer to know that the kids in the AP Posse had tried to gaslight him into believing Kevin was guilty. Mannen wanted him to know that Kevin was no killer.

He said it felt to him like the police were just looking for a scapegoat and the Shaker kids were only too eager to hand them one.

Chapter Twenty-Eight

THE BLACK GLOVE CULT

COURT RECONVENED ON JULY 1 and Chris Jones, one of Dan Dreifort's closest friends, took the stand. Assistant Prosecutor Karl Wetzel handled direct questioning for the prosecution, while Carmen Marino watched from his chair.

"Chris, how old are you?" asked Wetzel.

"I'm nineteen," said Chris.

"How did you know Lisa?"

"We went to the same high school. We became good friends sophomore year."

"How would you describe your relationship with Lisa?"

"We were very good friends," said Chris. "We talked to each other every day, shared everything together, I guess."

"Chris, do you also know Kevin Young?"

"Yes, I do."

"Do you see him in the courtroom today?"

"Yes, I do."

"For the record, would you please describe what he's wearing and point to him for the jury, please?"

Chris pointed to Kevin and said, "He's wearing a gray coat, dark pattern tie, white shirt."

"Chris, how did you come to know Kevin Young?"

"I met him at various parties. We had some friends in common."

"Do you remember September 13, that day of school?"

"Yes, I do."

"Do you have a recollection of seeing Dan Dreifort that day?"

"Yes. Lisa brought him to my tenth-period English class because he had just gotten home from the hospital and she knew I would want to see him."

"Was it your understanding that you would go to Dan Dreifort's that night?"

"Yes, it was."

"Had you called him?"

"Yes," said Chris. "He said that Tex was there and that Lisa would be stopping by later. I called him back at eleven-thirty and told him that I wouldn't be able to come over. I had to finish an English paper and it was late. I just wanted to go to sleep, basically."

"Did you, in fact, go over to Dan's that night?"

"No. I did not."

"Chris, on the day of the thirteenth, did you see Kevin Young at all?"

"Yes, I did. He was sitting on the high school grounds directly in front of his house. It was on my way to fencing practice. He asked me if I knew where Dan Dreifort was. I told him I thought that he'd gone over to the Rousch's house."

"Now, Chris, when did you become aware that Lisa Pruett had been murdered?"

"At six-thirty the next morning. Dan Messinger called me."

"When you heard the news, what was your reaction?"

"I didn't believe him. I thought he was joking or something. So I stopped talking to him. Then Kathryn Schulz called me and told me the same thing."

"Did you proceed to Kathryn Schulz's house?"

"Yes."

"Did there come a time, Chris, that you went to the Dreifort residence?"

"Yes, later in the afternoon."

"Who was with you?"

"Jennifer Margulies, Judy Miller, and Rachel Lowenthal." He explained that when they arrived, nobody was home, so they waited until Deb came back.

"Did you remain at the Dreifort home that night?"

"I spent the night there."

"Now, Chris, could you please describe Dan Dreifort's emotional state at that time?"

"I think he was in shock," said Chris. "He was pretty torn apart. He had just been, like, interrogated by the police, so he was extremely tired. I think we were all pretty numb. He seemed very crushed."

Wetzel asked Chris to explain a message they'd found among Lisa's things. It was a drawing of a black hand with a mouth full of sharp teeth in its palm. It was a flyer Dan and his friends had made for the Black Glove Cult, their gang of student fencers. There were some things written on the flyer that had caused alarm.

"Chris. 'Gynecologists of Death.' What is that acronym?"

"G.O.D."

"Why did you pick that?"

"It came from a Monty Python skit."

"There are teeth here on the gloves. It says, 'Beware. It bites. It leaves big hickies.' What's this in reference to?"

"Kathryn Schulz and Lisa had stolen Jeff Stear's glove because they thought our cult was silly," said Chris. "So I wrote, 'I bit this glove.' I bit the teeth on the glove in the picture to make the glove look dangerous so that Lisa would give the glove back to Jeff."

"So Lisa had taken Jeff's glove because she thought the cult was silly?"

"Yes."

"Chris, just for reference sake, did you have any thought about sacrificing a virgin?"

"No," said Chris. "I don't believe I ever had that thought, actually."

"Chris, showing you what's marked as State's Exhibit 15. If you can please look at the front of that envelope. Tell me if you recognize the words on that envelope."

"I do."

"Could you please read them slowly?"

"It says, 'I want to hit you with a really big stick. I want to poke your eyes out with my favorite pocketknife because your poison is running through my veins. I can't stand the sight of your brains. You're poison and you smell bad, too. I hate you.'"

"Where are those words from, Chris?"

"They're lyrics from a song that Dan Dreifort made up for his band."

WHEN WETZEL WAS done, DeVan handled the cross-examination for Kevin's defense.

"Mr. Jones," said DeVan, "you have referred here to this letter with the inscription 'Gynecologists of Death.' Now, the three people who were in that group were Dan Dreifort, you, and who else?"

"Jeffrey Stear."

"Jeff Stear, at one time, dated Lisa Pruett, correct?"

"Yes."

"Now, the three of you, in regard to this group, the Black Glove Cult, got together and talked over things that you were doing, correct?"

"Yes."

"Now, Dan was aware, was he not, that Lisa had taken one of the gloves, correct?"

"Yes," said Chris. "I think he was aware that Kathryn Schulz and Lisa Pruett took one of the gloves from Jeff Stear."

"And you talk about a virgin who must be sacrificed, yes?"

"Yes, that's also written on there."

"And you drew a knife, did you not, with blood dripping off of it?"

"Yes, I did."

"At the time you thought this was a joke, correct?"

"Yes, at the time it was a joke."

"In view of the way Lisa met her death, it's not such a joke anymore?"

"No. It's a bit macabre," said Chris.

"Almost pathetic," said DeVan.

"No. I would not say that, considering our culture, actually."

DeVan approached the young man. "Now, you've used Robo, haven't you?"

"I've used it once."

"And the effects of Robo on you were such that they made you have unrealistic thoughts?"

"The effects of Robitussin were sedative," said Chris. "Just similar to alcohol, in that things are blurred and you have trouble focusing on something or concentrating."

"How much Robo did you take when you had that effect?"

"I have no idea. Maybe half a bottle?"

"How about Dan Dreifort?" asked DeVan.

"I've never seen him take Robitussin, actually."

"So you don't know what kind of effect it would have on him, correct?"

"I would not have the knowledge, no."

"Now, sir, at the time that you talked with Dan in the evening, at around eight, it was clear, wasn't it, that he was trying to get together as many people as he could to come over to his house that evening?"

"No," said Chris. "I think it was more people he hadn't had a chance to see or talk to that much since he had been back."

"But he was talking about a number of people coming over, correct?"

"The only names I remember are Lisa and the fact that Tex was over there. I don't remember who else he would have invited."

"The impression you took from that conversation was that there was a firm plan that Lisa was sneaking out to come over, that she would come over?"

"Yes, that was the plan."

"In any event you decided not to go, correct?"

"Yes."

"Nothing further, Your Honor."

Judge Sweeney addressed the jury. "Ladies and gentlemen, I'm going to send you to lunch," he said. "Be downstairs at one-thirty. We'll get you up here as soon as we can. Remember, you are not to read, view, or listen to anything about this case. Do not discuss this case among yourselves or with anyone else. Do not permit anyone to discuss it with you or in your presence, and do not form or express any opinion on this case until it's finally submitted to you. We'll see you at one-thirty. Have a nice lunch."

AFTER LUNCH WETZEL called Daniel Messinger to the stand. Daniel painted a thorough picture of his friend for the jury. He talked about how affectionate Dan Dreifort and Lisa were when they were together. Then he told the story about how he'd been at Dan's the night before Dan was committed and how they'd stayed up past 3 A.M., shooting the shit in the Howling Commando Room. And how, after Dan was admitted into psychiatric care, he'd called him every day.

"One time we found out that Dan was going to be bowling with the people from the hospital," Daniel said. "So Lisa and I went and we asked to get the lane right next to him. We said it was our lucky lane and we sat down next to him, and Lisa and him got to talk. But we had to pretend we didn't know who he was."

Wetzel had Daniel walk the jury through the events of the day of the murder. He claimed to have had no knowledge of a party at Dan's that night.

"When was the next time that you became aware of anything involving Lisa Pruett?"

"Around five in the morning, the next day," he said. "My parents woke me up because we had received a call from my German teacher saying that she had been murdered."

"What did you do?"

"I sat on my bed for a few minutes, put on music, and I wrote in my journal."

Later, Chris Jones called and asked him for a ride to Kathryn Schulz's house. They met up with their friends there and discussed the murder. Then they went to Dan Dreifort's.

"Did you have an opportunity to observe his demeanor?" asked Wetzel.

"Yes. He . . . We were all very depressed. I mean, he was. I was. We all were. I mean, he was very shocked and very depressed, as we all were."

Wetzel then asked about the conversation Daniel had overheard at Arabica. "At that time you had a conversation with Kevin Young. What did Kevin relate to you regarding Lisa and Dan?"

"He said that he hated them and . . . First he said he hated them. I don't know why. He said he hated them and then he said he wanted to kill them."

WETZEL SAT AND then J. Michael Murray stood for cross-examination.

"Now, you've indicated that there was a time when Kevin made some statement to you at Arabica," said Murray. "And your testimony was that it occurred in the afternoon, I believe, correct?"

"I don't really recall when it was. I wasn't totally sure."

"And it was outside, correct?"

"I believe it was outside. We had been walking somewhere."

"With Kevin?"

"Yeah, I think it was with him. I mean, at some point I saw him."

"Today, as you sit here, you are certain that Kevin said that to you, is that your testimony?"

"Uh-huh."

"Two years ago you were not sure of that, however, were you?" said Murray.

"I believe I was," Daniel replied.

"Isn't it a fact, sir, that on September 18, you gave a lengthy statement to the Shaker Heights police?"

"Yes."

"And among other things you answered to the best of your ability, and as truthfully as you could, all of the questions that they asked you, correct?"

"Uh-huh."

Murray read from Daniel Messinger's official statement. "'I had heard either from Kevin Young or someone else that he, Kevin Young, had liked Lisa and that he hated both Dan and Lisa and that he wished that he could kill them both.' Isn't that what you told the police that night?"

"You see, the thing is . . ."

"Excuse me, Your Honor," said Murray.

"Wait," said Daniel. "Can I show you something, sir? You see, because at the time I also—"

"Here. Hold it, Mr. Messinger," said Judge Sweeney, cutting him off. "If you can answer the question."

"What was your question?" asked Daniel.

"My question is, did you not say to the police that night what I just said?"

"Yes, I did."

"That you had heard it from Kevin or from someone else? And that this statement is a statement that you were given an opportunity to read in its entirety?"

"Yes."

"Okay," said Murray. "And so, isn't it true that in September of 1990, over two years ago, at a time when your recollection was much fresher, you didn't know for sure whether you actually had personal knowledge that Kevin Young said those things or whether you were just reciting hearsay. Isn't that so?"

"That was what I said at the time."

"Now, you mentioned the group of high-school students that you hung around with was called the AP Posse?"

"Yes."

"And that was a certain clique, for lack of a better term?"

"You can call it that."

"And it's true, is it not, that after the killing of Lisa, that clique pretty much hung around twenty-four hours a day?"

"We were together a lot."

"You were together quite a bit," said Murray. "As a matter of fact, you had sleepovers."

"Yes," said Daniel.

"And that would include Dan Dreifort, correct?"

"Uh-huh."

"This clique, the AP Posse, was hanging out together on the fourteenth, the fifteenth, the sixteenth, probably even into the seventeenth."

"We hung out with each other quite a bit. I mean, I remember the couple nights afterward. We were always together."

"You consoled each other?"

"Yeah."

"And this group is close in the sense that you would try to make sure that each one of you could depend on the other, correct?" said Murray.

"We were good friends" was Daniel's answer.

"Dan Dreifort, for example, can certainly count on you to be a friend that would come to his aid if he were in trouble, correct?"

"Uh-huh."

"He's someone who could count on you to try to protect him from danger if you were in a position to do so, correct?"

"Yeah."

Murray moved on. "Isn't it a fact that Lisa and Dan broke up once?" he asked.

"They broke up right after the band went to Germany."

"Were you aware of any relationship that Dan Dreifort had with Becca Boatright (the girl Kevin was planning to take to prom) during that period of time?"

"Objection!" said Marino.

"Overruled," said Judge Sweeney.

"Not that I recall right now," said Daniel. "I think they might have, but I really don't recall."

"AP POSSE TESTIFIES in Pruett slaying," wrote McCarty, summarizing what had happened in court for the half-million *Plain Dealer* readers through the lens of his two subjective eyes. "They called themselves the AP Posse, an exclusive, loose-knit club of a dozen or so smart, rich kids from Shaker Heights High School who labored through advanced-placement classes together.

"By the time the reunited posse had finished talking, Dreifort's wounded reputation appeared to have been healed."

Chapter Twenty-Nine

I STAND CORRECTED

THE NEXT MORNING, A FRIDAY, Assistant Prosecutor Wetzel stood and said to the court, "The State of Ohio would call Dan Dreifort to the witness stand."

Dan walked around to the seat beside the judge and swore on the Bible that he wouldn't lie. Then Wetzel got some small talk out of the way: Dan was nineteen, a student enrolled at Ohio University. He currently worked as a handyman for the school.

"Do you have any other employment?"

"Yes," said Dan. "I teach Sunday school at the Unitarian Fellowship. I also babysit, give guitar lessons, and I have a band that I make a little money with, every once in a while."

"You're a graduate of Shaker Heights High School, is that correct?"

"No, I'm not," he said. "I didn't graduate from high school."

"Dan, when did you first meet Lisa Pruett?"

"I met Lisa in the seventh grade."

"When you had met Lisa, did you develop a friendship with her at that time?"

"Yeah. I was her friend throughout middle school."

"Did there come a time that your friendship changed?"

"Yeah," he said. "We went on a trip with the marching band to Germany in the tenth grade."

"You and Lisa continued this relationship up until a point in July, is that correct?"

"This is correct."

"In July, does something occur where you and Lisa break up?"

"Yes."

"Who initiated the breakup?" asked Wetzel.

"I did."

"For what reason did you initiate the breakup?"

"Well, I was under the impression that I was no good for her, or hurting her in some way, simply because I led somewhat of a more wild life, being in a rock-and-roll band and whatnot."

"It's been suggested in this courtroom that either that breakup, or during the time that you were dating Lisa Pruett, that you had sexual relations with Becca Boatright. Is that, in fact, true?"

"No," he said. "I was never intimate with Becca."

"Prior to you dating Lisa, what was your relationship with Becca Boatright?"

"Becca and I partied a lot and we were known to kiss every once in a while, but this was just in the partying sense, whatever that means."

"But during the time you were with Lisa, what has been suggested is that you were with Becca, is that incorrect?"

"Right. That's incorrect."

"You and Lisa get back together after this two-day stint?"

"Correct."

"When did the relationship end?"

"Our relationship ended with her death," said Dan.

"During the time of your relationship with Lisa, from March through September 13, 1990, excluding the two days of the breakup, how would you describe your relationship with Lisa?"

"Perfect."

"How did you come to know Kevin Young?"

"Through band, or possibly through my sister. I don't recall. Kevin is two grades ahead of me."

"Did you and Kevin Young develop any type of relationship?"

"Yeah, we became fairly close friends."

"Did there come a time that this relationship begins to diminish or start to end?"

"Yes."

"When is that, Dan?"

"I believe it was sometime around when he threatened to kill me."

"What are the circumstances in which Kevin makes this threat?" asked Wetzel. "Where does it take place?"

"I couldn't tell you."

"Do you remember exactly what Kevin says to you?"

"No. I do not."

"What do you do in response to the threat?"

"I called his father," said Dan. "His father reassured me that everything was okay and said that he'd take care of it."

"When this threat is made by Kevin, are you at that time dating Lisa?"

"I'm not sure," said Dan.

"When do you enter the Cleveland Clinic?"

"Probably August 10, 1990."

"When you enter the Cleveland Clinic, at whose impetus was it that you go in?"

"My parents."

"What's the reason you went to the Cleveland Clinic?" asked Wetzel.

"I wasn't going to bed when my parents told me to," said Dan. "And I wasn't paying attention to them, basically."

"It was suggested that it was part of a chemical dependency problem. Is that, in fact, true?"

"No."

"What was the diagnosis at the time of your release?"

"Adolescent adjustment, something or other," said Dan. "I had trouble getting along with my parents."

"How long were you in the Cleveland Clinic?"

"Thirty-three days."

"Dan, digressing a moment. You mentioned your father. Prior to you entering the Cleveland Clinic, it's a fair statement you and your father did not get along well?"

"Right."

"There were many disagreements between you and your father, many shouting matches and so on. Is that a fair statement?"

"Yes."

Wetzel then asked Dan if Becca Boatright came to his house the night of the murder.

"No, she didn't."

"Do you know whether she was coming over or not?"

"I knew that she was not coming. She said she was tired and wanted to go to sleep."

"Did there come a time that you are aware that Chris Jones was not coming to your home?"

"Yes. I believe sometime around ten maybe. He said he had to do some homework."

"So both Becca and Chris declined for various reasons?"

"Correct."

"What else are you doing, besides having dinner and calling people?"

"Well, a little later, my parents went out. At which time I called up Kim Rathbone and asked her to come over and cut my hair."

"Do you know how long Kim was over at your home?"

"About half an hour."

"When Tex came over at eight o'clock, do you have a conversation with him at that time?"

"Yes. We were talking outside under the awning."

Dan explained how he gave Tex some money to buy a pack of smokes that they could share. So Tex borrowed his bike and pedaled to Shaker Square. While he was gone, Dan talked to Lisa on the phone, and she said that if she was coming over, it would be between 12:30 and 1 A.M.

"Do you know what time Tex returns?"

"Ten-thirty, eleven. No. Later than eleven. He came up to the back door, gave me the cigarettes. I don't remember his reasoning, but he wanted to go home rather than stay over. I had invited him to spend the night." If the jury was counting, that made three people who had said they were going to hang out at Dan's the night of the murder, only to cancel later.

And now, at last, they had come to the murder itself.

"Sometime around twelve-thirty, I heard screaming," said Dan.

"Are the screams . . . Is it a scream? Screams? How would you depict it?"

"Many screams, lasting maybe fifteen seconds. As I was going to my window, my father called to me, 'Did you hear that?'"

"Do you respond?"

"I said yes. I believe I opened the window. There was a screen in the window. I looked around, still heard the screaming as I was opening the window. Then my father said, do you have your shoes on, or are you dressed, or maybe he saw that I was dressed. I remember him saying, 'Oh, good, you're dressed,' at which time we agreed that we should go down and see what happened."

Dan said his father was right behind him as he ran down the stairs. He walked out the front door, to Lee Road, and looked both ways, but didn't see anything out of the ordinary. Then, Dan said, his father went to bed, and he returned to his room and continued to unpack. About fifteen minutes passed before he started to wonder if the scream might have been Lisa. He decided to go back outside, without his father, to check again. This time he slipped out the back door so his parents couldn't hear him leave. He got to Lee

Road again and began walking toward South Woodland. That was when he found Lisa's bike, he said, propped against the bushes about twenty feet from his property line.

"I recognized it fairly quickly. I grabbed it with one hand to reassure myself that I recognized it."

"You're fairly certain at that time it's Lisa's bike?"

"Correct."

"What do you do?"

"I dropped it immediately, ran back inside to my house." Dan explained how he first called Lisa's house, but hung up without leaving a message before dialing 911. He walked the jury through his recollection of the conversation with the officer who came over and how, while everything was going on outside, he went back to bed.

"Why did you go to sleep?" Wetzel asked.

"Everything was a little too much for me to handle," said Dan.

After about two hours a police officer returned to his house and asked Dan to come to the station for an interview. It was during this interview that he was told Lisa was dead.

"What are your emotions at that time?"

"I blacked out for the most part," he said. "I remember someone putting a blanket around me."

WHEN WETZEL WAS finished, DeVan stood and walked around the table. For years DeVan had wanted to question this young man. Now it was finally happening, in front of so many people. And so much hinged on the answers he was about to give. During the course of the last few years, DeVan had developed his own theory about what had happened the night of Lisa's murder. He believed that Dan had planned a Robo party at his house to celebrate his release from the psychiatric ward, and had gotten high and lost control. Robitussin has the effect of making a person become extremely tired. That could explain why, when the police were processing the scene of his girlfriend's murder, he was compelled to go to sleep. But DeVan had never posed this theory directly to the boy. He was playing a hunch. And he was doing what lawyers are told to never do: He was asking questions he didn't know the answers to. If this didn't work, he risked losing the jury's confidence in the narrative he was building.

"Mr. Dreifort," said DeVan.

"Mr. DeVan," said Dan.

"You have admitted to taking Robo, correct?"

"Yes."

"And you said you had only taken it twice, correct?"

"Yes, that's correct."

DeVan asked Dan if it was true that he'd had Daniel Messinger sneak a bottle of Robitussin into his room in the psychiatric ward. Dan admitted it was.

"Obviously, Robo is not an accepted medication at the Clinic, unless it's prescribed by one of the doctors there," said DeVan.

"This is obvious," said Dan.

"Now, what's the recommended dosage on a package of Robitussin?"

"A tablespoon. A teaspoon. A couple."

"Would you agree it's probably two teaspoons?"

"Okay."

"Showing you what's been marked as Defendant's Exhibit X, sir. Do you recognize the contents of this bag?"

"Yes, I do," said Dan. "These are the twelve Robitussin bottles that were taken from my room."

"Would you look at the box and see what the recommended dosage is, please?"

"Two teaspoons, every six to eight hours."

"Now, you say that you've taken up to six ounces at a time?"

"I took six ounces once."

"Now, how many teaspoons are in an ounce, sir?"

"I couldn't tell you."

"Would you say it's twelve teaspoons in an ounce?"

"If you told me so."

"All right. Well, in six ounces then, you're dealing with . . . let's see. Seventy-two teaspoons, right?"

"I trust your math."

Dan shouldn't have trusted the math. There are actually six teaspoons in an ounce. Six times six is thirty-six, not seventy-two. However, that still meant that Dan had been taking eighteen times the recommended dose.

"You have described for us the effects of Robitussin. Isn't it true, sir, that you told Tex at one time about the effects of Robitussin?"

"Yes."

"And you told Tex that the effects of Robitussin were that you would go crazy, it would make you feel strong, correct?"

"It can," said Dan.

"And you also told him that one of the effects was that you were in a kind of trance?"

"You can put yourself or be put into a trance, just as when you are sober."

"You also told him it was like being in a hallway. Correct?"

"No."

"Do you deny that, sir?"

"I did tell him that, but not in that context," said Dan. "I told him that being in a trance is like being in a hallway."

"Go ahead," said Judge Sweeney. "You can explain."

"One time when I took Robitussin with Tex, I told him a story about a hallway, and he was walking down the hallway . . ."

"And you also said to him at that time that when you were under the effects of Robitussin and in this trance and were in a hallway, that you would kill anyone at the end of the hallway. You said that, didn't you?"

"No."

"Isn't it true, sir, you said that sometimes you just knock the person out of the hallway, correct?"

"I might have said that."

DeVan asked Dan to read from a letter that he'd written to Lisa while he was at the hospital, in which he discussed the effects that Robo had on him. Sometimes it felt like he was crossing into another world, he wrote.

"*Midworld,* correct?" said DeVan.

"That's a book by Alan Dean Foster," said Dan.

"And then *Glory Lane*?"

"Another book by Foster."

"Riverworld?"

"A book by Philip José Farmer."

"Those are things you were thinking of during your trip, trance, hallucination?"

"I prefer if you use the words 'Robitussin experience,'" said Dan.

"You saw yourself in a river world, a dorm, a cave, right?"

"I think these were just brainstorms of mine for things we could do to entertain people at a Robitussin party."

"You hoped to experience nudity there, didn't you?"

"No," said Dan. "That was in reference to a person in Virginia who tranced while he was drunk and all he could talk about was nude women."

"I see," said DeVan. "Now, among the things that are listed toward the bottom of that page, are things to do during this experience, and things to take with you, correct, sir?"

"Correct."

"Included in there is 'screw d,' correct?"

"Yeah."

"What did you mean by 'screw d'?"

"I have no clue."

"Across from that, you wrote, 'Lisa uncon,' right? What did you mean by that?"

"I have no clue."

"Now, what are these initials down here, 'S.I.' and . . ."

"S.I. is 'Summer Institute.' Summer Institute is the name of the ward where I was staying at the Cleveland Clinic."

"So this was written from the Clinic?"

"Not necessarily," said Dan. "It wasn't written from a cave and the word 'cave' is on there."

But DeVan knew that this letter—the one with "Lisa uncon" written on it—had been confiscated by police immediately after the murder, the day after Dan got out of the Clinic. So if it hadn't been written in the Clinic, it could only have been written on the very day of her murder.

"Well, how did you know what ward you were in if you weren't already in the Clinic?"

"This was either written in the Clinic or past the Clinic."

"Past the Clinic. The day you came home was the day Lisa died."

"So it was probably written in the Clinic," said Dan. "I guess it was written in the Clinic."

Here, DeVan asked the young man if he'd ever visited Shaker Square during his weekend passes from the hospital or even the day he got out. Dan was adamant that he had not. This was important to DeVan, but apparently Dan did not yet know why.

DeVan asked if Dan had been sexually active with Lisa. He said they'd had sex at least four times. But when DeVan asked where those encounters took place, the prosecutor called for a sidebar, and when they returned from the judge, DeVan dropped it.

"Isn't it true, sir, that in the presence of Jerry Eisenberg, on the day you got out of the Clinic, you went to a drugstore at Shaker Square and bought a two-pack of condoms?"

"No, that's not true," said Dan. "Not on that day."

If it wasn't Dan's condom that had been found in the Dreiforts' driveway that night, whose was it? DeVan left that alone for the moment.

"When you first heard that scream, you're telling us that it did not occur to you that it might be Lisa," asked DeVan.

"Correct."

"The girl you had not been close to physically for at least five weeks."

"Correct."

"When you went outside, it still did not occur to you that those screams might be related to Lisa?"

"Not in the slightest."

"Were you afraid to go outside?"

"No. My father and dog were at the door. I wasn't afraid at all."

"Did it occur to you that there might be danger out there?"

"No, it didn't."

DeVan asked Dan what led him to sneak back outside fifteen minutes later. "You went outside?"

"Yes," said Dan.

"You didn't call for Lisa?"

"No, I didn't."

"You found the bike, correct?"

"Correct."

"You're nearly certain it was her bike, correct?"

"Nearly certain."

"You didn't call out for Lisa, did you?"

"No, I didn't."

"Now, you grabbed the bike and took a closer look at it, correct?"

"I grabbed it with one hand."

"One hand. And you still didn't call out Lisa's name?"

"No, I did not."

"And then you ran inside. While running inside, did you call out Lisa's name?"

"No."

"And you would agree, sir, that the place over near the bushes, the residence behind the bushes on Lee Road where her body was found, is, in fact, a pretty good make-out spot?"

"No, sir," Dan countered. "I don't know what a pretty good make-out spot would be."

"Then after that, you went inside the house, you had some discussion with your father, and you were confused, so you went to sleep, correct?"

"I was confused, scared, worried, hurt, and bedazzled. I could use a lot of words," said Dan.

"So going to sleep was going to alleviate everything?"

"It was a way of escape."

"Escape from something that you knew about?"

"Escape from fears of what might have happened that I had no clue of."

Maybe it was that flippant answer, but this was when DeVan made his move.

"Mr. Dreifort, you testified that the Robo that was bought and was found in your room after the murder was all bought in one drugstore in Virginia?" Dan had told police that all the empty bottles found in his room had come from Virginia months prior to the murder, and that he hadn't used since he'd come home from the hospital.

"Correct."

"Would you please pull out the contents of that bag?"

Dan reached into the grocery bag and began to remove the empty cough syrup bottles. Suddenly he stopped short. "I stand corrected," he said.

"Now, Mr. Dreifort," DeVan continued, "amongst that collection of cough medicine is a variety of other brands of cough syrup besides Robitussin, correct?"

"Correct."

"Besides Robitussin, what kind of cough medicines were you taking? What's the brand?"

"Finast."

"Are you aware, sir, that Finast is a local food chain here in Northeast Ohio?"

"That's correct."

"Which means all those bottles did not come from Virginia."

"I stand corrected."

"And this is your collection of bottles you claim was consumed, correct, sir?"

"All these bottles were consumed."

"When you were in the hospital, you sent Lisa a list of things to do, including the purchase of Robitussin, correct, sir?"

"Yes."

It was a startling admission, that he'd asked Lisa to bring him Robitussin when he got out of the hospital. If, in fact, it was Lisa who had purchased the bottles at Finast, then she'd either given them to Dan at school, or she'd done it under her father's nose when she visited Dan's house before her flute practice . . . or she'd brought the bottles with her that night and Dan had interacted with her when she arrived.

"You were thinking about a Robitussin party when you got out of the hospital, right?" DeVan continued.

"That's incorrect."

"You were just going to do Robo with Lisa alone?"

"No. That's incorrect, too."

DeVan then established, based on the expiration dates on the bottles, that the cough syrup in the bag had to have been purchased very near the day of the murder. He came back around to the night of.

"You made a point of telling the officer that you had already touched the bicycle, correct?"

"Yes, I did."

"So it was on your mind at that point, sir, that your fingerprints might be on that bicycle right?"

"I was perfectly aware that it was evidence for whatever had happened and that it was important that I put my hand on it."

"It was evidence for whatever had happened," said DeVan, giving those words a moment before moving on. "Now, when you went into the police department that morning and began to be interrogated by the police, you went with your mother and father, correct?"

"Correct."

"You mentioned at that time that you had been talking with your sister, Debbie, until approximately twelve-thirty, correct?"

"Correct."

"You later found out based upon telephone records that you reviewed that this conversation ended at approximately twelve-nineteen in the morning."

"I believe it was twelve-eighteen."

"You made a point of telling them that you were talking with your sister until twelve-thirty. Correct?"

"Correct."

"Well, that's not true, is it?"

"No," said Dan. "It was a mistake on my part."

"Essentially, what you were trying to do, sir, was occupy your time until the hour of twelve-thirty, correct?"

"No, that's incorrect."

"Now, the second time you went out and you saw the bike, you touched the bike, you ran back inside without calling for Lisa, correct?"

"That's correct."

"For all you knew, Lisa might have been around the other side of your house, right? You didn't know, did you?"

"Well, no, I didn't know."

"Now, sir, when you were in the hospital, you had a considerable amount of anger pent up inside of you, didn't you?"

"Yes."

"And that anger, among other things, sir, was directed at your parents, correct?"

"Correct."

"Showing you what's been marked as Defendant's Exhibit L, sir. Do you recognize that particular letter?"

"Yes, I do."

"You sent it to Lisa as part of a longer letter, correct?"

"Yes, I did," said Dan.

"And you say, do you not, sir, 'I keep having these flashings of me choking my parents. I'll just lapse out and all of a sudden it's five minutes later.' You said that, didn't you?"

"Yes, I did. I wrote it."

"And what kind of reference did you make to your father?"

"I said my dad's an asshole."

"What else did you say?"

"He told me to shut my goddamn mouth or I'd pay for it."

"APPROACH THE BENCH for a second," said Judge Sweeney.

DeVan walked to the judge and had a short conversation. They were still being recorded by the stenographer, but the jury could not hear what they said.

"Your Honor," said DeVan, "these letters contain numerous threats by Dan to physically hurt his parents. He talks about punching his father in the mouth, hurting both his parents and enjoying it."

"So what?"

"He sent these to Lisa," said DeVan. "He sent these letters to Lisa and they express a pent-up rage in him. It's our theory that it boiled over at the time that he was released from the hospital."

"Okay," said Judge Sweeney.

"It shows he has a violent character and it's certainly relevant to the charges of this case because it shows this young man very well may have assaulted Lisa himself."

Judge Sweeney decided to release the jury so he and the attorneys could discuss the issue further. Once the jury left, the conversation continued.

"These letters show that he had a pent-up rage," DeVan continued. "He refers to nurses in the hospital. He says, 'I almost lost it today. I was so very close to clocking one of these amazon bitch nurses in the head.' In the next letter Dan refers to his mother.

Quote, 'My mom visited me today but she was being a real cunt so I kicked her out.' The next one he makes a reference at the bottom of it. 'I will hurt my parents severely. I will have fun hurting them. They have hurt me.' In the next one he says, quote, 'I keep having these flashes through my head. Allow me to tell you a few. In one scenario, they won't let me talk to you. I start breaking things, punching people. Then it phases out. Another is Friday my dad comes and informs me I'm not leaving. I ask to speak to him in my room. I punch him in the face, breaking his jaw and drawing blood. That's for putting me in here. I hit him again, break his lip and say, here's for keeping me here longer. I then open the door and say, Mr. Dreifort needs medical attention. He's hurt, bad. Ha, ha, ha, ha, ha, ha, ha.'"

"Do any of those letters have any reference to Lisa Pruett that is, in the least way, derogatory or threatening?" asked Judge Sweeney.

"No," said DeVan. "I cannot say that they do."

"I will tell you what," said Judge Sweeney. "Have copies made. Give them to the court reporter in case there's a decision adverse to you on appellate review. I see absolutely no relevance to these and I won't let them in."

DeVan wasn't done. "The state is being allowed to bring into evidence statements of our client to the effect that he was mad at the world."

"He's the offender," said Judge Sweeney.

"He's the *defendant*," DeVan corrected.

"I have made my ruling," the judge said. "You know, I've been wrong before. Maybe I'm wrong now. That's the ruling."

SWEENEY CALLED THE jury back and Dan's cross-examination continued.

"When you talked with the police, you gave a lengthy statement, did you not, sir?" asked DeVan.

"Yes, I did," said Dan.

"And nowhere in that statement did you mention any threats by Kevin Young directed at you, correct?"

"Correct."

"Mr. Dreifort, amongst the correspondence that you and Lisa exchanged, you wrote her a letter in which you describe your relationship with other girls?"

"Yes, I did."

"And it's true, is it not, sir, that in that letter you go into graphic description about your relationships with other girls?"

"Yes."

"And in that letter you say to Lisa, do you not, sir, that you wrote the letter to make her jealous and to hurt her, correct?"

"That's pretty much correct."

"Excuse me?" said DeVan.

"Correct," said Dan.

"What was the reason you wrote that letter?"

"Just to give her some background and to let her know . . . Oh, what's the word? That I was vulnerable," he said.

"To let her know the kind of guy you really are, right?"

"More or less."

LATER, OUTSIDE THE courtroom, a familiar face with a trademark mustache approached Kevin and DeVan. It was Carl Monday, the reporter who'd made Kevin famous.

"I want to say, I'm sorry," Monday said to Kevin.

But not every journalist in town had changed their minds about Kevin.

"Boyfriend confronts his words," wrote McCarty for the next edition of the *Plain Dealer.* "It was hard to figure out who was on trial yesterday for killing Lisa Pruett. The defendant, Kevin Young, meanwhile, was almost an afterthought to the day's events, silently observing his former friend, Dreifort, an accomplished fencer parrying the defense lawyer's questions."

Chapter Thirty

THE DOG THAT DIDN'T BARK

On Tuesday, July 6, Wetzel put Bob Dreifort on the stand to talk about the circumstances that led to Dan being committed to the psychiatric unit at the Cleveland Clinic, where Bob was employed as the administrator for the Department of Pediatrics.

"What caused you to seek some type of program for Daniel?" asked Wetzel.

"During the early part of that year, Dan was becoming less accepting of our parental concerns for his comings and goings and demanding more freedom than my wife and I were willing to give him."

"Would you and Daniel have shouting matches over these disagreements?"

"I'm sure that our discussions devolved into shouting matches from time to time," said Bob.

Dan was in the hospital for thirty days that summer, he said. Meanwhile, the rest of the family was participating in therapy, too. Ultimately, Dan was diagnosed as having an unspecified "adolescent adjustment problem."

"You were present when Dan gave his statement to the Shaker Heights police?"

"We were with him the whole time," said Bob.

"Mr. Dreifort, when was the first time that you became aware that Lisa Pruett had been killed?"

"The first time I knew for sure was about four in the morning. We were sitting at Sergeant Gray's desk. They wanted a statement from Dan and they wanted to read him his rights and to have him sign a piece of paper. It was at that point that Dan, and I think probably all of us, questioned why this was necessary. Sergeant Gray talked about aggravated murder and said that Lisa was, in fact, dead."

MURRAY TOOK THE cross. His mission out of the gate was to get on record that Bob had been present for his son's entire statement when it was given to Detective Gray—the implication being that it had allowed Bob to paint the details of his own statement to police, later, so that his story matched up with his son's.

"Mr. Dreifort," Murray began, "you were present throughout the questioning of your son at the police station, were you not?"

"I was in the building. I wasn't with him. I don't believe I was with him when he actually made a statement to the police."

"You and your wife actually signed as witnesses. Did you not?"

"We were there when he signed it."

"Mr. Dreifort, this is your signature, is it not?"

Murray showed him his signature. "Yes."

"And it's a signature to your son's statement, correct?"

"That's right."

"At four-fifteen A.M. on September the fourteenth. Now, you were questioned at approximately ten A.M., were you not?"

"As I say, I can't remember the precise times. I was in isolation with Detective Mullaney. He took my statement. There was a period of time waiting for a stenographer. Then they got it typed up and brought it back and I read it and finally signed it. So a lot of time transpired, yes."

Murray moved on. He asked Bob about his job at the Cleveland Clinic. He had worked at the hospital until February 1992, but was currently unemployed.

"Do you have any medical training?"

"No."

"You're not a psychologist?"

"I'm not a licensed psychologist."

"You're not a licensed social worker?"

"I'm not a licensed social worker."

"You're not a medical doctor?"

"I'm not a medical doctor."

"Your training is more concerned with how you manage . . ."

"I'm a health care administrator, you're right," said Bob.

"Now, as I understood your testimony, it was you, together with your wife, who decided it was necessary to hospitalize your son, correct?"

"That's partly true."

"In consultation with some of your colleagues and friends at the Clinic," Murray prompted.

"That's correct," said Bob.

"Did I understand you correctly when you said that the reason that Dan was put into the hospital was, and you'll correct me if I'm wrong, I tried to write it down as accurately as I could, because at age sixteen he was becoming less accepting of your parental concerns and he was more demanding of freedom than you were willing to give him. Did I get that pretty accurately?"

"That's probably what I said, yes. Sounds like what I said."

"Now, wouldn't you agree, that probably describes ninety percent of sixteen-year-olds?"

"Objection!" said Marino.

"Overruled," Judge Sweeney replied. "Go ahead."

"I should answer that?" asked Bob.

"Yes, if you can."

"Do I think that describes ninety percent of sixteen-year-olds? I have no idea what percentage it would describe," said Bob.

"Was he . . . Was the decision for Dan to be hospitalized a joint decision in which he participated as well?" asked Murray.

"No," said Bob. "At that point I, in consultation with the professionals, decided that would be best."

"And so he was placed in the hospital on an inpatient basis. He was there twenty-four hours a day, except for the weekend pass, correct?"

"Yes."

"What are some of the rules that he was breaking?"

"The rules that he was questioning, and not necessarily breaking, involved a great deal about the hours he kept, or wished to keep, and how he would keep us informed as to where he was and who he was with."

"Do you think that was unusual for a sixteen-year-old?"

"I'm told it happens."

"Is it true that you and [Dan] had shouting matches over these issues?"

"[We] have shouted at each other over the years, yes."

"And who did most of the shouting?"

"Hard to say."

"I take it you did your share of shouting, you do recall that?"

"I just said I've shouted at Dan over the years."

"Did you scream at him from time to time?" asked Murray.

"Screaming defined as a high-pitched sound?"

"Yes."

"I don't know that I have been known to scream," said Bob.

"Was there physical violence between you?"

"There was a time when Dan raised his hand at me, yeah."

"And what happened?"

"He pushed me aside."

"Did you defend yourself?"

"Well, yes," said Bob. "Anybody that tried to strike me, I would defend myself, yes."

"What about any violence directed from you to him?" asked Murray.

"My violence toward Dan was probably verbal."

"After your son gave his first statement to the police, you arranged to have him represented by a lawyer, correct?"

"At some point during that morning, I called the family attorney and explained to him what was happening and he advised me that none of us should talk to anybody without him being present from that point forward."

"By the way," said Murray, "did your dog bark at the screams?"

"No," said Bob. "Our dog was quite aged and was almost deaf at that point and arthritic."

"So the dog... Did the dog hear when the doorbell would ring?"

"I think that depended on where she was in the house."

"In any case the dog didn't bark at that piercing, shrieking scream of a kind that you had never heard before, correct?"

"Not to my recollection."

"Now, Mr. Dreifort," Murray continued, "the police are there. You know that your son has found what appears to be Lisa's bike. The Pruetts are there advising you that there may be a dead girl behind the bushes. Police are all over. And it's your testimony that in the face of all of that uncertainty, your son goes to sleep because he's got to get up to go to school the next day?"

"My testimony is that at some time during that period, we advised him to get some rest."

"And so neither you nor your son was demanding to know what had happened to this young girl before your son left with the police?"

"Au contraire," countered Bob. "We did. From the very instant we thought something was wrong and we tried to determine what was going on. At that point the police were telling us things like, 'There's been foul play and we can't talk about it. We don't want to talk about it. Come to the station and we'll talk about it.'"

"No further questions, Your Honor."

Chapter Thirty-One

CONFIDANT

THE NEXT DAY THE PRINCIPAL of Shaker Heights High, Jack Rumbaugh, took the stand.

"Now, Dr. Rumbaugh," said Wetzel. "In late spring of 1990, did you have a discussion with Kevin Young regarding Lisa Pruett?"

"Yes," said Rumbaugh. "Kevin and I talked after the band trip to Germany."

"And what was the impetus for Kevin to arrive at your office? What brought Kevin to your office?"

"My memory is he just wanted to talk to me."

"Do you remember what specifically Kevin said, in regard to Lisa Pruett?"

"Yes. He was angry and hurt over Lisa's attention to a boyfriend who also was having some type of psychiatric problem, and was wondering why his treatment was so different."

"And Kevin said the name 'Lisa Pruett' at that time?" asked Wetzel.

"He said 'Lisa,'" said Rumbaugh.

"Would you consider yourself a confidant of Kevin Young's?"

"I think so."

"Did you have further discussion with Kevin in late August 1990?"

"Yes."

"Did the topic of Dan and Lisa come out again at that time?"

"Yes," said Rumbaugh. "Kevin mentioned to me that he was bewildered by how Lisa could still love Dan, and how Lisa would be so nurturing to Dan, and when he was ill, no one was nurturing or cared for Kevin."

"Okay, and in the discussion Kevin again expressed anger toward Lisa and her boyfriend and the way she was treating him."

"Objection, Your Honor," said DeVan.

"Sustained," the judge replied.

Wetzel tried a different approach. "In August of 1990, did Kevin express a similar anger?"

"Objection."

"Overruled. Go ahead."

"I think Kevin's issues in August were more, in my opinion, hurt feelings," said Rumbaugh. "Not so much anger."

DeVan took point on cross.

"Kevin did not threaten Lisa or Dan during either of these conversations, to the best of your recollection, did he, sir?" asked DeVan.

"No," said Rumbaugh.

"Now, Dr. Rumbaugh," said DeVan, "I take it that you were notified early on the morning of the fourteenth that Lisa had been murdered."

"Yes, that's correct. Mr. Pruett telephoned me early in the morning and told me that Lisa had been killed."

"Approximately, what time did you receive a telephone call?"

"Very, very early. One-thirty A.M. Somewhere in that range."

Rumbaugh explained that he and his wife got up then, and in those early-morning hours, he organized a crisis response team of clergy and child psychologists to be present at the school in the morning. Then he personally went to the Pruett home, where he stayed for several hours. Later, he was called by Mr. Dreifort and got to their house just in time to see them leave.

"And isn't it true, sir," said DeVan, "that at that time you told the crisis intervention team that Lisa had been stabbed, but it did not appear as though she had been raped?"

"Yes, that's true."

"You told them that, so as to spread some consolation amongst them and the students they would be talking with throughout the day?"

"Yes."

With the principal's testimony DeVan had just shot holes in the state's assumption that Kevin Young could *only* have known that Lisa had not been raped if he was at the scene of the crime. Not so. Pretty much every student at Shaker Heights High School knew this through word of mouth, a chain of gossip that Mr. Rumbaugh had started himself.

In the courtroom DeVan was racking up win after win, but you wouldn't know it if you weren't there. "Trial's focus shifts to Young," McCarty wrote in the next day's paper. "Witnesses drew a portrait of the defendant as a jealous, troubled, and lonely youth preoccupied with the girl he is on trial for killing."

Chapter Thirty-Two

A STORY FOR DAVID LYNCH

DEBBIE DREIFORT TOOK THE STAND on July 8. Besides being Dan's sister, Deb was also dating Tex Workman at the time of the murder, and Tex had been on a short list of suspects for a time. And she'd been close with Kevin as well.

"When you attended Shaker Heights High School, did you know Kevin Young?" asked Wetzel.

"Yes," said Deb. "We were buddies."

"When did you come to know Lisa Pruett?"

"After my brother started dating her."

"And how did you know Tex Workman?"

"He was my boyfriend."

"When did you first become aware that Lisa had been murdered?" Wetzel asked.

"When I went to my eight-to-ten class, Tex called and left a message on my answering machine saying that something terrible had happened."

"What did you do in response to that?"

"I went back to Cleveland."

"Who did you first see when you got to Cleveland?"

"Tex and Kevin Young."

"Where did you meet Tex?" asked Wetzel.

"At the Rapid station in Shaker Square."

"When you arrive, Tex and Kevin Young meet you, correct?"

"Yes."

"Is there a discussion regarding the murder of Lisa Pruett at that time?"

"Yes."

"Do you remember who said what at that time?"

"No."

"How would you characterize Kevin's demeanor?"

"Nervous and frightened."

Debbie said that after she spoke with Tex, she went to the police station, where she met up with her family. Then they all rode back to the house together. The prosecutor circled around to her prior conversations with Kevin Young.

"Was there a time specifically, if we could, in 1990, when Kevin Young said something regarding your brother, Dan?"

"Yes," said Debbie. "Early summer at Arabica. Kevin was very jealous of Dan and Lisa's relationship. He had a crush on Lisa."

"What did he say specifically regarding your brother?"

"That he hated my brother, that he wanted to kill my brother."

"Did Kevin give you an indication what the impetus was behind the threats, and why he said the threats concerning Dan?"

"Yes," she said. "The incident that Kevin focused on was my brother had jokingly offered to let Kevin pinch Lisa's bottom, Lisa's behind, and Kevin thought that this was the most terrible thing, that this was hideous, that my brother treated Lisa so bad."

"MS. DREIFORT," SAID DeVan, beginning his cross-examination, "you say that in the week after the murder of Lisa Pruett, you spoke with Kevin about the murder, at Arabica, correct?"

"Yes."

"You knew that Kevin was planning on attending Ohio State that fall, correct?"

"Yes."

"Did you know that classes started on the Monday following the murder of Lisa Pruett?"

"No."

"Well, if classes did start on the Monday following the murder..."

"Then I talked to him during the weekend," said Debbie.

"Excuse me, ma'am," DeVan interjected. "I am not done. If classes started on the Monday following the murder of Lisa Pruett, and Kevin began attending classes, he would not have been in Cleveland during that week."

"No."

"Which means that your recollection is mistaken."

"Then I talked to him at Arabica during the weekend," said Debbie.

"That means your recollection is mistaken during that week?"

"Objection," said Wetzel.

"Sustained," said Judge Sweeney.

"Thank you," said DeVan. "Yes or no, ma'am."

"The objection is sustained," said the judge, "so ask another question."

DeVan obliged. "Now, during the months preceding the murder of Lisa Pruett, it's true, is it not, that you were dating Tex?"

"Yes."

"In fact, Tex slept over at your house almost on a nightly basis during that summer prior to the murder, did he not?"

"Yes."

"And your parents did not know that he was sleeping over there during that period of time, did they?"

"No."

"They, of course, would not have approved, correct?"

"No, they would not have."

"In fact, your father and mother would have been extremely angry [if they] had found that out, correct?"

"They would have been upset, yes."

"So, basically, it's true, is it not, that during that period of time, there was at least one person who was able to get in and out of that house without your parents even knowing, correct?"

"Yes."

"And your brother was very familiar with your parents' sleeping patterns, and the ins and outs of that house, correct?"

"Objection!" said Wetzel.

"Overruled."

"Would that be a safe assumption?" asked DeVan.

"Yeah, it is," said Debbie.

"One of the topics of conversation at the Shaker Rapid stop on the day of the fourteenth was Tex's concern regarding his alibi for the night before, right?"

"Objection."

"Overruled," said Judge Sweeney.

"I don't remember if that was an issue when I had first gotten to the Rapid stop, but yes, that was an issue for him," said Debbie.

"He was also concerned about the knife that he had left at your home previously, correct?"

"Yes."

"And that particular knife, what kind of knife was that?"

"It was a butterfly knife that was in Athens with me at the time of the murder."

"So he was concerned at that particular point that his knife, which he thought he left at your home, might somehow be implicated in this murder?"

"He thought he was going to be framed."

"He thought he was going to be framed?" asked DeVan.

"Yes."

"Now, since that time, you and Tex have broken up?"

"Yes."

"And there came a time, did there not, in the spring of 1991, in which the breakup between you two became somewhat violent, correct?"

"I'd call it messy, not violent," said Debbie.

"In any event there was a time, was there not, when Tex assaulted you, correct?"

"Objection!" said Wetzel.

"Sustained," said Judge Sweeney.

DeVan asked for a sidebar. He and Wetzel stepped to Judge Sweeney's bench.

"Your Honor," said DeVan, "the evidence will show that if we are allowed to get into this, that in the spring of 1991, Tex and Debbie broke up, and in the ensuing breakup, at one point Tex stopped her on the street by using his car and he reached through the window at her, and that later on, she reported this to the police and she was told by Detective Gray to forget about it."

DeVan pressed on. "Also, Tex was told that this entire thing would be put aside, and Tex got the impression that as long as he continued to cooperate with the police in regard to Kevin Young, that this entire matter between him and Debbie would be forgotten about, and so it goes to a number of issues here. Additionally, Your Honor, Tex will deny that he assaulted her. If, in fact, he did not stop her and she lied about being assaulted, it shows, number one, that her credibility can be impeached, and number two, that she will lie for someone she may have been in love with at the time and that she would change her story later on. We have her on tape, saying—"

Judge Sweeney stopped him. "What's your position, that he assaulted—"

"She wasn't assaulted, no," said DeVan. "She lied about being assaulted. Number three, that when the police found out about this, because Tex was at that point an essential witness against Kevin Young, they conveniently forgot about this charge."

"The objection is sustained," said Sweeney. "If you can get Mr. Workman up there, and if you can show that the police offered not to prosecute, you can show that bias."

But neither DeVan nor the prosecution wanted to put Tex on the stand. To do so would complicate the stories each side was trying to tell. Tex was a wild card that nobody knew quite what to do with.

DEVAN TURNED BACK to the witness. "At this particular time in the week or two following the murder of Lisa, your brother was still a suspect, wasn't he?"

"Yes, he was," said Debbie.

"And you certainly love your brother and would want to help him if you could, correct?"

"Yes."

"Now, early on following the murder of Lisa Pruett, you and Becca Boatright began to talk about writing a book about all this, correct?"

"Becca and I began writing a movie script that we were going to send to David Lynch."

"And David Lynch is a producer who does rather weird and crazy movies, correct?"

"Uh-huh."

"And he did *Twin Peaks,* correct?"

"Yes."

"And it was your idea and Becca's idea to begin to write a movie script based upon the murder of Lisa Pruett?"

"No," she said. "Based on Shaker Heights."

Chapter Thirty-Three

THE RUNAWAY JUROR

Becca Boatright took the stand next. Wetzel again led the direct for the prosecution while Marino looked on. "I knew Lisa since third grade, since we both attended the same elementary school," said Becca. "I got to know her in high school, during marching band. I was her squad leader and, of course, her relationship with Dan brought me closer to her."

"When did you first come to know Kevin Young?"

"I first began to know him really well my freshman year," said Becca. "We became friends."

Wetzel asked what she remembered of the day of the murder.

"Dan called me about eight-twenty that evening and told me that a few people were coming over to his house that night and asked me if I would be interested in coming over," said Becca.

"Did he indicate to you who would be coming over?" asked Wetzel.

"He mentioned Lisa, Chris Jones, [Daniel] Messinger. A few other names."

Curiously, this was the first time Daniel Messinger's name had popped up on that list of friends who had been invited to Dan's the night of the murder. Daniel had said nothing about it to detectives.

And he'd testified that he'd never known about the party. It's always possible that Becca was mistaken, but it's also easy to believe that Dan would have wanted to see his best friend the night he got out of the hospital. Daniel Messinger, after all, was dependable, a friend willing to sneak bottles of Robitussin into the Cleveland Clinic and go undercover at a bowling alley.

"Did you reply to Dan whether you would be able to come over that night?"

"I told him I wouldn't be coming over," she said.

"When did you become aware that Lisa had been murdered?"

"That would be first period the next day at school. Eight oh-five, I believe. Dr. Rumbaugh came over the PA system and said that Lisa had been involved in a homicide the night before."

"When did you leave school that day?"

"I left school around ten-thirty."

"Where did you go?"

"I went up to Arabica at Shaker Square. I knew Debbie was going to be coming home and I thought that might be one place she might go."

"Did you see anyone at Arabica at that time?" asked Wetzel.

"Kevin Young was there," she said. "I told Kevin what I had heard at school was that Lisa had been bludgeoned and raped, and he said that it was his knowledge that she had not been raped and that she had been stabbed rather than bludgeoned."

"Did he indicate anything else to you regarding the rape?"

"No. Just that he was fairly sure that she had not been raped."

"What is his demeanor at that time?"

"He acted nervous and he was chain-smoking."

DEVAN WAS READY for cross. "At the time that you heard of the murder of Lisa Pruett," said DeVan, "you were attending classes at John Carroll, as well as at Shaker Heights High School, were you not?"

"Right," said Becca.

"At the time you were taking German at John Carroll, correct?"

"Correct."

"And Professor Bartsch was your professor?"

"Yes, he was," said Becca.

"And your classes were on Monday, Wednesday, and Friday, correct?"

"Correct."

"The day of Lisa's murder was Friday, the fourteenth of September, correct?"

"Correct."

"And your classes would begin at one P.M. at John Carroll, correct? And it's true, is it not, that you said you met Kevin at one-thirty P.M. on that day, correct?"

"I may have said that," she said.

"Ms. Boatright, do you recognize this particular statement of the Shaker police, which you made to them?"

"Yes, I do."

"And that's your signature, correct?"

"Correct."

"And isn't it true that on the first page, that you describe going to school that morning? 'Later, around 1:30 P.M. I went up to Arabica at Shaker Square and since I was waiting for Debbie to come in and since Kevin Young was the only one I knew up there, I sat down and talked to him.' Correct? You said that."

"I said that, however it's—"

"And you were given an opportunity to check for any inaccuracies, correct?"

"Correct."

"And you said that you were at Shaker Square at one-thirty, correct?"

"Apparently."

"'Apparently' is your answer. You said this to police?"

"It's been three years."

"Yes or no. 'Apparently' is your answer?"

"Yes."

"If you had been at class that day, that would contradict with your statement that you had met Kevin at one-thirty, correct?"

"Yes, it would," she said. In fact, DeVan had already spoken to Becca's professor, who would later testify that Becca had, in fact, been in class that day. He remembered the day specifically, because she was so upset about Lisa's murder.

But DeVan moved on. "Now, Rebecca, in the spring of 1990, there was a time when you and Kevin made plans to go to the senior prom, correct?"

"Correct."

"And your idea was to go as friends, correct?"

"Correct."

"And it's true, is it not, that Kevin apparently mistook that as something more than just friends, correct?"

"Correct."

"And when he suggested that there was some sort of relationship between you and him, which was more than just friends, you made it clear to him you were planning on just going as friends, right?"

"Right."

"And Kevin then broke up that arrangement to go to the prom, correct?"

"Yes, he did."

"Now, following that particular episode, you, did you not, become somewhat close to Dan Dreifort, correct?"

"Correct."

"And when you say 'close to Dan,' without getting into any details, it was less than sexual, but was more than friends, correct?"

"For maybe an hour."

"'For maybe an hour'? Dan, as you later came to learn, bragged about that with some of his friends, correct?"

"Objection!" said Wetzel.

"Sustained."

"May we approach sidebar, Your Honor?" asked DeVan.

"Sure," said Sweeney.

"Becca threatened that she could cause a mistrial in this case," DeVan said when he was out of the jury's earshot.

AUTHOR'S NOTE: Some context is required in order to understand what DeVan is talking about here. Sometimes, especially in big cases, sometimes there is a coincidence that is so absurd, you're left to question the very nature of free will. What DeVan is talking about here is the weird happenstance wherein Becca Boatright was called for jury duty just as Kevin Young was preparing for trial.

Two weeks before Becca testified that day, Joe Booker, the jury bailiff, contacted Judge Sweeney's office. Booker worked for the common pleas court. His job was wrangling prospective jurors for criminal cases, way down on the fourth floor. One of his jurors, a young woman named Becca Boatright, had gotten angry with him. She had been sitting near jurors from Kevin Young's case and she'd overheard them saying nice things about Kevin. Becca reported the conversations to Booker and claimed that what she'd overheard was enough to cause a mistrial. When Sweeney learned about this, he brought Becca in to speak with the prosecutors and defense attorneys in a private session. So we'll call this a flashback as we travel two weeks into the past, of the past, of the past...

"I'm Judge Sweeney," said the judge, in his chambers. "This is Carmen Marino. Karl Wetzel, Mark DeVan, Mike Murray, and these other folks are court personnel and the court reporter. Now, I'm told you indicated to our jury bailiff downstairs that you heard some remarks about this case?"

"I hear people talking about it all the time," said Becca.

"Have you heard anyone who is a juror on this case talking?"

"No," she said. "It's all people who have been, I guess, excused."

"Okay," said Sweeney. "Well, so you are absolutely sure that no one associated with this case has been talking about it?"

"I'm not absolutely sure," said Becca. "I don't know who's on and who's not."

"You guys want to ask any questions?" asked Sweeney.

"Can you tell us what was said that you overheard?" asked DeVan.

"Just . . ."

"Your Honor," Wetzel interrupted. "I'm going to object until we know who said it, whether it was an excused juror or a juror who is following the case."

"Miss Boatright," said Judge Sweeney, "when I talked to Mr. Booker, he told me that you said that you heard some things that would cause a mistrial."

"No," said Becca. "I said that because I was mad at how rude he was being."

"So you were just snapping back?"

"Yeah."

"And you didn't really hear anything that would cause a mistrial?"

"I don't know what would cause a mistrial."

"Did you respond to those jurors?" asked DeVan. "Did you say anything to them?"

"No. I tried not to listen."

"Listen," said Judge Sweeney, "you heard a lot of comments. What was the worst thing you heard?"

"I mean, there were people saying nice things, like Kevin looked very nice. 'He looks like a nice boy.'"

"Did you hear anyone make any comments concerning his guilt or innocence?" asked the judge.

"Well, there were a couple of people who were talking about how they couldn't be jurors for the case because they thought he was guilty for the past two years and so it would be—"

"Those obviously weren't jurors in our room," said Judge Sweeney.

"We don't know that, Judge," said DeVan. "How did you distinguish between jurors you thought were excused versus jurors who are still on the panel as potential jurors up here?"

"I didn't," she said.

"This young lady apparently would go so far as to say to a jury commissioner that she is threatening to cause a mistrial because he was rude," said DeVan. "Who knows whether or not she said something to someone? I mean, really."

Judge Sweeney excused Becca from any further jury duty and sent her home.

BACK TO THAT sidebar during Kevin's trial . . .

DeVan continued: "I believe Becca Boatright is directly important in this case because she threatened to cause a mistrial because of a perceived slight, and that goes directly to her character and the extent to which she will do something and react, and perhaps, for that matter, obstruct justice or lie. I would ask the court to allow me to go into this and cross-examine her on the testimony that she gave to the court."

"Well, I'm sure it's part of the record during the jury selection process," said Judge Sweeney. "However, I would ask you not to inquire."

"You are ordering me not to, Judge?" asked DeVan.

"Yeah."

"Well, please note our objection for the record."

"Sure."

"No further questions."

Chapter Thirty-Four

THE AP POSSE RIDES AGAIN

JENNIFER MARGULIES HAD MADE THE most of her time since graduating Shaker Heights High. She was nineteen years old now, and when she wasn't attending classes, she worked for the ACLU as a community organizer. She sat in the chair beside the judge, tucked her legs up under her body like she was lounging on a sofa at home, and sipped from a bottle of water as Carmen Marino questioned her. He asked Jenny to tell the jury about the kind of things she'd heard Kevin say at the coffee shop.

"He stated that he would not let people ignore him," said Jenny. "And I believe it was Rachel who asked him, 'Well, what can you do if someone ignores you? They are going to ignore you.' He repeated, 'I won't be ignored. There are ways of making an impression on people. It's been done.'"

"What was your reaction to this conversation?" asked Marino.

"I found it rather chilling," said Jenny. "Actually, I went home and told my mom about it because I thought it was a disturbing statement to make."

Marino asked Jenny to recall another conversation with Kevin that took place in August 1990, a month before the murder.

"Ken Mitsumoto and Kevin had come over to the table where Rachel and I were sitting," she said. "We began to talk about where

Dan was and set Ken straight on some rumors he had heard about why Dan was at the Clinic. Kevin said, 'I'm sorry that he's in there.' And then he went on to say that he was sorry because he had some unfinished business to take care of."

"Did he say what he meant by that?" the prosecutor asked.

"No, he didn't."

"What was your reaction to it?"

"Well, I thought it sounded kind of ridiculous. To be honest, I think I laughed at the time. Then he said he had unfinished business to take care of with Dan and the slut. He said, 'I was going to mess with him real good, but now he's not around.'"

DeVan found this young woman off-putting, something about the insouciant way she used the water bottle as a prop, the way she sat in the stand. It was disrespectful to the process. She didn't seem like she was taking it seriously. Meanwhile, Kevin sat beside him, quietly listening to it all.

"Ms. Margulies, you're working at the ACLU?" DeVan asked at cross.

"Yes."

"As an employee of the ACLU, you certainly understand the need for everybody in a controversy to have a fair opportunity to interview witnesses, correct?"

"Yes," said Jenny.

"On several occasions within the past six months, investigators have, on behalf of the defense, attempted to interview you, correct?"

"To my knowledge, that's correct."

"You're aware, are you not, that your parents would not allow for you to be interviewed, correct?"

"That's not exactly correct. I made that decision myself," said Jenny.

"You chose not to speak to a defense investigator and give him this version of what you say occurred, on your own volition, correct?"

"Yes."

"You said that, knowing full well the benefits to both sides to know the full story prior to a witness testifying, correct?"

"Yes. I said that with a belief in the judicial process."

"'The judicial process,'" DeVan mused. "As long as you weren't interviewed, correct? Now, you spent the evening of September 14 in the presence of Dan Dreifort, correct?"

"Among others, yes."

"And at whose house was that?"

"Rachel Lowenthal's."

"Who were the people that stayed at Rachel's?"

"The people you mentioned before," said Jenny. "Judy, Kim Rathbone. Brian Keating was there. Kim Cole was there. All of us that had been friends with Lisa and that were grieving together at the time."

"And Dan Dreifort spent the evening there also?"

"Yes."

"And did Dan Dreifort sleep over that night at Rachel Lowenthal's?"

"Yes."

"All this time you were aware of these alleged statements by Kevin Young?"

"Yes."

"But you did not give your statement to the police until October 9, roughly three weeks later, correct?"

"Yes."

DeVan pointed out that Jenny's parents were good friends with Kevin's parents and they had both spent Friday, September 14, at the Young household while she was at Dan's. He wondered if her parents would have really done that if Jenny had told them about the threats Kevin had made.

"Are you familiar with Chris Jones?" asked DeVan.

"Yes," said Jenny.

"Since the time he testified in this trial, he has appeared at your house, has he not?"

"Yes."

"You didn't talk about the case?"

"No."

"You didn't talk about the case?" he asked again. "You didn't talk about his testimony?"

"I asked him if he did all right and he said he did fine. That was the extent of our conversation."

During a trial witnesses are kept out of the courtroom until they've testified so that prior testimony by other people does not influence what they will say on the stand. Having secret discussions with witnesses outside the courtroom kind of defeats the purpose of this rule. It's underhanded.

"You've talked to Kathryn Schulz?" said DeVan.

"Yes."

"You talked about the case?"

"Again, about how I'm dealing with it, how she's feeling."

"In fact, her mother, Mrs. Schulz, has been in the courtroom continuously, has she not?" Kathryn's mother, Margo, sat by the Pruetts every day. The defense team had taken to calling her "Madame Defarge" for her habit of knitting during the proceedings and ostensibly relaying what she learned at the trial to others, like the character from *A Tale of Two Cities.* It had become apparent to DeVan that the teenage witnesses had intimate knowledge of prior testimony.

"Yes," Jenny replied.

"She's been sitting with the Pruetts throughout this matter?"

"Yes."

"Objection!" said Marino.

"Sustained."

"Throughout the investigation of this case, your mother has also received reports through Rosemary Herpel, public relations director for the city of Shaker Heights?"

"Objection."

"Overruled."

"Correct?"

"I don't know from whom my mother has been getting information."

JENNY'S GOOD FRIEND Rachel Lowenthal came to the stand next. She backed up Jenny's testimony about the conversation at the coffee shop and then added a story about overhearing Kevin complaining about how he couldn't get a girl "to suck his cock."

Murray handled the cross for Rachel. He established that Rachel had also waited weeks to report her suspicions about Kevin. Then an interesting detail emerged: On the day that Shaker Heights police had held their big press conference to announce that Kevin Young was their prime suspect, there had been a second, secret conference organized by Detective Gray for Dan's close friends.

"And do you know, among your friends, who was there?"

"Yeah."

"Could you please name them?"

"Let's see. Chris Jones, Kim Rathbone, Dan Messinger, Kathryn Schulz, Kim Cole, Judy Miller, Jennifer Margulies. I'm sure there were more. He gave us . . . He sent messages through the school, so we each got a little card."

"You got a little card from Sergeant Gray?" asked Murray.

"Yes."

"You were all members of the AP Posse?"

"I believe so."

"And it was this conference at which the authorities from Shaker Heights suggested that they thought they had the right suspect, Kevin Young, but they didn't have any evidence to prosecute him, correct?"

"Objection," said Wetzel.

"Objection!" said Marino.

"What was the point?" Murray asked Rachel. "Were you called there to wait for the press conference to happen and be over?"

"No," said Rachel. She said they just talked to Detective Gray about the evidence against Kevin. Murray wondered if it had all been a clever maneuver by Gray to get everyone's stories straight in case they were interviewed by the media after the announcement.

"Young's outbursts recounted by friends," wrote McCarty, for the *Plain Dealer*. "Heard individually, the snippets of conversations recalled by witnesses from the summer of 1990 carried little weight. But considered together, the stories formed a compelling cloud of suspicion over Young.

"In articulate and descriptive testimony, the youths recalled how Young, now 21, transformed his unrequited love for Lisa into a deep, dark hatred for the sixteen-year-old and her boyfriend, Dan Dreifort."

Chapter Thirty-Five

SHADES OF GRAY

IT WAS FINALLY TIME FOR Detective Tom Gray to take the stand. Together with Detective Mullaney he had built a compelling circumstantial case against Kevin Young. But, in a way, Gray was the lone dynamo that powered the engine of the entire investigation. Nobody else had poured so much energy into proving that Kevin Young had killed Lisa Pruett.

"How were you first made aware of the murder of Lisa Pruett?" Marino asked the detective.

"I received a phone call at home," said Detective Gray. "I had been asked by the deputy chief to come in and conduct an interview with a possible suspect."

"About what time of night was it?"

"It was after two in the morning," said Gray. "I responded to the police station. I then went to the scene, got a basic description of the crime scene and the information we knew at the time, and then accompanied Detective Mullaney and Dan Dreifort back to the Shaker Heights Police Department."

Gray told the jury a story about how he'd traveled to Quantico to visit the FBI's Behavioral Analysis Unit for tips on how to obtain a confession from Kevin the day before he interrogated the defendant in Columbus. The FBI BAU profilers had suggested that Gray talk to Kevin about how the media was covering the case—something that both Detective Gray and Kevin could agree was the real problem at hand.

"I told Kevin we had been under a lot of pressure from the media to attempt to resolve the case and we wanted to come to some resolution."

"And why did you use the explanation that you were under media pressure to solve the case?" asked Marino.

"It was a discussion with Jim Wright and his staff at Quantico that the media was an issue that concerned a lot of the witnesses in the case, and that would be a good approach to bring it down to a common level."

"As a practical matter, did you feel any media pressure to solve the case?"

"No."

WHEN IT WAS time for the cross, Murray started pushing the detective, hard, right out of the gate.

"Sergeant Gray," said Murray, "I understand from your testimony that your first involvement in this investigation was in connection with looking at Dan Dreifort as a possible suspect. Is that correct?"

"That is correct," said Gray.

"Were you the one who found the pocketknife in Dan's bedroom?"

"I recall it sitting there. I am not sure if I was the first one who saw it, but we recovered it from his bedroom."

"But, again, you recovered that knife and seized it because it could be evidence connected to the crime, correct?"

"Correct."

"And later you had that knife examined by the coroner, to determine whether or not it could or could not be excluded as the murder weapon, correct?"

"The police department did, correct."

"And as you came to know, the coroner could not exclude that as the murder weapon, correct?"

"I believe so," said Gray.

"Well, you had available to you all the information in the case before you went down to Columbus," Murray reminded him. "Maybe that doesn't occur before you went to Columbus, but if that determination had been made prior to September the twenty-sixth, you would have been aware of that, correct?"

"That's correct."

"May I approach the witness, Your Honor?"

"Yes," said Judge Sweeney.

Murray stepped toward the detective.

"Dr. Challener examined a knife, which he was unable to exclude as the murder weapon, on September 24, correct?"

"That's correct."

"Two days before you went to Columbus, correct?" said Murray.

"That's correct," said Gray.

"And as a matter of fact, it was a day before you went to see the FBI in Quantico, correct?"

"That's correct."

"And before you went to the FBI in Quantico, you gathered together all the information that was available in the case thus far in order to present it to the FBI, correct?"

"That's correct."

"So, given all of that, you probably were aware by that juncture that Dr. Challener had made the determination that Dan's knife could not be excluded as the murder weapon, correct?"

"Correct."

And yet his focus remained on Kevin Young alone.

"Every single decision that was made, you would agree, would you not, Sergeant, as to who would conduct this interrogation, and how it would be conducted, was made with a view toward maximizing the likelihood that a confession would result from it, isn't that true?"

"That's correct."

"And you drove alone with Kevin to the hotel, correct?"

"Correct."

"And you tried to put him at ease, didn't you?"

"Correct."

"And all of that was done before you ever advised him of any of his constitutional rights, correct?" said Murray.

"Correct."

"And the plan was to take him out of there before anybody could serve him with any copy of the search warrant, correct?"

"The plan was to take him and remove him for the interview and do the search simultaneously," answered Gray.

"Because if somebody had gone and given Kevin a search warrant and explained to him that his room was going to be searched for evidence of a crime, that might cause him to be sufficiently concerned that he'd actually call his parents or refuse to be interrogated, isn't that so?"

"That's possible."

"And that was a risk that you didn't want to take?"

"That's correct."

Murray asked Gray to recall the moment during the interrogation when he asked Kevin to imagine how the murder may have occurred. Kevin had said he thought Lisa was stabbed "once, twice, maybe more." In fact, she'd been stabbed at least nineteen times.

"You can interpret his statement however you want," said Gray.

"Do you think 'once, twice, maybe more' means 'once, twice, maybe nineteen'?"

"I didn't ask any further than that."

"Now, throughout this entire period of time, Kevin kept insisting that he was innocent?" asked Murray.

"That's correct," said Gray.

"He didn't kill Lisa Pruett, he kept telling you on a number of occasions?"

"Correct."

"You were playing with his mind, weren't you?"

"You could describe it that way."

"Well, you knew he had emotional problems, didn't you?"

"Our profile of both the killer and Kevin showed some serious emotional problems."

"And after some twenty hours, you engage in a very lengthy monologue, give him a little speech about how you didn't believe him, did you?"

"That's correct."

"He told you, over and over again, he didn't do it," said Murray. "And you told him that he'd never escape it. You told him that until it was resolved, he couldn't go back to Shaker because everybody in Shaker would think of him being a suspect. He couldn't go back to college because everything in college would now remind him of Lisa. He couldn't go back to anything until he told the truth. You told him he had to clear his conscience and tell the truth, right?"

"Correct."

"He could have told you that he had done it, spent a couple years in a hospital, and then gone on with his life, but he had to tell you the truth, 'and this is the truth, and if I don't tell you this, I don't know how I could ever live with myself.' That's what he told you, correct?"

"Correct."

"Referring to that, throughout this, he had been telling you the truth, right?"

"Referring to whatever he was about to say."

"That's the suggestion you want to leave with this jury, that he was on the verge of telling you the truth rather than insisting that he had been telling you the truth. Is that your testimony, sir? You suggested the possibility that he might even be executed for this crime, didn't you?"

"Correct."

"That's how you played with his mind after twenty hours. And it's at that point, after hearing you continually mention getting help, 'tell the truth and you'll get help by confessing,' with the notion that 'if you don't, you'll go to prison for the rest of your life, you might even be executed,' it's at that juncture that Kevin breaks down and he says he could have told you that he did it, spent a couple years in a hospital, then got on with his life, but he said, 'I've got to tell you the truth and this is the truth. And if I don't tell you this, I don't know how I could ever live with myself.' That's when he says that, correct?"

"Correct."

"And isn't it a fact that he was telling you that it would have been easier for him to falsely confess to this crime than to tell you the truth that he had been telling you and risk the possibility that you're going to send him away for the rest of his life or even execute him?"

"He didn't refer to the truth that he had been telling us," said Gray. "He referred basically to the truth that he was going to tell me right then."

"And the young man, because you won't believe him after twenty hours that he's innocent, he's driven to the edge of suicide, isn't that so?"

"Because he's confronted with the facts as I presented them to him."

"And that's when he says, 'I'm going to kill myself,' correct?"

"He says, 'I feel suicidal, I need to be in a hospital,' correct."

"He was waiting for his doctor to call, you started up with him again in the hopes that you'd get a confession from him at that point, didn't you?" asked Murray.

"We continued the interrogation at that time period, sure."

"Did he ever deviate from his position that he was innocent and didn't kill Lisa Pruett?"

"No," said Gray.

"So you failed in your mission, with all the advice you had and all the training, to get a confession from Kevin Young?"

"We did not get a traditional confession."

"You didn't get a confession," Murray corrected. "But you did drive him to the edge of suicide, didn't you?"

"Something did."

Chapter Thirty-Six

THE CURIOUS CONFESSION

A WOMAN NAMED EDYTHE HEINZ came to the stand on July 13 in Judge Sweeney's courtroom after lunch. She was the reason this trial was happening at all, and she was, perhaps, the most important witness for the prosecution. It was Edythe who claimed that Kevin had confessed to her that he killed Lisa Pruett.

"What is your educational background?" Marino asked.

"High-school education, couple years of college," she answered.

"And have you worked recently?"

"I haven't worked for three years. I'm starting my own business."

"Did there come a time when you had some difficulty in your life where you entered into Laurelwood Hospital?"

"Yes."

"Would you explain that to the jury?"

"My father died," said Edythe. "My sons had graduated and joined the navy and I had lost a job."

"When did you go there?"

"November 13 to December 12, 1990."

"And when you went in there, were you taking some medication?" asked Marino.

"Yes. I was taking lithium and clonazepam, and I was being phased off the clonazepam and put on Depakote." These medications are primarily used to treat psychiatric conditions such as bipolar disorder. Clonazepam is helpful for panic attacks.

"Were you able to understand, relate, and function with the rest of the people who came to see you, the people who worked at Laurelwood and the people who were there?"

"Yes."

"So your perception of reality wasn't clouded?"

"No, sir."

"About how long were you there before you met Kevin Young?"

"About a week," she said. "I was asked by one of the staff members if I wanted to go out for a walk around the grounds and we were introduced on the walk."

Edythe said that Kevin seemed to have his own set of rules inside Laurelwood and wasn't pushed to participate in group therapy. He mostly played computer chess all day. He didn't act "crazy." She wondered why he was there at all.

"I'm going to direct your attention to the early part of December of 1990, approximately fifth, sixth, seventh, in that area," said Marino. "Describe to the jury what happened."

"I heard a man scream, another patient, and it reminded me of the screams of my father. My father was a Japanese prisoner of war and was tortured during World War Two, and . . ."

"Where were you when you heard the screams?"

"I was in my room, in my bed," she answered.

"Did you have a roommate?"

"Yes, I did."

"Do you know from where that scream came?"

"The room next to us."

"So you hear this scream," said Marino. "What effect did it have on you?"

"I had a flashback and I thought that I was at home. I thought it was my father screaming and I thought I was at home, as a younger child, and I cried a lot, wanting to know what happened to my daddy."

"Was there a time that you got up and left your room?"

"Yes."

"By that time, had you calmed down?"

"Oh yes, yes."

"So you were no longer feeling the effects of the emotional trauma you suffered from hearing that scream?"

"No."

"Can you estimate about what time of the evening it was?"

"Three or four in the morning."

"Did any of the nurses do anything for you, once you came out of the room and left the station?"

"The one nurse asked me if I wanted to listen to a relaxation tape and I said yes."

Edythe then took the relaxation tape into the common room and sat, listening to it.

"Kevin Young came from behind me and sat down. We had some small talk and I asked him why he was there."

"What did he say?"

"He told me that his father put him there to keep him from the police. I asked him why and he answered because he was accused of killing someone."

"Then what did he say?"

"He said, 'Wait.' He got up and he left me. He came back with some news clippings."

"What were the news clippings of?"

"They were all about Lisa Pruett's murder."

"What did you say when he showed you these clippings of Lisa Pruett?"

"I asked him if he killed her and, without any hesitation, he said yes."

There is no mention in the transcripts of an audible gasp from the gallery, but this is right where it would go. She'd said it directly, confidently, and without hesitation. Kevin had confessed Lisa's murder to her. It was the most damning moment of the entire trial. How would his defense recover?

Marino continued. "Mrs. Heinz, during your treatment, did you keep either a record or a journal of certain things?"

"Yes, I did."

"And did you write some things down about this incident concerning Kevin Young?"

"Yes, I did."

"I'm going to show you what has been marked as State's Exhibits 13-A and 13-B. Take a look at each one of those, please. Do you recognize those?"

"Yes, I do," said Edythe. "They're from my journal."

"Would you start with 13-A and read it for the jury, please?"

She obliged. The passages verified her testimony thus far, reflecting the details of the events that she had told the attorney and the courtroom.

"Did there come a time when you decided to come forward with this information?" asked Marino.

"Yes. I came forward last September, 1992, when I saw Bill Younkin on Channel 5 doing a special on the anniversary of Lisa's death, and I had no idea that this was still an open case. I thought it had been closed."

"Well, what did you do once you realized it was still an open case?"

"I called Bill Younkin. I didn't know where to call to get in touch, what community to get in touch with anyone. So I called Bill Younkin. He directed me to the Shaker police."

"And who did you talk to there?"

"On Friday night I spoke with Sergeant Mullaney. And on Saturday I went down with my husband and I made a statement to the police."

"Nothing further at this time, Your Honor."

"YOU MAY INQUIRE," Judge Sweeney said to Mark DeVan when Marino had finished. DeVan knew that the verdict hinged on this woman's testimony. And her testimony was compelling. DeVan understood that he could win or lose the case based on this cross-examination. Careers hinge on such brief conversations in open court. It happens every day.

"You roomed with Sue, correct?" asked DeVan.

"Yes," said Edythe.

"And when did she leave the hospital, if you recall?"

"December 5."

"That would have been around the time that you say you had this hallucination about your father?"

"It was not a hallucination."

"Excuse me, flashback about your father?"

"Yes."

"Now, you would agree, would you not, ma'am, that when you had this flashback about your father, that was a very terrifying experience, correct?"

"It most certainly was."

"Was that the first time you ever had a flashback?" asked DeVan.

"Yes."

"However, this was not the first time that you had been hospitalized?"

"No."

"You had been hospitalized the previous spring, was it?"

"The previous November. The anniversary of my father's death. I was severely depressed and suicidal."

"And you believe, do you not, that this flashback regarding your father occurred sometime around the fifth, sixth, or seventh of December, 1990?"

"It was after December 5."

"And in that flashback, it's true, is it not, that you could actually see your father's suffering, as if you were a child again, correct?"

"I heard his terrorized scream, yes."

"And while you were doing that, isn't it true, ma'am, that you had another flashback of actually being able to see your father being tortured?"

"Wrong."

"Well, explain to us what you saw in this flashback."

"I heard my father's terrorized scream that no TV movie, theater, anybody, could ever re-create."

"I'm sure it was very memorable," said DeVan.

"And I could not ever begin to understand what they had done to him or others like him. And I felt as if I was a young child, crying as a young child."

"So you saw yourself once again as being a young child, being terrified about what was going on with your father?"

"Yes, sir."

"Now, when you had this flashback, you would agree, would you not, that this was very realistic to you, correct?" asked DeVan.

"Yes, it was."

"However, you realized that it was, in fact, a flashback, and it was a mental process, which was not realistic. It wasn't the real world."

"When I came out of it, I realized it was a flashback."

"But at the time you were living that experience again, weren't you?"

"For a short time, yes."

"So, for that short period of time, you were out of touch with reality, weren't you?"

"Yes, I was."

"It's true, is it not, Mrs. Heinz, that in your statement to the police, which you gave on September 19, 1992, that you describe this event with Kevin as occurring in the last two weeks of November 1990?"

"The days ran together."

"And you were basing that upon your journal entry, were you not, in which at the top of each of these pages, it says 'November '90' or 'November.' "

"I didn't write that for anybody else, other than myself," said Edythe.

"I understand, ma'am, but there's a significance to writing dates on journal pages when you're a psychiatric patient, isn't there? For keeping track of time?"

"There might be."

"And it's important to keep track of the events in your progress, in terms of your treatment, in terms of time, correct?" asked DeVan.

"Yes."

"Now you're saying that although you wrote 'November '90' at the top of that page back then, you are saying that this actually occurred on or after December 7 or after December 5, for that matter?"

"Yes, sir."

"And you knew, did you not, when you went to the police and made your statement that, in fact, Sue had been your roommate until December 5, correct?"

"Yes."

"And Sue could, could she not, ma'am, corroborate or contradict your claims of what occurred regarding this conversation with Kevin Young—if she was still your roommate at the time. You knew that, didn't you?"

"I didn't know that at the time, no."

"But you since figured that out, correct?" asked DeVan.

"Because the date was important to the police," said Edythe.

DeVan continued. "And, of course, since the time you've written that, you realized that Sue was discharged on December 5, correct?"

"Since speaking with the police."

"Since the time that this has occurred, the date has now gone from sometime in November of '90 to after December 5, correct?"

"That's correct."

"And December 5, coincidentally, is the very day that the woman who could contradict you left the hospital. Right?"

"She was discharged."

"She left on December 5, right?"

"That's established."

In fact, Edythe Heinz was now contradicting her own testimony. She'd already told Marino that, at the time of Kevin's confession, she still had a roommate.

"Now," said DeVan, "if you would please turn to 13-B. This particular document in your journal begins with November, Tuesday, correct?"

"Yes."

"Now, isn't it true that the very first line is 'Kevin was different'?"

"Yes."

"You used the word as though this had been written after the fact, correct? Past tense, as we say."

"It may have been written that way, but . . ."

"You didn't say, 'Kevin *is* different,' did you?"

"No, I didn't."

"Now, you also say, 'Kevin was treated different,' correct?"

"Uh-huh."

"You did not say, 'Kevin is treated different,' correct?"

"That's what I wrote."

"You knew back in November or December of 1990, depending on which of these we choose to believe, that Kevin Young was the suspect, correct?"

"I knew after December 5, Kevin Young was the killer, and I believed it and I still do."

"Now, throughout that period of time, you made no effort to call anyone in a law enforcement capacity to report what you claim occurred, correct?"

"I made no effort to tell them what Kevin told me, correct."

"You called a news channel, correct?"

"Because I figured they could tell me where to get in touch with what community, whatever."

"And your only goal was to obtain the name of the proper law enforcement agency, is that what you are saying in calling this journalist?"

"Yes."

"Mr. Younkin came out to your house, did he not?"

"Yes, he did."

"And he brought a cameraman with him, correct?"

"Yes."

"Now, at that time you consented to going on camera and relating this story, which you have given us here in this courtroom, correct?"

"It's not a story," she countered. "But I did consent to the taping, yes."

"Knowing full well that would be broadcast sometime by Channel 5, correct?"

"In cooperation with the prosecutor," said Edythe.

DeVan held up a black spiral notebook. "Now, Mrs. Heinz, do you recognize this item that I'm putting in front of you?"

"Yes."

"This is your journal."

"It was one I used at the time."

"And it's true, is it not, that State's Exhibits 13-A and 13-B you claim came from this journal, correct?"

"They came from that book."

"It's true, is it not, that the page after this page, 13-A, says, December 4, 1990, correct?"

"Correct."

"It's true, is it not, that the preceding journal entry is specifically dated December 2, 1990, correct?"

"Yes."

"So, what you have written down as November of '90 is in between two pages [that] are dated December 2, 1990, and December 4, 1990, correct?"

"That's correct."

"Now, it's also true, is it not, ma'am, that the page on which is written 'December 2' and the page on which is written 'December the 4th' are exactly alike in terms of the type of paper, correct?"

"Yes."

"However, State's Exhibit 13, which you saw was written and put in there in between, is a different type of paper, correct, ma'am?"

"That's correct."

DeVan pounced. "You realized, after you went to the police, that Sue was the one person in this world who might contradict your story if she was still your roommate then, didn't you, ma'am?"

"Objection," said Marino.

"Sustained," said Judge Sweeney.

"You knew in September of 1992, when you went to the police and you recalled your journal, you knew that journal would suddenly become a very important item in a criminal trial, didn't you?"

"No, I did not. The police felt the black book was important and I was just trying to do the best I could."

"You would agree, would you not, ma'am, that looking at those two journal entries, and based upon the difference in the paper and the inability of you to write down a specific date, it's as though those were written long after the fact? You would agree with that?"

"I would not."

"You would not?"

"I most certainly would not."

"You certainly didn't even remember that you had written this down until after you had gone to Bill Younkin of Channel 5, gone to the Shaker police and made a statement, correct, ma'am?"

"I walked in there with one page in my hand, and Lieutenant Gray found the other page, looking through my journal."

In court this turn of events was momentous. The state's biggest witness had admitted to hallucinating the night of the alleged confession, and the journal that she used as proof appeared to have been written after the fact, and the date corrected to make it appear the incident occurred when Edythe Heinz no longer had a roommate, who could have discredited her story.

But you wouldn't know that reading the *Plain Dealer,* which ran this concise headline the following day: YOUNG ADMITTED KILLING LISA PRUETT, WITNESS SAYS.

Chapter Thirty-Seven

THE FINAL WITNESS

DeVan may have been able to cast reasonable doubt on Edythe Heinz's testimony, but she was not the only person from Laurelwood who claimed that Kevin had confessed. And the second witness was not a patient. She worked there. Her name was Anastasia Tressler, and according to those who were present in court that day, she entered the room like a movie star taking the red carpet. She was escorted by two officers, head high, aware of the cameras.

"What is your educational background?" Marino asked after she had sworn on the Bible and given her name.

"I have a degree in clinical psychology and also a bachelor's degree in biochemistry."

After college, near the end of August 1990, Tressler was hired at Laurelwood, but she only worked there for a few months before moving on.

"When you were hired at Laurelwood, what was your position there?"

"I was a mental health technician."

"What was your job?"

"Various duties. Taking vital signs. Doing room checks to check for sharp objects. Talking one-to-one with the patients, recording progress notes so as to communicate with the doctors and nurses."

"Describe the type of facility that Laurelwood is," asked Marino.

"Laurelwood is an acute-care psychiatric hospital, where the average length of stay for a patient is approximately thirty days."

"Do you know about how much it costs to keep a person there?"

"It runs about six hundred dollars a day," she said.

"Would there be times that you would report the notes that you had taken pursuant to your interviews with patients to either a nurse or a psychologist or psychiatrist there?"

"Generally, my notes were recorded in a chart. Rarely, would I talk directly with a doctor or nurse, unless something outstanding happened."

"Did you come to learn the name of an individual named Kevin Young?" asked Marino.

"Yes, I did."

"Would you state for the jury when, and under what circumstances, you first met Kevin Young?"

"Your Honor," said Murray, "may we approach the bench, please?"

Judge Sweeney turned to his court reporter. "Sue, bring the machine."

"YOUR HONOR," SAID Murray, quietly, to the judge, "just for the record, so it's clear, at this time we would object to the testimony that is about to be elicited from Ms. Tressler concerning her interaction with Kevin Young, concerning conversation she had with the defendant, and concerning statements made to her by the defendant on the grounds that [this] is part of the treatment that Kevin received at the hospital and, therefore, it represents privileged communications between Kevin and those who were employed by his doctor to assist his doctor in his care and treatment, and we will object."

Sweeney looked to the prosecutor. "Do you want to be heard?"

"I believe the testimony will show that there was actually no treatment going on at all," said Marino, "and the reason will be given during her testimony." If Marino could prove that Kevin's stay at Laurelwood had all been a ruse to keep him away from the police, then the information would be admissible. Otherwise, it should be covered under the umbrella of patient/doctor confidentiality.

"Go ahead, Mr. Marino," said Judge Sweeney.

Both lawyers returned to their corners.

"WHEN AND WHERE did you first meet Kevin Young?" Marino asked.

"I first met Kevin when I was working on a unit of the hospital called the stabilization unit. Kevin was playing chess by himself."

"Describe the stabilization unit for the jury."

"The stabilization unit is a unit of the hospital where people are taken that are, quote unquote, 'out of control.' Generally, they've had a violent outburst, or they are a danger to themselves, or they're very psychotic."

"Describe to the jury how many staff members it takes generally to take one patient to the stabilization unit."

"Generally, what happened in the hospital was, a code would be called telling all available employees to physically restrain and bring the patient in."

"So it was not a situation where a person would just walk from one area of the room to another?" asked Marino.

"Yes, that's true."

"Were the patients doing something that would require extraordinary attention like this? In other words, what were they acting like?"

"Crazy," said Tressler.

"That a technical term?" asked Marino.

"No."

Tressler explained that the stabilization unit at Laurelwood had eight to ten beds. There was a main corridor, a small activity room, a nurses' station, and four or five padded rooms, where violent patients were put under restraint. These rooms had video cameras so the nurses could observe them.

"When you first saw Kevin Young, where was he?"

"He was in the activity room," said Tressler.

"Was he in any way acting up?"

"No, not at all. In fact, he was the opposite. He was very calm and cool, playing chess with this computerized chess game. I approached him. In this situation you never want to confront a patient, because it's not a real pleasant circumstance in which to meet someone."

"Describe what you mean by 'confront.'"

"You never want to go up to a patient and flat out say, 'So, why are you here,' that kind of thing. It might come up in conversation to ask them what landed them in the hospital, but on first meeting I wouldn't want to do or say anything to scare the person."

Her job was simply to gain their confidence, to get the patients to open up. To trust her. Then she would report that interaction to the doctors. That day Kevin taught Tressler how to play chess.

"Did there come an evening when you were in the community room and an article appeared on television?" asked Marino.

"Yes," said Tressler. "It was something related to a murder in Shaker Heights and Kevin's picture was shown on television."

"What was the reaction of the people watching?"

"There was a certain amount of quiet and then there was hell breaking loose. People were very frightened."

"Was Kevin there?"

"Kevin walked off to his room."

"What did you do?"

"I waited a bit to kind of put the other patients at ease and then I went to Kevin's room to see how he was doing. I just asked if he wanted to talk, and he refused, so I respected that and left."

"Was there another time after this TV interview where you had a discussion about Shaker Heights with Kevin?"

"Yes. I remember over a chess game talking with Kevin about how the people in Shaker Heights were trying to get him out of there, and that he just wanted to go back to school, and they were all against him."

"Was there an order given to you and other staff members as to how you should treat Kevin Young?"

"There was a very clear, stated order not to ask Kevin or to talk about anything going on in Shaker Heights regarding the murder."

"Compared to the therapy given other patients there, would you describe the therapy given to Kevin Young at that time?"

"There was a complete lack of therapy given to Kevin in the hospital."

"I want to call your attention to an incident sometime around the end of October 1990 when you were playing chess with Kevin. Did Kevin make an odd comment about killing a little girl at that time?"

"Out of the blue, Kevin said, 'They think I killed that little girl.' And that threw me for a loop. I didn't know how to react to that. And in the back of my mind, I kept hearing the staff saying not to discuss this with Kevin. So I kind of just let this go and kept playing chess."

"Did you make a note of this and include it in his notes?"

"Yes, I did."

"Do you recall the first of two incidents where you and Kevin were talking and he walked off and you followed him down the hallway?"

"Yes, I do."

"Describe that for the jury."

"I remember walking down the hallway with Kevin, and I remember him abruptly kind of turning away and talking, almost as if he was in a daze, and saying, 'I didn't mean to hurt the little girl. I didn't mean to hurt the little girl.'"

"Was he talking to anyone in particular?"

"To himself."

"Was there a second incident similar to this one?"

"Yes, there was," said Tressler. "Again, walking down the hall, I can't recall the circumstances prior to this outburst, but I remember

Kevin hitting a wall very hard and then saying, again in this kind of dazed mumbling to himself, 'Well, maybe I did hurt the little girl, maybe I did hurt the little girl.'"

MURRAY STOOD FOR the cross. "It would be extremely important for you, since you weren't the doctor, to record in the chart what your conversation was with a given patient, correct?"

"Correct," said Tressler.

"And, in fact, it's true, is it not, that you wrote down in the progress notes at Laurelwood Hospital the discussions and the incidents that you've described here in court today?"

"Yes, I did."

"When is the last time you had an opportunity to see those notes?" Murray asked.

"Before I left Laurelwood."

"Now, may I approach the witness, Your Honor?"

"Yes."

"Ms. Tressler, I'd like to place in front of you a document. You have pretty distinctive handwriting, don't you?"

"If you say so."

"May we approach sidebar?" said Marino.

"Sure," said Judge Sweeney.

THERE WAS A discussion between Murray, Marino, and Judge Sweeney at that time. Marino had caught on to what Murray was after. If what Tressler said was true, her story would have been written down in Kevin's chart. Both lawyers had copies of Tressler's reports. And Marino knew that nothing about a confession was in there. Marino argued that the records they had were incomplete. The full file was still under lock and key at Laurelwood. Her note about the confession must be there.

Judge Sweeney allowed Murray to continue his line of questioning.

"Ms. Tressler, it's true, is it not, that you would write in Kevin's chart in your own handwriting, correct?"

"I don't think I can do it in anyone else's handwriting," Tressler quipped.

"I want to hand you what has been marked for identification as Defendant's Exhibit U. Now, you recognize the handwriting at the bottom of that page as your handwriting, correct?"

"Yes, that's correct."

Murray asked her to go through the entire document and identify all her notes. It became clear that Tressler could find no record of Kevin's so-called confession.

"And it's true, is it not, that there is not one single word about Kevin saying anything remotely resembling, 'I didn't mean to hurt the little girl. I didn't mean to hurt the little girl' on this particular page?"

"Without the benefit of seeing the whole chart, I do not see that written here."

But there was one troubling story that did appear in the document. And Murray got around to it then.

"You asked Kevin whether he would feel better, more positive about himself, when the legalities were finished, correct?"

"Correct," said Tressler.

"And he said, 'No, this torment will never end. I don't know. Maybe the police were right. Maybe I did kill the girl. Maybe I do have three personalities, but I would know that, wouldn't I?' That's what you wrote down?"

"That's what I wrote."

AT THAT POINT another sidebar was requested. Everyone agreed that they needed the complete file from Laurelwood to know for sure if what Tressler alleged was true. The judge asked DeVan's investigator Peter Gray to drive out to Laurelwood and pick them up. (Author's note: He was not related to Detective Tom Gray.)

"You tell those people that I sent you out there," the judge instructed. "And that I want them here, and that if they don't produce them, I'm going to have the sheriff go out there and bring them down here. Tell them that. It's for the entire hospital record."

The judge told Marino that when the file arrived, he could review it for Tressler's notes, but he absolutely could not consider the rest of the contents, which would include every private detail about Kevin that had been discussed with his doctors during his stay. Then Judge Sweeney sent everyone to lunch.

AFTER SOME TIME DeVan's investigator returned with a hefty file. Tressler was allowed to sit with it to review her notes. When she was done, the jury returned and Murray continued his cross-examination.

"My question is, Ms. Tressler, did you, or did you not, write anyplace in this entire chart the fact that Kevin Young said to you, 'I didn't mean to hurt the little girl. I didn't mean to hurt the little girl'?"

"We've both gone over those transcripts," said Tressler. "And I do not see it written anywhere in these charts."

Anastasia Tressler walked out of the courtroom, deflated. That infectious confidence, that assured swagger, had disappeared.

Chapter Thirty-Eight

THE MOSAIC

CLOSING ARGUMENTS BEGAN MONDAY MORNING, July 19, 1993. The prosecution had presented a compelling case against Kevin Young. It was now Carmen Marino's job to sum it all up for the jury in one simple narrative that would inspire them to look past the lack of any physical evidence and find Kevin Young guilty of murder. Everything that had transpired since September 14, 1990, had led to this day. Every phone call. Every police interview. Every polygraph.

Judge Sweeney explained the procedure for the jury. "Ladies and gentlemen, as I indicated to you Friday, at this time the attorneys are going to present their final arguments. Now, in a case like this, since the state has the burden of proof, the state will have an opportunity to argue twice. So Mr. Marino will argue, Mr. DeVan will argue, and then Mr. Marino will have a rebuttal argument. After that, the court will instruct you as to the law. Remember, these arguments are not evidence. Mr. Marino?"

"GOOD MORNING, FOLKS," said Marino. He brought his chair out so that he could sit in front of the jury as he spoke. Normally, he would stand to give his closing argument, but that day his back wasn't having it. He was in pain, quite a lot of pain, in fact. So he did his best from his chair.

"I'm going to talk to you a little bit about this case now," he said. "Closing arguments are designed to give you an appreciation not only of the evidence that you have heard, but of the state's conclusions and the inferences we think you should draw in this case.

"The defense has pleaded not guilty, and in simple terms what they are saying is there's a reasonable doubt. 'I didn't do it. I'm innocent. I want to leave this courtroom not guilty with no societal restrictions on my conduct.'

"There is a lot in this case that goes to state of mind, the intent of which, if not all of it, deals with Kevin's mental aberration, if not outright psychotic behavior."

"I will object," said DeVan.

"Sustained."

Marino continued. "There have been no facts presented to you in this case that anyone other than these six people knew about that meeting between Daniel and Lisa that night, and we've listed them here: Daniel Dreifort, Lisa Pruett, Kevin Young, Christopher Jones, Tex Workman, and Rebecca Boatright.

"Nobody who has testified sees or hears anybody on the street. They don't see any cars, any motorcycles. No one is walking around, and, indeed, when you consider just how desolate this area is at that time, and that it's Friday morning, a school night, there's no commercial area here, there is nothing to attract anybody if a killer decides to, say randomly, go someplace to kill somebody just for the heck of it.

"Now, at about twelve-thirty, screams are heard. It's the state's position and our contention that Lisa Pruett rode her bike to this location and was slain, that there was no intermediate meeting with anybody.

"They are not just screams of youngsters in rivalry. You know that unquestionably they are the screams of a young girl in dire straits. They are the screams of a young girl being murdered as the killer continually assaults her.

"There were a number of stab wounds. The final stab wounds to her back, four in a row, were with such sufficient force that a rib was severed. You may even reasonably decide, consistent with the state's contention, that not only was she murdered there, she was not raped, but the killer with bloody hands disrobed her ignominiously and displayed her.

"And you have to use your recollection of the facts, along with your common experience of how long you think it would take to do something to this person who has just been murdered, to take her clothes off and display her that way, to take one shoe off so that the other part of her clothing can be taken off of her.

"What state of mind is that killer in at the time he's doing that? And how long does he stay there? And you will realize what an extraordinary stroke of luck it is that [the] person was able to do that and leave the scene without anyone recognizing him or even knowing about his presence. By any standards, that's extraordinary.

"What did you think when you saw that scene? That's not the work of a normal human being. That's a psychotic killing. The mind of that killer expressed a desire to do an extraordinary amount of violence to Lisa."

"Objection," said DeVan.

"Overruled."

"I'm going to take you through it as best we can, based on the testimony of everybody who has testified in this case," said Marino. "Lisa's state of mind is a happy one. She wants to see her boyfriend. There's nothing in the case about her ever being in fear of her boyfriend. There's no record that she went to the police and said, 'My boyfriend threatened me one time, I'm in fear of him, but now we're back together.' Unquestionably, she's in a happy state of mind. She wants to see her boyfriend that night and she rides to this scene. She gets off of her bike and leans her bike into the bushes.

"The state contends nothing happened on the sidewalk. That's not definite. We don't have to prove that beyond a reasonable doubt, because the only issue we have to prove beyond a reasonable doubt is that Kevin is the murderer. And in any case it's described, I think most appropriately, as a mosaic. The portrait of Lisa's killer is made up of different pieces of evidence put together reasonably to the point where you have no doubt, no reasonable doubt, that Kevin is the killer.

"You know the killer's on the other side of that bush. That person waiting back there knew what he was going to do. He got there on foot and he escaped on foot. That makes it a neighborhood crime. He sees her getting off her bike. He has his knife out. He hates that person, that sex, that human being. For whatever reason he hates her.

"Is there a reason to hate Lisa Pruett? Is she a bad person? Is she a slut? Is she some reprobate that no one would care if she were killed? Always go back to the scene when you have a difficult time reconciling an issue presented to you by a witness. What does the scene tell you about the killer? Does the killer have a demented psychosis he can't control? Or is he on Robitussin? We'll get to that at a later point.

"He went there knowing what he was going to do. This is not an accident or a mistake. It's purposeful and intentional. It was purposeful and intentional with prior calculation and design, meaning premeditation.

"You tell me, as a jury, how long it takes to inflict nineteen stab wounds. You can go through this. You can pretend you have a knife in your hand. How long would it take to stab a girl to death, a girl that is fighting for her life, a girl whom the killer has grabbed by her blue shirt, pulled it around her neck so tight that it left the imprint of the collar in her neck? Who has testified in this case and described to you, witness, after witness, after witness, building the mentality of the killer, the mentality of Kevin Young? Who fits the mind of the killer?

"Who has a motive? Daniel Dreifort doesn't have a motive. He's investigated as a possible suspect right away for this reason: where there's a boyfriend/girlfriend–type relationship, always the survivor is looked at, because human nature tells you, ladies and gentlemen, the other side of the love coin is hate.

"Who focuses on their relationship in an unnatural way? This girl didn't mean anything to Kevin Young. I mean, she never dated him. There was no reason for him to be so concerned about why Dan has a better relationship with women than him. Not in a normal mind.

"And when we get to the statements he made while he was in Laurelwood, when asked 'did you do it, did you kill her,' and he says 'yes,' he's in a lucid moment. He's not imagining. He's not in a trance. And Mrs. Heinz said, 'Why did you do it?' And his statement is verbatim, 'I did it because.' There's no reason. 'I did it because.' If you take a psychological approach to it, the answer has to be 'I did it' because the killer is nuts. 'I did it' because the killer is demented, but when he says, 'I did it because,' that's consistent with the scene. There's no reason for this murder. He wants to get back at the rest of the world.

"Another interesting note that you can consider, he's got no women friends his age. He's got no girls that he dates. He doesn't have the ability to develop a rapport with a woman his own age. That is a problem throughout this case. This girl represents something to him that he can't have, he doesn't know how to get. And I don't mean sexually. He doesn't know how to do it. It must be very frustrating.

"So when you see these girls testify, remember their age. Remember their age at that time. Sixteen years old, folks. You're immortal. You're never going to die. Even if Kevin says he's going to kill Lisa, who believes that wacko? Why do you think we send our youngest and best to go to war? We're all old enough to know that you don't want to go to war if you don't have to. Send the youngest. They don't believe they're going to die.

"The next witness was Daniel Dreifort, the central focus of the defense case, whose main effort was made to get you to believe that Daniel Dreifort killed Lisa Lee Pruett, the girl he liked, the girl he wanted to see, the girl he has been friends with—a man who has no criminal violence in his background, no record, no evidence in this case that he has ever hurt anybody.

"And before I go into his testimony, let me tell you what the defense is. Anticipating meeting Lisa and wanting to have a Robitussin party, Dan took the Robitussin, put it into the Hawaiian Punch bottle. He's got twelve bottles in his room, but he doesn't want his parents to know he's drinking Robitussin that night.

"So he drinks the Robitussin. He goes outside. Now they're going to have consensual sex with a condom outside in the neighbor's lot. They do that. He goes through his trance, pulls his knife, and stabs her nineteen times with her screaming at him. Washes himself off with the hose, goes back inside the house, sees his father, goes back outside the house to look and see where the screams came from. That's a really stupid scenario. That's really pretty silly.

"Look, the Robitussin, they make it sound like it has alcohol and half cocaine and half heroin in it. It's cough syrup that has alcohol in it. Anytime the pharmaceutical companies want to sell us anything, they put alcohol in it. It makes you feel good, makes you high. The guy drinks it. He's trying to get high, right? So at one time in his life, he goes through a bout with his father and he drinks Robitussin, and now he's a murderer?

"Could Dan Dreifort have killed the girl and ran back home for no reason at all? That could have happened, folks. What does the state concentrate on? What did happen.

"So now we have this attention on Daniel Dreifort," said Marino. "The defense can do with him what they will. It's the state's contention and position he's not the killer. He's innocent in the true sense of the word 'innocent,' as it applies to the identity of the killer. And I don't like the idea that they are going to suggest these things to you, but I can't stop it, because someone may say, 'Well, this is just quiet Kevin. Let him go and maybe the state will try somebody else.' That's not the way we do things in this community. You got one shot, and one shot only, at the killer of Lisa Lee Pruett."

"Objection," said DeVan.

"Sustained," said Judge Sweeney.

"This is our opportunity to show you who killed Lisa Pruett. And it's not Daniel Dreifort.

"Now, Anastasia Tressler was criticized because some of what she said she made notes about are not in the documents that defense counsel had available to cross-examine her on. Here is her November 28, 1990, entry: 'Patient met with lawyer.' What is the significance of this? You have information before you that not only did Mr. Young come and see him at Laurelwood, but that his attorney came to see him there. His attorney was telling him to keep his mouth shut."

"Objection!" shouted DeVan.

"Sustained."

"Your Honor, I ask he be reprimanded for his conduct," said DeVan.

"I'm referring to a fact in evidence," said Marino. "And I'll point it out to the court if you wish."

"Come on up here," said the judge.

Marino and DeVan joined the judge at sidebar and had an off-the-record conversation. Then Marino was allowed to continue.

"What's in evidence is that Kevin said his lawyer told him not to talk to anybody," said Marino. "You may even be posed with the argument—and it's a fair one, because it's the same analysis a good investigator goes through when they look at evidence—look at Daniel Dreifort and look at the defendant. Both were in hospitals, both have fathers who provide an alibi, both have access to knives, both are in the neighborhood. 'How can you say my client did it when Dan Dreifort could have done it?' It's the same thing that juries across this country, down through history, have done. You look at one person's action and his background and what people say about him, and another person, what he says he did, and you make a decision, one person didn't do it, one person did do it.

"And when you go through these facts, the state is confident you will find the defendant guilty of murdering Lisa Lee Pruett. Thank you, folks."

"Thank you, Mr. Marino," said Judge Sweeney. "Mr. DeVan, you may begin."

Chapter Thirty-Nine

FORGET IT, JAKE, IT'S SHAKER HEIGHTS

If G. Gordon Liddy hadn't sent his goon squad into the Watergate Hotel to tap the phones at the headquarters of the Democratic National Committee, someone else would have presented closing arguments for Kevin Young's defense. That crime was the first link in a long chain of events that led to Mark DeVan becoming Kevin's lawyer. For every action there is an equal and opposite reaction.

"If it pleases the court," said DeVan, "you have been chosen as a jury to witness one of the greatest travesties of justice ever seen in an American courtroom. The State of Ohio is attempting to prosecute this young man, not on evidence, but on theory. Wild speculation as to his mental processes. No physical evidence. Supposition as to whether or not he hated Lisa Pruett because he had arguments about Dan Dreifort.

"The prosecution of this case is an injustice to the memory of Lisa Pruett and it is an injustice to Kevin Young. Kevin Young is innocent. He did not kill Lisa Pruett. He was at home that night with his parents—after eleven-ten P.M. until at least one-fifteen A.M., when his father turned out the light.

"Lisa was murdered sometime around twelve-thirty, but Kevin's emotional problems and his naïve and childish ways brought him to the attention of the authorities. They made him an easy target for those who would prey upon him, those who preferred to twist the facts of this case to fit him. It's as though the Shaker Police Department decided, 'Hey, let's write a story, only we'll do the last chapter first, and then we'll fill in the rest of this case.' And that's what has occurred here.

"I'm glad that Mr. Marino has that crystal ball and knows what I'm going to tell you, but you already know what I'm going to tell you, much of it, because it came out in this courtroom.

"The investigation into Lisa's death began with a desperate attempt to find someone, anyone, to charge with her murder, and when they focused on Kevin Young, the Shaker police suffered from tunnel vision for the next two and a half years.

"Now, if we are to understand the state's argument about why Kevin Young is guilty, I think we should address it point by point. First they say the killer had a certain emotional makeup and was an enraged killer. Well, this bare argument is based upon the speculation that because Kevin Young had emotional problems, he must be the killer. But it seems that every one of these young people had emotional problems, Dan Dreifort included.

"To focus upon Kevin Young's mental problems is like focusing upon a grain of sand at the beach and ignoring the beach.

"The state relies upon the testimony of the AP Posse. Let's go back to the very genesis of the AP Posse in this courtroom. We saw the claims of [Daniel] Messinger. Remember that? Oh, Kevin threatened Dan and Lisa. And on cross-examination, he admitted, well, he really couldn't remember if that was based upon what he heard or what someone told him.

"When Lisa was found dead, the AP Posse got their heads together, they started thinking about this. Oh yeah, he threatened Dan and said something about Dan and his slut. Must have meant Lisa, and the term 'slut' was converted to Lisa. They speculated that 'slut' meant 'Lisa Pruett,' and that speculation turned to fact when they spoke with the police, but what the state has ignored was the statement of Ken Mitsumoto and Debbie Dreifort herself.

"Ken Mitsumoto said, yep, Kevin used to call somebody a slut. Was it Lisa? Oh no. It was Becca Boatright he was talking about. And Debbie Dreifort used to talk with Kevin, and she said he never talked bad about Lisa. What Kevin used to say was how he hated her brother, thought he was a real jerk, but he never talked bad about Lisa.

"And then it came on the news that Kevin Young was the prime suspect, and the AP Posse's rightness was confirmed in their own minds, and these children told each other how right they were, and what they did was the right thing to do. After all, they are the best and the brightest Shaker Heights has to offer. And in all this righteousness, the truth got lost."

After a moment DeVan continued. "Now the next item of evidence that the state claims supports their theory was that Kevin knew Lisa was going to Dan Dreifort's house that night. So did Tex Workman. So did Chris Jones. So did Kim Rathbone. So did Jennifer Margulies. So did [Daniel] Messinger. And most importantly, so did Dan Dreifort. And who knows who else each of them told?

"To believe that this has some relevance to this case is to believe that Kevin Young went over there to murder Lisa Pruett in the midst of a crowd at a party, which is what he thought was planned, and that's just ludicrous. That's absolutely ridiculous. Kevin went home that night. That's where he went and that's where he stayed.

"But Rebecca Boatright, her lies are symptomatic of a greater evil that prevails in this case. The lies show the lengths to which certain parties will go to manipulate the truth. They changed their testimony to fit the Shaker agenda. Rebecca Boatright can join the rest as perjurers.

"The most important thing about Kevin's interrogation in Columbus is that not only did Kevin not confess, he vehemently denied any involvement in the murder of Lisa Pruett. That was a considerable feat for him to do. He was a vulnerable young man with a history of emotional problems at the hands of a skilled interrogator. That, in itself, shows his innocence.

"And then Kevin supposedly hid out at Laurelwood and received special treatment. Let's clear the air here of one basic fact. Kevin Young was hospitalized at Laurelwood as a direct result of the actions of the Shaker Heights police. That's what happened.

"As developed during cross-examination of Detective Gray, Kevin was driven to near suicide as a result of his interrogation. He was told he could never go home to Shaker Heights.

"You know, I thought Americans fought a World War so we wouldn't have to live under Nazi rule. I really thought that. That's what this was tantamount to. I know a lot of you might remember shallow graves and rice paddies so that we could stand here in America and live here, be treated fairly, but you hear things like that, and it rips your stomach out!

"The officers of the Shaker Heights Police Department forgot what their roles were, and I guess also they had no code of decency. None at all. But the torment did not end there in Columbus. The police went to the Young residence and spoke to Mrs. Young, Maryanne. They told her that her son was very sick, that he should be hospitalized, and they knew things, and they needed him hospitalized, but they wouldn't tell her what they knew. What they knew was how they treated him. They wouldn't reveal that.

"So they stomped off and they left the Young home and proceeded on their way. What was the effect of this band of storm troopers? They drove Kevin to the brink of suicide, and they reached inside his mother and ripped her heart out. And when this didn't work, the mayor called her and threatened her. That's Shaker Heights.

"What is really appalling here is that the officers of the city of Shaker Heights caused Kevin to be hospitalized, and now the State of Ohio has the gall to come into this courtroom and claim that he was hospitalized to warehouse him. The State of Ohio has lied to you—out and out lied to you.

"And lastly the state bases its case on statements made to patients and a mental health worker at Laurelwood Hospital. Let's analyze that. Anastasia Tressler was a trained mental health worker who swore to an oath from that stand, 'Oh, I wrote this all down, if only I can see my notes. It's all in my notes.' Only there were two things that she never counted on in this courtroom. Number one, the power of a subpoena. Number two, the ability of J. Michael Murray to cross-examine, because when confronted with those notes, she tried to claim, 'Oh, it doesn't look like all of them.'

"So we gave her the entire chart. And guess what? She said, 'Well, if I didn't put them in my notes, I must have told the doctor.' She amended things. The truth of the matter is, she got caught lying. That's what she did. She jumped on the Shaker bandwagon, thinking she would never get caught in the act of lying. 'Once the pen has writ, it moves on.' That's exactly what happened.

"So now we have dealt with what has been the state's part of this case. Let's get back to reality and away from theory. The state's proof of guilt is based upon theory. Our proof of innocence is based upon physical evidence.

"You have before you a chart showing the physical evidence in this case, the physical evidence the state does not want you to think about, but it's there and cannot be ignored. Let's start right at the top.

"First, Lisa's body. Lisa's body was found next door to the Dan Dreifort house, with nineteen stab wounds. And then there are Lisa's clothes, pants, and panties around her right ankle, her shirt pushed up over her bra, and her left shoe was off. It was also untied. Then there was Lisa's wounds. When Chief Brosius arrived on the scene, his first conclusion was this was a neighborhood crime. You can't get much more neighborly than Dan Dreifort, less than a hundred feet away.

"Secondly, pants and panties around her right ankle, her shirt pushed up over her bra. You know what this was? This was a couple of kids sneaking off to have sex. That's what this was. There's no doubt about it. And what's most interesting is, and you'll see that in the photos, her left shoe was untied.

"Now, why would she untie her left shoe? The state has this theory that the killer undressed her after she was murdered, after she was stabbed—and it's just a theory. But I want you to ask yourselves the very basic question that apparently the police never asked themselves. Who is the one man in this world on September 14, 1990, for whom Lisa Pruett would take her pants off? Dan Dreifort. And where was he? One hundred feet away in the house next door. Supposedly.

"And bear in mind, neither the pants nor panties are torn, and her shirt is pushed up over her bra. She knows what was going on.

"Then we come to the two hairs on the victim's shirt. Her shirt was scraped at the county coroner's office. Hairs were found. They didn't match Kevin Young, but the police weren't satisfied, so they sent those hairs down to the FBI lab. And they were inspected by an agent there. Well, that agent excluded Kevin Young. And you know the police have come into this courtroom and made a point of telling you several things about how conscientious they were. 'Oh, we're sure we had the right suspect. We excluded all other suspects. We did everything we could.' They did everything they could to pin it on Kevin Young, and anything [that] might clear him, they never bothered with. They never even tested those hairs to see if they were Lisa's.

"Now, if those two hairs turned out to be the hair of Lisa Pruett, fine, then it's a couple of hairs of Lisa Pruett and it means nothing. Clearly, it wasn't the hair of Kevin Young. And what if it wasn't the hair of Kevin Young and wasn't the hair of Lisa Pruett? Then what do you have? You got the killer's hair, very possibly. Nobody bothered to do it because it did not fit their agenda. They also found animal hairs on Lisa. And you will remember that the animal hairs have never been compared to Dan's dog. Right? The State of Ohio didn't bother. Shaker Heights police didn't bother. They didn't want to know.

"The blood at the crime scene, it was not Kevin Young's. Lisa's bicycle, it was leaned against the hedges, ten feet from her body. It was grabbed by Dan Dreifort. There were no fingerprints of Kevin Young. You know what's really interesting about that particular bicycle? They were unable to make any comparisons of fingerprints at all. It appeared to have been wiped clean.

"Footprints were found on the south side of the Dreifort property. There was no match to Kevin Young.

"And that brings us to [Dan] Dreifort. [Dan] Dreifort spent five weeks in the Cleveland Clinic away from the one woman in this world that he wanted to be with. He had two thoughts on his mind for five weeks. One, get out, and number two, be with Lisa.

"He claims that his only plans were tentative with Lisa. If she could get away, she would sneak out. But other witnesses who spoke with them that night—Jennifer Margulies, Kim Rathbone, Chris Jones—all testified that Dan planned on her coming over. It was a given. It was a done deal. She was coming over.

"So Dan Dreifort lied to you. He got out. He planned that night. He planned that rendezvous, and then he claims that after being away from her for five weeks, he forgot she was coming over? That's ridiculous.

"And then he said he heard screams. He still didn't remember that Lisa was coming over. He thinks nobody in this courtroom remembers being young and being in love and wanting to be with someone and being intimate. He thinks he buffaloed the police, so he can buffalo these jurors. He thinks that you people will actually believe that he's going to forget about Lisa Pruett coming over that night.

"And then the pocketknife. Less than a hundred yards from the body, there was found in Dan Dreifort's bedroom his pocketknife, the only weapon in this case that the coroner said cannot be excluded as the murder weapon.

"Now, also found in Dan Dreifort's bedroom as a result of his, as he likes to call it, 'Robitussin experiences,' are what he claims are souvenirs. The average dosage is two teaspoons. He would take six ounces. And then he tried to tell you, you know we did this in Virginia. Until he was confronted with the fact that Robitussin also comes in a generic brand sold at Finast, and suddenly he was caught in a lie. And he said, oh, 'I stand corrected.' Twelve empty Robitussin bottles. And what's really, really interesting in this case is that from the hospital he sent Lisa Pruett a shopping list. Why would he send her a shopping list like this unless he planned on doing Robo that very night?

"Since he left the witness stand here, Dan has yet to show his face in this courtroom. He has never come back. And you think he'd have the decency to come back and check in on the trial of the man accused of killing his loved one. It's because he's ashamed. He's ashamed that he knows more about this murder than he's telling.

"This is the person Shaker police chose to ignore, the person who lied to them when he said to one officer, he did not hear any screams, and then to another officer, he said he did hear screams, then to another officer, he said, 'Oh, both Mr. and Mrs. Pruett and my parents knew Lisa was coming over,' and then later on he says, 'Oh no, they didn't know. They didn't know she was coming over.' The person who got out of treatment the very day of her murder, set up a party, and in whose room they found twelve Robitussin bottles.

"It's clear that Dan Dreifort was going to do Robo that night, and this was a longstanding plan of his. He knew Lisa was coming over and he never had to leave the house when he heard screams because he was right next to it.

"The AP Posse decided to saddle up and come to his rescue. And the police were forever barred from chasing this Shaker Heights intellectual, this talented student.

"Ladies and gentlemen, you will soon retire to deliberate this case. It is a very important day today because you will be deciding the fate of a young man, Kevin Young. It's a day that Kevin and his family have looked forward to for more than two and a half years, because this is the day that he prays an American jury will clear him.

"We believe that when you look at all the evidence—not just the theories of the state, but the hard evidence in this case—you will agree that none of it leads to Kevin Young. What has happened here is the State of Ohio has created a second victim besides Lisa. It has created a victim of Kevin Young. What they have done is to destroy Kevin's life.

"The evidence in this case cries out for you to acquit him, to find him not guilty. It's now up to you."

Chapter Forty

THE VERDICT

McCarty's headline the next day: YOUNG FATE IN JURY'S HANDS. "To acquit Young the jury would have to discount testimony about Young's repeated threats against the couple, and later his tacit and sometimes direct admissions of guilt."

On the first day of deliberation, the jury foreperson—a young woman who worked in debt collections—called for a vote to see where everyone in the group stood. She ripped pages from a notebook, passed them around, and everyone wrote "guilty" or "not guilty" on their piece before passing it back. The vote came out ten to two in favor of an acquittal for Kevin Young.

The foreperson then led a discussion about the evidence against Kevin, or lack thereof. They went through all the testimony from Dan's friends again. And they debated the believability of Kevin's alibi.

At 11 A.M., the foreperson called for another vote. This time it came out eleven to one, not guilty. There was a single holdout, and he was digging in his heels. They debated whether they should declare a hung jury, but that would just pass the responsibility on to another group of citizens, and it would put Kevin and everyone else through another long trial. No, they couldn't bear to do that. So they debated some more.

At 3 P.M., the foreperson rang a buzzer, announcing that the jury had reached a unanimous verdict.

Judge Sweeney sent out word to the prosecutors and to the defense team. The Youngs were called in. Quickly everyone returned to the courtroom. DeVan was optimistic. He felt his closing argument had gone over well. Just as they were about to begin, the judge noticed that the Pruetts were not present. Someone had forgotten to notify Lisa's family, so the police were dispatched to give them a ride downtown.

Finally, at 4:30 P.M., with the Pruetts in the audience surrounded by supporters, the jury was brought in. The verdict was read: "Not guilty."

An audible gasp was heard in the courtroom. Someone clapped.

Kevin grabbed Michael Murray in a bear hug as he wiped away tears.

The jurors immediately exited through the rear door, accompanied by deputy sheriffs, who escorted them downstairs and into waiting cars.

Marino and Wetzel left without speaking to the throng of reporters standing in the back.

"When a young man is innocent, he's acquitted," said DeVan as microphones pressed around him. "Kevin is a young man who never sought notoriety. It was thrust on him. He has lived through this. He has survived and now he's going to go on with his life."

That night DeVan celebrated with the Youngs. Dozens of friends and well-wishers had gathered at their house in Shaker Heights. As the evening began, Tal made a short speech. "Let's not forget that a young lady is dead and the killer is still out there," he said.

MCCARTY HAD THE final word, of course. He wrote one last article that ran in the oversized Sunday edition of the *Plain Dealer* on August 1.

"Verdict left jurors frustrated," he wrote. "They felt a gnawing sense that, during the three-week trial, they hadn't heard the entire story of the troubled young defendant from Shaker Heights. They were right.

"The rules of evidence prevented the jurors from hearing about the three lie-detector tests Young flunked—or about the one he passed. Nor could the jurors possibly have heard the macabre whispers of Young's neighbors, to police: that Young, as a youth, had drowned his family's pet cat.

"'We all felt sick to our stomachs,' said Nancy McMurtrey, a Lakewood businesswoman who was the jury's foreperson. 'There was a chance [Kevin did it], but there just wasn't the evidence. I went in with reasonable doubt and I came out with more reasonable doubt.'

"Young is now free, cloaked in immunity from double jeopardy.

"The last holdout to join the majority now says he believed all along that Young was guilty, but switched his vote under pressure. 'Mr. Kevin Young will be judged again by someone up above,' said the juror, who asked not to be identified. 'But when that happens, he won't have his fancy lawyers with him.'"

Kevin read the story, of course, along with half a million other subscribers. The thing about the cat stung deeply. There was simply no truth in it—just rumors from neighbors treated as fact. He'd been found not guilty, sure, but this article proved he would never be seen as innocent.

Later that night Kevin drove out to Ridgebury Boulevard, in Maple Heights, and parked his car beside the bridge over Interstate 271. He got out, climbed onto the railing. Ten lanes of traffic whizzed by, below him.

Kevin hesitated.

At that moment Sergeant Clifford Uzell, of the Mayfield Heights Police Department, arrived. The officer got out and slowly approached the young man.

"I'll jump!" Kevin warned him.

But Uzell spoke calmly and persuaded Kevin to climb down. As soon as Kevin's feet touched the pavement, Uzell grabbed him. Kevin burst into tears. He was released to his parents that night. But his car was impounded. And everyone read about it the next day.

LATER THAT WEEK Judge Sweeney received a letter in the mail:

> Judge!
>
> How much did you make on this dirty low life verdict? The sooner that numb brained punk murderer hangs himself, the better. If not, someone will get him. This is the most rotten piece of justice ever by a money-hungry judge and lawyers. Revenge is coming soon.
>
> *Lisa's Friends*

Part Three

JUDGMENT

Chapter Forty-One

I HEAR YOU PAINT HOUSES

I SPOKE WITH KEVIN YOUNG just once before his terrible and untimely death. This was in 2008. I had just turned thirty and I was working as a reporter for *Cleveland Scene* (that's the free *Village Voice*–type paper for my city). I lied to get Kevin to meet with me. Or, I should say, his friend lied for me.

I was researching the Lisa Pruett cold case for a feature article timed around the eighteenth anniversary of her murder. But I couldn't get Kevin to return my calls. Luckily, word got around—Shaker Heights is still a small, weird world, after all—and a man who was friends with Kevin got in contact with me. "Meet me at the coffee shop in Cleveland Heights," he said. "I'll bring Kevin. Pretend you're interviewing house painters."

Since the trial Kevin had found occasional work painting houses on the east side of Cleveland, eking out a living despite being a quasi celebrity pariah. Though he'd been acquitted, the general consensus in Shaker Heights was that a fancy lawyer had tricked the jury, and a guilty man had gone free. The media in Cleveland never ran articles about the hunt for Lisa's real killer, like they did with other local unsolved cases. The Shaker Heights police were not investigating the case. It was over. The bad guy won.

I had my doubts about Kevin's guilt even then. Through a retired journalist I had come into possession of boxes of police reports related to Lisa's case, and what I'd found inside made me see the case in a different light. When you lay out the interviews in chronological order, it's easy to see that Kevin was not a suspect until Dan's friends went to the police and said that he should be. And there was not one piece of evidence that connected Kevin to the crime scene.

Kevin was five minutes late to our meeting. I was talking with his friend at the coffee shop on Cedar when he finally came through the door in white pants spotted with paint. He was still handsome. Square jaw. Wide shoulders. But his hair was salt-and-pepper now, and there were deep wrinkles at his eyes.

I stood and shook his hand.

"I'm James Renner," I said.

He remembered my name from the messages I'd left for him, I guess, because he turned to his friend and said, "Why did you do this?" Then he walked away in a hurry.

I caught up with Kevin in the parking garage behind the shop.

"I don't think you did it," I told him.

Kevin stopped at the door to his car, keys in hand. I stepped closer. He didn't look at me at first. "People write about me and it's on the Internet now," he said. "And it doesn't matter I was found not guilty. I've been on four dates in the last year. They Googled my name and there was never a second date."

"I want to hear what you think happened," I said.

"You already know what I think happened," he said. "Keep at it."

And then he got into his car and drove away and I never did see him again. I finished the article later that week and it was published in *Scene* at the end of July. They ran a full-page photograph of Lisa's hand on the cover. The picture was taken at the morgue the day she died. Her fingers are curled into a loose fist, her nails painted pink, a friendship bracelet still wrapped around her wrist, two spots of blood on her skin.

I put the police reports and my notes into a box and the box went in my basement. They were destroyed when my house flooded in a storm. That was twelve years ago, and while I can't say that I've thought about Kevin every day since then, I never forgot about him for long. At times, mostly while lying in bed at night, I found myself trying to figure it all out, how it had gone so wrong, and if maybe there was still a way to learn the truth.

Chapter Forty-Two

THE SERIOUS PROBLEM OF INTERNET SLEUTHS

I NEED TO TELL YOU about one of the worst days of my life and you're going to think it has nothing to do with Kevin, but it does. At least I think it does. And anyway, it's how I ended up getting pulled back into the Lisa Pruett mystery.

Can I begin this story with a "What had happened was"? I've always wanted to say that.

What had happened was, I had just written a book called *True Crime Addict.* It was about a UMass student named Maura Murray, who disappeared under mysterious circumstances. The book came out in May 2016. A couple weeks after its release, I woke up and checked my email to find a note from one of my mentors, true crime author M. William Phelps. The subject line read simply: *New Yorker. If it's any consolation,* he wrote, *I've been hammered like this before. I don't understand it. Why even write a piece that only attacks a book writer?*

That's a bullshit way to start the day, let me tell you. I pulled up *The New Yorker* online and there it was: "*True Crime Addict* and the serious problem of Internet sleuths," by Michelle Dean. It was an indictment of armchair detectives in general and of me in particular. Here's just a snippet: "Renner, who was a reporter for an alternative weekly in Cleveland until he was fired in 2009, has no particular connection to the case other than an apparent obsessive streak that previously was laser-focused on the disappearance of a ten-year-old girl named Amy Mihaljevic." Fucking yuck.

The article was weirdly personal and left out mitigating context, like how Amy and I were the same age when she was abducted from the town next door, in 1989. And how I've been trying to find her killer since I was eleven years old. And sure, I was fired by the CEO who owned *Scene.* I told him to go fuck himself when he'd spiked a political exposé I'd written that embarrassed one of his fellow Republicans.

But more than that, this was a major literary magazine punching down. I wasn't big enough for a review in *The New Yorker.* It would be like Charles McNulty blasting a high-school production of *Our Miss Brooks.* It felt personal, but I had no truck with Michelle Dean, as far as I knew. She was a former *Gawker* writer—that bastion of journalism that was sued into bankruptcy after they released Hulk Hogan's no-holds-barred sex tape. And she already had a reputation for fabulism; in 2014, the *Washington Post* had devoted an article to Michelle's lax relationship with the truth. From *Gawker* to the literati's inner sanctum in two years. Harold Ross was spinning in his grave.

What I thought to do was reach out to other writers who had recently covered true crime for *The New Yorker.* I wanted to know what their take was on *True Crime Addict.* Was it really as offensive as she'd said?

The New Yorker had recently run a story about the phenomenon of the Netflix docuseries *Making a Murderer*. It was quite good and raised some solid points about sensationalism and the lack of thought given to the subjects of these documentaries. I emailed the author and asked if I could send her a digital copy of my new book. She wrote back right away: *I'm surprised that you enjoyed my piece on "Making a Murderer," as it specifically indicts projects like your own.*

I had come across your work before and been appalled by how irresponsible it is. Sincerely, Kathryn Schulz.

I stared at the name and some old synapses, dusty and damaged from pot and neglect, sparked a bit. I knew that name. But from where? And then it hit me. Of course.

The day after Lisa Pruett was murdered, her friends had gathered at a classmate's home to share memories of Lisa and to discuss their theories about the killer. That was Kathryn Schulz's house. It had been Schulz's father, the president of the school board, who'd answered the phones at the Pruetts' house, keeping the reporters at bay.

What are the chances?

I'll probably never know for sure how Michelle's article made its way into *The New Yorker*. Maybe it's a shitty coincidence, evidence of a very small world. But is the world really that small?

Kathryn's response got me thinking about Lisa's case again. There was so much more to the mystery than I was able to fit into the article for *Scene*. If I dug deep enough, could I find something that would clear Kevin's name in the court of public opinion? He was still out there, somewhere, painting houses in Shaker Heights. Maybe a book could at least get the guy a date.

But I got busy with other writing projects, stuff that paid. The most I did was put in a public records request for the prosecutor's file. Over a thousand pages of documents arrived in my Dropbox one day. I told myself that I'd get to it soon. The story had waited twenty-six years, after all. It could wait a little longer.

But then Kevin Young died.

Chapter Forty-Three

TIME ENOUGH AT LAST

I WAS TOLD IT WAS SUICIDE. But it wasn't. Not really. I mean, yes, okay. In a way you could say it was suicide. But not like you imagine when you hear that word.

On February 21, 2017, a local reporter called me and said they'd heard that Kevin Young was dead. It was still unverified. A rumor. But the scuttlebutt was that Kevin had finally succeeded in killing himself and had left behind a note confessing to the murder of Lisa Pruett. I called the medical examiner's office and verified that Kevin Young had, indeed, passed away. I asked them to email me the autopsy report.

At the time of his death, Kevin was living in Cleveland Heights, on the top floor of a ramshackle house that had been converted into apartments. On January 14, the landlord, a guy named James White, who lived on the second floor, realized he had not seen Kevin in several days, even though his car was parked outside. Concerned, he checked the footage from his driveway security camera. The recording showed Kevin walking inside at 9:11 A.M. on January 6, but it didn't look like he'd ever come out again.

Fearing the worst, James called his buddy Ralphie Tudor. Together they went up the stairs to Kevin's apartment on the third floor. They knocked, but there was no answer, so they used a hammer to pry off the door. Inside they found Kevin's body laying faceup on the floor. James immediately called the police.

Officer Lewis Alvis responded. What he found inside Kevin's apartment was disturbing. The floor was littered with wine bottles and Mike's Hard Lemonade cans. Clothing was strewn about, unwashed. In a tiny bedroom they found a mattress covered in dirt. The mattress, itself, had become embedded into the floorboards. The bed was surrounded by more hard lemonade cans.

In a cupboard the officer found two crack pipes. One still had residue in it.

There was no suicide note.

Like Lisa Pruett before him, Kevin Young's body was transported to the Cuyahoga County Medical Examiner's Office and placed upon a stainless-steel table, and his body was undressed and attended to by unnamed leichendieners.

The ME noted in the report that Kevin had a history of crack cocaine abuse and his body showed the damage it had inflicted. His liver was enlarged and fatty, indicating years of alcohol consumption. Official cause of death: chronic ethanol abuse.

I was angry. Angry at myself for dicking around with the Maura Murray case when I could have written this book, instead, and had it out before Kevin died. The main goal of this book was always to show how Kevin had been mistreated. But what good was any of that if he was dead? I was also angry at Kevin for treating himself like shit. I wanted to tell him that the best revenge is living a good, long life. Don't let the haters get you down. I was angry at every person who was whispering about Kevin's death, especially those asking about a suicide note.

You know who killed Kevin? The little, crazy children of Shaker Heights. That's who. Kevin had a goddamn trial. He was found not guilty. And still, those kids made his life hell. And why? Because he was the weird kid in school, because they didn't want it to be Lisa's boyfriend, because they didn't want it to be their friend.

I was being selfish—narcissistic even. Who the fuck was I to care? Who the fuck was I to think I'd have any bearing on this case or this man's life? This isn't my story. Never was. This is the sort of behavior *The New Yorker* had dressed me down for. And I wasn't up for another fight at that time. I was still licking my wounds.

For a while after that, I thought about Kevin a lot. And then a little. And then not at all.

Then, in 2018, I helped research a three-part documentary on the Amy Mihaljevic case for ID Discovery. I worked well with the producers and they invited me to host my own miniseries for the network, *Lake Erie's Coldest Cases*. I got to pick five unsolved crimes from the Greater Cleveland area to feature. I wanted to devote an episode to Lisa's case, but they wanted a source who was good on camera and was close to Lisa. Once again I reached out to Kathryn Schulz. Once again she declined to talk. We were forced to replace Lisa's episode with another case.

It was about that time that something wonderful happened in the world of true crime. On April 24, 2018, armed deputies with the Sacramento County Sheriff's Office arrested seventy-two-year-old Joseph James DeAngelo, one of the most prolific serial killers in modern history, better known by his nom de guerre, the Golden State Killer. GSK is in that upper echelon of modern real-world horror, alongside Zodiac and the Anthrax Killer—one of those mysteries that everyone assumed would never be solved. And they only caught him by first inventing an entirely new forensic tool: genetic genealogy.

Back in 1980, DeAngelo had broken into the home of Charlene and Lyman Smith, of Ventura. He murdered them both. A deputy coroner used two rape kits on Charlene's body. The kits were kept in the bottom of a freezer for thirty-eight years. Flash-forward to 2017. A detective with the Contra Costa County Sheriff's Office, Paul Holes, contacted a genealogist named Barbara Rae-Venter and asked if she could help him compare the DNA profile they'd obtained from the Ventura murders with profiles on public genealogy databases. He wanted to use genealogy to catch their monster. Rae-Venter uploaded the data points from the suspect's DNA onto a site called GEDmatch, which is like a clearinghouse for genetic data that people use to track down ancestors. Rae-Venter found several people who shared a great-great-great-grandparent with the Golden State Killer. Now came the hard work of building out family trees to locate a descendant who happened to be in Ventura, California, at the time of the murders. That led her to Joe DeAngelo. To confirm they had their man, police took a fresh DNA sample from the door of DeAngelo's car and from a tissue found in his garbage can. These samples matched their Ventura profile. DeAngelo was the Golden State Killer.

DeAngelo confessed to the murders in court in order to avoid the death penalty. He claimed there was an evil entity inside him named Jerry that made him rape and kill. "He went with me," he said. "It was like in my head. I mean, he's a part of me. I didn't want to do those things. I pushed Jerry out and had a happy life. But I did all those things. I destroyed all their lives. So now I've got to pay the price."

Paul Holes got his man and he'd opened a Pandora's box in the process. Genetic genealogy was the first new tool for cold case detectives since the discovery of DNA itself. It was better than fingerprints. And suddenly every department with an unsolved homicide went looking for genealogists.

I wanted in on it. In the spring of 2019, I formed a nonprofit, The Porchlight Project, to raise money to hire genetic genealogists to work on Ohio cold cases. There was a line in that *New Yorker* article that had cut deep: "Cold cases have long attracted hangers-on like Renner, who work for years on 'solving' the crime but never do." She was right. I had been trying to solve Amy Mihaljevic's murder since I was eleven, and it was still unsolved. But I saw an opportunity to do better.

There was this one murder I'd never gotten around to writing about. In Cleveland there's no shortage of unsolved murders, and this was just another one in the to-do stack at *Scene,* but something about it called to me. The victim's name was Barbara Blatnik. She was just seventeen years old in 1987, and there's this photograph you'll find with a quick Google search, a school photo, and Barbie looks like the quintessential 1980s party girl: dark eyeliner; floofy, blow-dried dirty-blond hair; hoop earrings. Five days before Christmas, Barbie went out drinking with friends. After they partied, Barbie's friends dropped her off at the corner of Warner Road and Grand Division, a central hub of Garfield Heights. It was very late at night, but Barbie wasn't going far. She was planning to stay with her boyfriend at his apartment there, but she never made it inside. Her nude body was found the next morning, a half hour away, on a maintenance road leading into Blossom Music Center, a popular venue for outdoor concerts in the summers. The Cuyahoga Falls Police Department asked if the Porchlight Project could help fund new DNA tests. It became our first case and in a week we had a sample of DNA taken from under Barbie's fingernails sent to a private out-of-state lab.

This genetic genealogy thing was so interesting and new that Hollywood was eager to capitalize on it. Who would be the first to create a new police procedural about genealogists solving crimes? Well, for a minute I thought it might be me.

I was hired to write a pilot for a new TV series on Paramount called *Blood Relative,* a fictional take on the life of Dr. Colleen Fitzpatrick, a NASA contractor-turned–genetic genealogist. Think *Bones* meets *Monk.* They brought me out to New Orleans for the shoot in March 2020. Melissa Leo was set to star. We were three days away from filming when COVID shut down the Big Easy and I was sent back to Ohio. I had planned to work on *Blood Relative* for the rest of the year. Now, like so many others, I didn't know what the fuck to do with my life.

When I got home, I started drinking heavily again and I never stopped. I went to Acme, got me some Stoli. I drove over the border into Michigan for legal weed, some hybrid stuff called Chocolate Diesel. If this was the end of the world, I had no intention of going out sober.

And in the midst of this entitled ennui, in order to not go crazy from sheer boredom, I opened the Dropbox file the Cuyahoga County prosecutor had sent me, all those police reports from the Lisa Pruett case. There was a book in there, somewhere. And now, as Burgess Meredith once discovered, there was time enough at last.

Chapter Forty-Four

SOCIALLY DISTANT

ONE OF MY FAVORITE NOVELS is this little mystery that was published in 2012, *The Last Policeman* by Ben H. Winters. The conceit is, the world is ending (an asteroid coming in hot, no way to stop it), but one New Hampshire detective decides to keep working a homicide case. I love that idea. It's at once so ridiculous and so human: We are all the Last Policeman, after all, going about our jobs, doing what we know how to do, as we wait for our death, which may come tomorrow or fifty years from now. We're all living on borrowed time.

I thought about that book a lot as I sifted through Lisa Pruett's case file, arranging police reports in chronological order. While I worked, my kids' schools closed and the shelves of toilet paper at the local Acme supermarket emptied out and Minneapolis burned. Why was this book important at all compared to what was happening to the world? The answer was simple. Because it was mine.

I constructed a new routine. Like Detective Gray, I understood that routine provides momentum when things would otherwise grind to a halt. Routine separates us from the fear and emotion of a traumatic event—from the rising tally of the sick and the dead on Twitter. When you are faced with life-altering events, it's best to rely on routine to get you to the next day, and the next, until you find your footing again.

In the mornings I researched. In the afternoons I wrote. In the evenings I got lit. Rinse, repeat. And when it was time to conduct interviews, the first person I contacted was Mark DeVan.

I didn't have great expectations when I reached out to Kevin's defense attorney. We had gotten into a heated conversation on the phone years ago. He represented a suspect in the Amy Mihaljevic case and I wanted to know why the suspect wouldn't sit for a lie detector test. Of course, having survived the Kevin Young trial, DeVan knew how lie detector tests could be twisted by police.

But DeVan invited me to his office to talk. He worked on the twenty-second floor of a building downtown, on Public Square. It was a late-winter gray day when I arrived, and the wide window in the lobby of Berkman, Gordon, Murray & DeVan looked out at the cold concrete of Terminal Tower, which had been built by those eccentric brothers, the Van Sweringens, of Shaker Heights, back in the Roaring Twenties (fun fact: Terminal Tower was the second-tallest building in the country, until 1964). DeVan ushered me into a conference room where a statue of Don Quixote on his horse was tilting at the windowsill. We were both wearing those periwinkle-blue disposable masks.

It had been twenty-seven years since DeVan had saved Kevin from a life in prison. The lawyer's hair had receded and grayed, but otherwise his eyes were still alight with that puckish energy that had come out in court during his cross-examinations of the AP Posse. Since Kevin's trial, DeVan had served a term as president of the Ohio Association of Criminal Defense Lawyers and had sat on committees at the national level. He'd also become a fellow in the American Board of Criminal Lawyers and a fellow in the American College of Trial Lawyers. He often spoke at seminars on criminal procedure and law. The kid from Parma was now kind of a big deal.

DeVan had spoken to Tal Young, who gave his blessing to finally talk about the case, now that Kevin had passed and could not be exposed to further trauma. We had an off-the-record conversation, then, a simple introduction to the facts of the case. And he provided me with background I needed to begin tracking down sources. Everyone except his private detectives. Two of the investigators DeVan had used at trial had died. The third, Terry Sheridan, had never returned from Eastern Europe.

The one new thing I learned from DeVan that day was that evidence from the crime scene had been overlooked. A police officer had filmed the recovery of Lisa's body on an old camcorder, and when DeVan's team had reviewed the tape, they discovered that the police had stepped over a pair of sunglasses lying in the grass. He showed me stills from the video that had been enlarged. There was no denying that there was a pair of sunglasses on the ground at the crime scene. When he'd showed this to prosecutors, they'd told him that what he'd seen was actually a set of keys. A single key had been bagged and placed into evidence (it turned out to be Lisa's). But the image in the picture was no key ring. It was clearly a pair of sunglasses, possibly left behind by Lisa's killer. And that evidence was never collected.

KEVIN'S LITTLE SISTER, Maureen, became a lawyer. She tutors students on the bar exam these days, and early in my research, we met up at Winans Chocolates & Coffee, in Springfield, not far from her home. I had not been inside a coffee shop for several weeks. Ohio's lockdown had only just lifted. It felt good to be back in a room that smelled of freshly ground beans, talking about a mystery, even if there was only one other customer and the barista was wearing a mask.

Maureen has dark hair and a kind of gaze that seems to always be analyzing your biometrics. There's a resemblance to her brother, very subtle. It's in the mannerisms, mostly. This kinetic, jouncy movement of the body and hands. You'd expect it to be nerves, but it's not. She's confident. It's more like bottled energy.

We sat with coffees at the window.

"What do you remember?" I asked.

"I remember Lisa," said Maureen. "I remember how kind she was. She was two years ahead of me, and I remember getting on the bus in third grade and I saw Lisa and she patted the empty space in her seat and let me sit with her."

Maureen told me stories about her family and what it was like to grow up with Kevin, and why the family dog was named Molly. She and her brothers named it after their favorite babysitter, Molly Shannon, whom they later watched perform on *Saturday Night Live.*

"I lived in a house with a white picket fence," Maureen said. "We used to walk to the end of the street and meet our dad at the train stop and walk him home. He'd come inside and play 'The Spinning Song' on the piano and we'd all dance."

My twelve-year-old son, Casey, who reminds me of Kevin in some ways, had played that very song on the piano at home just the day before. I knew it well.

Maureen told me she had liked how diverse Shaker Heights was. The year she graduated, 1994, was the first year that whites were the minority of graduating seniors.

When she was little, Kevin would make up imaginary characters for her and their younger brother. He'd hide under a blanket and pretend he was a kid named Wiplow, who was shy and didn't want to come out and play. Maureen would have to coax Wiplow out and ask him what he needed. Kevin would say, "Powder and perfume!" and so she'd hit him with the powder. They had played endless games of *Dig Dug* on Atari. Kevin would sometimes invite his friends over and they would commandeer the Atari, and Maureen and her friends would have to watch them play. But she didn't care. Maureen had a crush on Dan Dreifort. And her friends crushed on Kevin.

Maureen learned about Lisa's murder in band class. She played the sax and was waiting for the big announcement about that year's class trip. Rumor had it, they were going to Mexico. So when she walked into Mr. Bohnert's room and saw *No Instruments* written on the chalkboard, she and her friends assumed that this was because the big announcement was finally happening. They whispered excitedly to each other until one of the older kids told them to hush.

"It's not a good news day," one girl said. That's when Maureen noticed that some of the other kids were crying. Something bad had happened.

During the remainder of that fall, as Kevin was first questioned and then became the target of the investigation, Tal kept reassuring Maureen that everything would blow over, that it was all just a big misunderstanding.

"We knew he didn't do it, because Dad was with him," she said. "Kevin wanted to submit his DNA. I remember, DeVan told my dad that if there's any chance he really did it, they shouldn't risk it. My parents told him to take Kevin's DNA."

Kevin's family always knew he was innocent, but they also understood there was something fundamentally wrong with his mind. Personally, I've always wondered if Kevin was autistic, but perhaps that's my own life influencing my perspective: My son is on the spectrum and had violent outbursts when he was young. Maureen won't offer an opinion. And neither one of us is a psychiatrist. Whatever was going on with Kevin, he did mellow out as he got older. By the time he was thirty, you wouldn't have suspected he was very different from anyone else.

Maureen and I talked about Kevin's life after his acquittal. When he was still a young man, Kevin had gotten engaged to an au pair from Norway. He'd even moved over there to be with her. But it didn't last. And after that, he'd had trouble getting a second date with anyone, because of the Internet.

Kevin left a message on Maureen's voicemail shortly before his death. Just a big brother checking in. She kept it and still listens to it when she wants to remember him.

Her parents didn't want to have a funeral service for Kevin in Cleveland because they didn't want the media attention it would bring. So they took their son's cremated remains to their vacation spot on the shore of New Jersey, a place where he'd loved to play as a kid. The family went to mass, then scattered Kevin's ashes across the waves.

They left a pair of Kevin's shoes on the beach. When Kevin was little, he used to leave his shoes on the beach until they were washed away by the tide. He was always leaving things behind.

And eventually the tide came. And the shoes and the last of Kevin disappeared from the world.

Chapter Forty-Five

REASON AND LACK THEREOF

THANKS TO MULTIPLE PUBLIC RECORDS requests, I had now amassed a couple reams' worth of documents related to the murder of Lisa Pruett. It took a week to read through it all. I selected Jazz Radio on Pandora and sat cross-legged on the floor of my home office, listening to Stacey Kent, as I organized the mess into something resembling a narrative.

I was searching for something very specific. Not some lost clue that would solve Lisa's murder—I had no delusions that I would be that lucky (not until later that summer)—but some explanation for why police and prosecutors had become so hyperfocused on Kevin despite his alibi.

My suspicion was that one of those AP Posse kids, one of those well-meaning but impressionable teens that had met at Kathryn's house to discuss the murder, one of them must have had a relative on the police force or inside the prosecutor's office. But I didn't find anything like that.

Instead, I found a list of items from the crime scene that was provided to DeVan during discovery. Here's all the police had to work with:

Lisa's navy-blue turtleneck had bloodstains, and the fabric had picked up some hairs and vegetation. There was a white stain on her sleeve. They tested the shirt, but found no semen or saliva.

Lisa had worn Guess jeans and they had grass stains on the knees and on the backside, as well as a grease stain on the right leg, from where her bike chain had rubbed against her.

They had tested her underwear. No semen.

Oral, rectal, and vaginal swabs showed no sperm.

They found two hairs on her body—one on her right hand and another on her left foot. And eventually they did get around to testing them against a sample from Lisa's scalp—they matched. The hairs were Lisa's.

A condom and wrapper were collected from the ground near the crime scene.

Spots of blood found on Lisa's body were tested. The samples were consistent with Lisa's blood type: A. Kevin's was O.

Detectives had also found a brown paper bag with a bloody shoe print on it. The print was from a shoe with a herringbone pattern on its sole. The FBI lab tested both Lisa's and Kevin's blood against the blood found on the paper bag. However, the DNA from the bloody bag was too degraded for them to match it to anyone. They also found a partial palm print on a newspaper found inside that brown paper bag, but they were unable to match that to Kevin.

Okay, so the answer to why the police focused on Kevin Young wasn't to be found in the evidence. There was nothing there to point to Kevin, or to Dan, for that matter. Yet, the grass stains on Lisa's knees could possibly suggest a consensual intimate encounter that night.

So, what the hell? Why Kevin all the time?

I finally found the answer in a series of internal memos from the Shaker Heights prosecutor's office.

IN THE FALL of 1990, the Shaker Heights Law Department posted a job opening. They were adding another prosecutor to their staff to handle smaller cases, while their big guns worked the high-profile Pruett and Porter homicides. The city received around two hundred applications for the position. One résumé was submitted by a prosecutor in Columbus named William Dwayne Maynard. He came highly recommended by Councilman Peter Lawson Jones, so Maynard was one of only twelve candidates personally interviewed by Law Director Margaret Anne Cannon.

During the course of Maynard's interview, Cannon explained that she was looking for a prosecutor who could handle the criminal docket while she was otherwise engaged. This is taken from a statement she later made to police:

"At that point in the interview with Mr. Maynard, he states that he was aware of the Pruett case because an attorney in Columbus was a good friend of his and had been retained to represent Kevin Young when our detectives went to Columbus to interview Kevin."

Cannon didn't ask for details and the conversation shifted focus. However, Maynard had a second interview that day, with Prosecutor K. J. Montgomery. After that interview Montgomery relayed to the law director what Maynard had just told her: Kevin's Columbus lawyer, a guy named Bill Meeks, had told him that Kevin had killed Lisa. Montgomery immediately wrote a note to the police chief, Walter Ugrinic. She told Ugrinic that Kevin's lawyer had said, "Kevin did it—killed that girl." She recommended they reach out to Meeks directly.

But she cautioned the chief: "Note whoever calls needs to be extremely sensitive to the fact that what Meeks did is probably grounds for disbarment. I understand that Meeks has a good reputation in Columbus and we might not want to fry him if it can be avoided. Will you give this some consideration and advise what you think we should do?"

Chief Ugrinic took the rumor to Cuyahoga County prosecutor Steve Dever. Dever wanted confirmation, so detectives were dispatched to Columbus to speak with Maynard and Meeks directly.

They found Maynard on the twelfth floor of the courthouse. When they asked the prosecutor to repeat what he'd told K. J. Montgomery, the man swore he'd never said such a thing. And when detectives tracked down Meeks, he told them that he'd never made such a statement to Maynard and only knew the man as a passing acquaintance. The police noted in their report that they believed Maynard had been trying to inflate his ego and self-importance so that he could get the job in Shaker Heights.

Maynard was never hired by them, but he did go on to serve as a muni court judge in Franklin County, until 2012.

K. J. Montgomery is now the muni court judge in Shaker Heights. I reached out to her through email and asked about the matter. She responded: *I have no recollection of a letter. And I don't remember who Maynard is . . . I wish I did . . .*

As far as I can tell, the Shaker Heights police never seriously considered any suspect but Kevin Young from that point on.

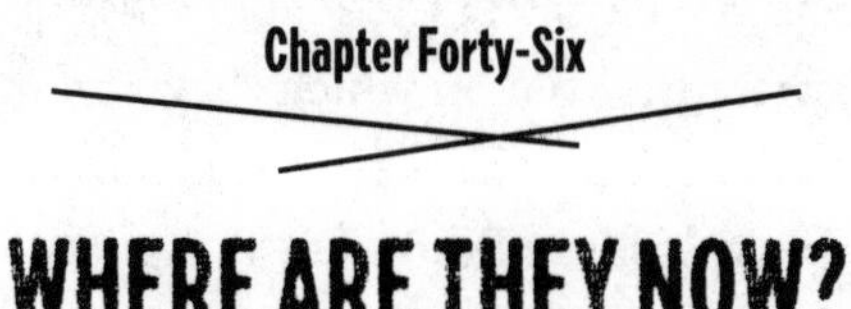

Chapter Forty-Six

WHERE ARE THEY NOW?

In June, the bar down the street from my house opened back up. It's this little pub in Wallhaven called Larry's. Same guy's worked the bar there for years. There was limited seating inside and an outdoor patio. I met journalist Jim McCarty there one afternoon. We didn't know how to greet each other and made do with an awkward elbow bump. Then we took off our masks and sat in a booth and ordered a couple beers. It almost felt normal.

McCarty is retired now. He leads bird walks in the Metroparks these days. He still has that sly energy about him, though, and that charm that got him the best sources. He walked me through what he remembered of Kevin's ordeal. Twenty-seven years later, he still believes that the cops had the right man. And he still bristles when he hears DeVan's name.

"DeVan is a street-fighter type of lawyer," said McCarty. "He'd do whatever it took to win an acquittal. What they did to Dan Dreifort was wrong. I'm not a defense lawyer getting paid to defend a young kid, but I don't think it's worth destroying the life of another boy to save your client."

He said the circumstantial evidence only pointed one way: at Kevin.

As we finished our beers, McCarty suggested some new avenues I might take, some sources I might contact. I brought up what happened with Kevin the day after the *Plain Dealer* ran his interview with the jurors after the trial, in which they said they had doubts about his innocence. After the article was published, Kevin had climbed onto the Ridgebury Boulevard Bridge with the intention of doing a swan dive onto I-271.

"I was actually working the desk when the call came in," said McCarty. "Kevin Young was threatening to commit suicide. I was like, holy shit. That story, it was one hundred percent newsworthy, but I never thought he would end up there, on that bridge."

IT WAS TIME to contact Lisa's parents, but I didn't want to. I dreaded that part. Years ago, when I'd written the article for *Scene,* Gary Pruett made it clear to me that he believed Kevin had killed his daughter. The detectives had convinced them of Kevin's guilt. And the Pruetts had been clear from the very beginning that they had no desire to speak to the media. Gary and Lynette had three children, and two of them died young. I didn't want to add any more grief.

Most of us will never understand what the Pruetts went through. I do not know what it's like to lose a child; hopefully, I never will. But I did get the briefest hint at such torment one day. This was in 2015. I had just returned home from a birthday party. My daughter, Laine, was two years old and still had to be strapped into a car seat. My seven-year-old son was in the back of the Subaru with her. It was just us three. It had rained that day. One of those fierce downpours that only lasts five minutes and leaves as quickly as it came.

We lived in an old Tudor that had been constructed from a Sears catalogue. It sat at the bottom of the neighborhood, and sometimes when it rained, our basement got wet. So I was expecting to have to turn on the dehumidifier when we got home and maybe mop out some water. I pulled into the driveway and parked by the garage, out back.

I got out and walked around to Laine's door. That's when it happened. It sounded like a freight train had jumped the tracks up the hill. I turned to Casey, my son, who was standing behind the car. He was pointing at the sky. I followed his gaze. A two-hundred-year-old oak tree was coming down on us. It was the neighbor's tree. One of those old picture-book trees with the wide canopy that shadows a whole yard. The tree still looked healthy. We'd learn later that its trunk had rotted from all the wet weather, and that last downpour had saturated what was left. It was falling toward us and there was but a second to respond.

I opened the door and had just enough time to look at my daughter. I realized there was no way I could get Laine out of the car before the tree crushed it. My fatherly instincts kicked in and I climbed onto the side of the Subaru, one foot in the open door, and held out my hands as if I could catch the tree.

When it hit, the branches threw me backward against the porch. I was knocked unconscious for a moment. Probably only a couple seconds. I came to and looked at the wreckage. There was no sign of the Subaru. All I could see was that tree's canopy over my driveway. The trunk had demolished the garage. I was sure the car had been flattened, with my daughter inside. I remember to this day the sound of my scream, echoing back to me before I realized I was screaming. Just a guttural *"Noooo!"*

I began digging through the leaves and branches of the tree. Casey came out of the basement stairwell, where he'd hidden at the last second, and he looked as shocked as I was. I climbed under the branches and found the car. The windshield had shattered. A large, knobby branch had stuck through the side window like a claw, digging into the seat where Casey had been. The only part of the vehicle that remained untouched was the space where Laine's car seat was. She was safe in that little space. Not even a scratch. And she didn't cry. She just sat there, staring back at me, until I snatched her up and held her tight.

For ten seconds I was certain my daughter was dead. It was the most terrible ten seconds of my life, and the whole time I was bargaining with God to take it back; to take me, instead. I was lucky. Others are not. So it goes. I never want to feel that despair again. I can't fathom it being real, the strength it must take to go on and live.

I stopped by the Pruett house in the early days of the pandemic. There was a brief conversation. Ultimately, though, Gary and Lynette Pruett declined to be interviewed for this book.

DAN DREIFORT LIVES in California these days. He has a Search Engine Optimization business. I haven't spoken to him since 2008. Back then, he agreed to an interview on the condition that Gary Pruett give his blessing first. After Gary did, Dreifort backed out. I left a message on his cell phone.

Debbie Dreifort is still in Athens, where she works as a finance and operations manager for a large firm.

I drove out to Robert Dreifort's house one day, early on in my reporting. He was sitting on his front porch, watching the day go by. His garage door was open and a restored VW Bug, the same kind that DeVan was driving the night he decided to become a defense attorney, was displayed inside.

Bob declined an interview, too. "Everything I have to say is in the reports," he told me. "I've forgotten most of it, anyway."

"Do you still think Kevin did it?" I asked.

"Oh yeah."

I REACHED OUT to a number of Lisa's closest friends, including Jenny Margulies, Rachel Lowenthal, and Daniel Messinger. Nobody wanted to revisit the tragedy.

Becca Boatright and Kim Rathbone became lawyers. Boatright is currently the executive director of legal affairs for the Seattle Police Department—certainly, one of the more stressful jobs in the country this last year.

I tried to talk to Kathryn Schulz again, too. She's still at *The New Yorker*. She won the Pulitzer Prize in 2016 for a feature story she wrote about the Cascadia fault line and the probability of a large earthquake in our lifetime. It was called "a masterwork of environmental reporting and writing." It's quite good. She also authored the book *Being Wrong*, in which she muses on how upsetting it can be when you realize you're wrong.

I did not engender any respect from Kathryn. I bungled the relationship at every step. Case in point: I had written Kathryn to let her know I was working on this book. After a couple weeks of waiting for a response, I went back and re-read the email I'd sent. I had begun the missive with *Dear Lisa.* Jesus Christ. I had been so deep into police files at that point that Lisa's name was always at the forefront of my mind. I remember writing the email after finding a particularly interesting bit of information and wanting to connect right away with someone who knew her, and so I wrote it and sent it off and didn't think to proofread it or anything. *Dear Lisa.* I'm not sure what she was supposed to do with that.

AFTER KEVIN WAS acquitted, Detective Tom Gray was transferred out of the detective bureau to an office position, where he worked until his sudden death, on January 7, 2002, at the age of forty-nine. He had a heart attack while shoveling the snow out of his driveway. After Gray's funeral Scott Frank, the Shaker Heights health director, wrote a letter to the Ohio Public Safety Officers Death Benefit Fund, in which he expressed his belief that Gray's work on the Lisa Pruett case had directly contributed to his demise. The stress of the media blitz and the pressure from the community had caused high blood pressure, which had blown out Gray's aortic valve during the investigation. He'd had it repaired, but it failed him again that day, in 2002. "I have no question in my mind that Captain Gray's disease happened as a result of the performance of his duty."

I tracked down Detective Richard Mullaney. He's retired now, living a quiet life on the west side. He was kind enough to speak about suspects for a bit, but he didn't want to go on the record. He knew better than anyone what the media circus did to Tom Gray.

TEX WORKMAN IS dead, too. He died the day before his thirty-eighth birthday, on December 19, 2011. He overdosed on antianxiety and depression medication. The autopsy report said that he took citalopram. Medical examiner ruled it a suicide. No note was left behind.

I met up with his wife, Rebecca, at a Panera in South Euclid, not far from where they had raised three boys. She gave me the rest of Tex's story.

After the trial Tex made a real good family for himself. He worked at an auto parts store for a while; then he got a gig selling PCs at trade shows. About ten years before he died, he became a tattoo artist. One of the first things he did was alter the "Debbie" tattoo he'd gotten into a skull with sunglasses.

There were times over the years when Tex talked about Lisa. He told his wife that he carried a lot of guilt over her death because Dan had asked him to walk Lisa over from her house that night. But he just had a feeling that something was wrong, so he'd decided to go home, and Lisa had to get to Dan's on her own.

In the early days Tex knew he was a suspect in the eyes of Tom Gray and the detectives at the Shaker Heights PD. Nobody believed that story about waiting for a bus for forty-five minutes. So a couple days after the murder, Tex had sat at the bus stop for hours, waiting to catch the guy who had driven his bus that night. He knew the police wouldn't bother tracking him down—and that dude was his alibi. And, luckily, Tex found him. The bus driver remembered him well, because he wasn't supposed to be picking up any more passengers, but he'd given the kid a break and had taken him to Shaker Square. Tex begged him to make a statement for the detectives. And he did. That's how the detectives ruled out Tex. Hard to tell what would have happened if Tex hadn't done their job for them.

His widow, Rebecca, didn't believe Tex committed suicide. Tex was kind of flaky, and he'd get so absorbed in his work or his video games that he'd forget if he'd taken his meds that day. Sometimes he'd skip several days and then take all the missed doses at once. She believed that's what happened. He just forgot he'd taken his pills and took more. And then more, again.

Oh, and in case you were wondering how he got his name: One day he'd walked into school wearing a cowboy hat and boots, and someone said he looked just like Matt Dillon in the 1982 movie *Tex*. The name stuck.

ONE OF THE first people who spoke to me on the record for this book was Tim Smith, who, at one time, was friends with both Kevin Young and Lisa Pruett. Tim is the son of Derwood Smith, the preacher at the Church of Christ at Forest Hill, which practices a very conservative form of Christianity to this day. Reverend Smith performed the services for Lisa's funeral.

Tim was close with Kevin for a long time and would often play at his house after school. "Kevin was a strange kid," he admitted. "But he was not harmful to anyone but himself. He just had no filter. Kids would make fun of him and he'd spaz out." He remembered how Kevin would get so upset at school sometimes that he'd hide in the coat closet and cry. When Tim would check on him, Kevin would tell him he wasn't sad, he was just hibernating.

"He was intense and that progressed as he got older. It was like he stopped growing socially around age ten." When Kevin started taking an interest in girls, he would call Tim nightly to debrief him about his attempts to get a date. "He'd get interested in some girl, she wouldn't want to go out with him, and he'd call me and cry. I'd say, move on to someone else. He'd say he didn't want to. So I'd just listen. After a while, when he called, I'd tell my mom to say I was out."

Tim recalled Dan Dreifort as a funny little kid with fluffy hair. "He was harmless," he said. "But his dad was a piece of work."

In regard to the murder, Tim believed that the level of violence perpetrated against Lisa's body suggested someone who wasn't on anyone's radar at the time. Someone with significant pent-up rage.

Tim kept in touch with Kevin after the murder. They had many long talks and, according to Tim, Kevin never even hinted at being involved.

Years later, after having not seen him in some time, Kevin called Tim one night and asked him to come to a pub on Lee and have a drink with him. Tim met up with Kevin and Tal and had a few beers. Lisa's name came up in conversation. He said Kevin expressed sympathy for the Pruetts, but he was perplexed about how he'd ever become a suspect.

"They think I did it," Kevin said. "How could they think I did it?"

Still, to this day, Tim believes Kevin was innocent, for all the good it did him. "He was convicted by the public," said Tim.

Chapter Forty-Seven

THE RELUCTANT FOREMAN

I STILL DON'T KNOW WHAT to do when I meet someone for the first time in this new world. It feels like if I offer a hand to shake, it's somehow declaring my loyalty to the antivaxxers. But not offering to shake a hand keeps me at a distance from a subject, makes me appear aloof. More aloof than normal. How did shaking hands become political?

This anxiety was tickling my brain when I was led into the office of the director of JP Recovery Services, in Rocky River. That's a big collections agency, one of those places where people call you up at weird times if you've let your credit run away from you. It's managed by a woman named Nancy McMurtrey, who, twenty-seven years ago, handed Judge Sweeney a note that said the jury believed that Kevin Young was not guilty. She came into the room and I extended my hand, then thought better of it and went in for the elbow bump, then just gave up and shook my head.

"We need a new greeting," I said.

"How about this?" said McMurtrey, sticking up both middle fingers.

"That'll work."

I took the leather couch across from McMurtrey's desk and got out my notepad and pen and asked her how she came to be the jury's foreperson at Kevin's trial.

McMurtrey explained that she'd received the notice to appear for jury duty in the mail at a very inopportune time. Her husband had lost his job, she was managing the paperwork for a different collections agency, and she'd just had her third kid. But she showed up at the Justice Center and she didn't complain. When I asked her why she didn't try to get out of it, she just shrugged. It was a job she was asked to do. She did it. Simple as that.

So McMurtrey sat in a waiting room with a hundred other residents of Cuyahoga County and waited to see if she'd be picked. Eventually she was brought into Judge Sweeney's courtroom and a lawyer asked her how she felt about the death penalty. She told them she could sentence someone to death if she thought they were guilty.

One by one, the other prospective jurors were dismissed until fourteen remained: twelve jurors and two alternates. McMurtrey was the second alternate and she figured she wouldn't even have to vote at the end. But two jurors were dismissed during Kevin's trial. One young woman was sent home after she told the judge she couldn't reconcile her personal beliefs with her duty as a juror. Another got kicked off for bringing books about jury selection into the courthouse. As a juror you're not supposed to do your own research or consider information not presented by the lawyers. So, by the time Marino gave his closing argument about the mosaic of guilt, McMurtrey was on the jury proper, and when it came time to pick a foreperson, nobody else wanted the job.

"I knew I couldn't find Kevin guilty as soon as the prosecutor gave his closing argument," she said. "I was like, *really?* You haven't proven anything. It was a great story, but they had nothing to back it up. But the same goes for the defense."

She thought that both sides were dealing in fiction, trying to convince the jury that they were telling the truth, when it was apparent that nobody knew what the hell had happened. The only person they felt they could trust was Judge Sweeney. One juror made buttons for them that said SWEENEY'S MEANIES, which they made sure to hide before going to the cafeteria for lunch.

McMurtrey was terrified that she might be the only one who thought Kevin was innocent. So the first thing she did was call for a vote. It came back ten to two, not guilty, and she relaxed. All they had to do was convince the two holdouts. So they discussed the case, again, as a group.

There were a couple things that gave McMurtrey reasonable doubt. One was that her father had been a lawyer. He'd drilled into his daughter's head that you never talk to police without a lawyer present. Kevin's dad was a lawyer, too. Surely, Tal Young would have given the same advice to Kevin. But Kevin still talked to the police. In her mind this meant that nobody at the Young house was worried that Kevin might be arrested for murder. If Tal was lying about being Kevin's alibi, there's no way he would have let Kevin talk to the police. Additionally, there was no evidence that Kevin had ever been at the scene of the crime.

"So, who do you think did it?" I asked.

"Well, I never thought it was Kevin. Or Dan, for that matter. I always thought it had to be someone else. But I don't know who."

One thing that bothers McMurtrey to this day is how Drill, the police dog, had picked up a scent on Lisa's bike and followed it around to the driveway of Kim Rathbone's house, on Sedgewick. "Whoever killed her ran around Dan's old girlfriend's house when they left. It had to be someone from around there."

Eventually there was that one lone holdout, McMurtrey recalled. "He was not convinced that Kevin was guilty, but he didn't want to take responsibility for his actions if he was wrong." For a moment it seemed like he'd dig in and cause a hung jury. But when they voted again, he switched to not guilty, too.

She remembered being escorted out of the building after the verdict. And later that night she got a call from McCarty at the *Plain Dealer* and she granted him an interview. She came to regret that. "Everything I said was taken out of context," she claimed, still fuming after twenty-seven years. "I felt so bad after Kevin climbed up on that bridge. I wrote to his parents. I was so pissed. I called McCarty and said, 'Are you happy now?'"

Before I left, I asked McMurtrey what she thought it would take to close the Pruett case. "Somebody's going to have to talk," she said simply. "If it was one of the local kids, someone knows." She shook her head. "Those kids were so spoiled. Their parents had no clue."

Chapter Forty-Eight

HIS OWN WORST ENEMY

Once I had read through all the documents obtained by the Cuyahoga County Prosecutor's Office, it became obvious to me that there was, after all, enough circumstantial evidence to get a conviction. But not against Kevin Young. If Marino had wanted, I believe he could have successfully prosecuted Dan Dreifort.

There's the placement of the body, just beside Dan's house. He got out of the psychiatric ward that day. There's circumstantial evidence suggesting Dan was high on Robitussin and possibly experiencing unexpected side effects due to mixing it with whatever medication they'd given him in the hospital. Dan set up the meeting with Lisa, but expected the police to believe that he forgot about it. Any juror who was once a horny teenage boy wouldn't buy that for a moment.

But the most damning piece of circumstantial evidence came directly from Dan himself. Inside Dan's house, and in Lisa's bedroom, the police found intimate letters between the two lovers that were at times quite sweet—and others that were quite troubling.

There's this, from a letter that Lisa wrote to Dan: *I, Lisa Pruett, a confessed sinner repent all sins and buy my soul back from whatever low life scum now possesses it and sell it to morally pious Dan. I will never sin again and I will devote my life to being nice and kind.*

She wrote in a letter delivered to Dan in the hospital:

> Hello Dan,
>
> I love your necklace. It's a good distraction. And I love your ring it makes me happy. And I love you and I think I must be crazy but that's ok. Maybe crazy is better. I am a very happy person then again I'm easy to please.
>
> P.S. This note was brought to you courtesy of the fucked up noodleloaf.

> Hi Dan,
>
> Read this fast. Well I just talked to you three hours ago and I'm still totally glowing. It made me incredibly happy. It convinced me that you're still alive. I swear any connection to you at all just makes me glow because that's all I have, ya know? About the phone call, I was seriously so happy I cried. I dream about you every night sometimes it's happy and sometimes not.

Lisa wrote in one letter that went on for several pages:

> I probably won't tell anyone else about this so listen carefully and give me a monstrously large hug next time you see me. When I got home, Dad wasn't there and when I asked my mom where he was she said she didn't know. My first thought was that he had gotten angry and left but my mom didn't seem upset (she's a great actress). At about 11:30 I heard my dad pull in the driveway so I went downstairs to say hi to him. He was sitting, no, lying on the couch in the library with all the lights off. I said hi to him, cheerily, and he told me that he took the cat and let

her go in the country. Shit, I'm crying again. Dan, I want you here right now because there's no one here who can comfort me. Dan, she doesn't have any front claws. She's going to die out there. How could he be so evil? I never even got a chance to say goodbye to her. The worst part is still coming, though. This isn't even bad compared to the rest of it. I went back upstairs, crying, and my mom walked into my room. She didn't even know what he'd done. Apparently, they got into an argument and my dad let out a long string of profanities and left. My mom was seriously afraid that he wasn't coming back. Now this is all happening in my perfect family where nobody dares swear and mommy and daddy are always perfect. I don't want to write the rest of it. I can't think straight. After you read this, take me someplace and make me tell you the rest of it. I want you here, Dan, I love you so much. I love you more than just about everyone in the world (right now I can't think of anyone I love more) so we'll just leave it at that. Whatever.

Lisa

Then, this:

Hi Dan,

I feel like shit (great opener, eh?). This whole thing is beginning to upset me greatly. I know how hard you can take things and I really don't want to hurt you. I know all of those things you told me—being drunk, seduced, accidental, and never again, but that's not helping how I feel inside, ya know? So I just have to get this out before I explode. Please don't be hurt or upset to any large degree. Just feel a little bit guilty. Ok here goes. I just talked to Kathryn and didn't tell her anything. I always tell K ev-

> erything. I feel like some sort of criminal. I want to be able to tell K stuff but she would take it too seriously. Maybe I'm not taking it seriously enough. Dan how could you do this? You fucking kissed another girl. And she's not even gorgeous or something.
>
> P.S. Keep in mind throughout this whole desultory barrage of madness that I love you anyway. I just keep picturing it and it's making me sick. I wish the whole thing would go away. I wish she'd go away. Fuck. I have to go to sleep.

Lisa wrote Dan again during band camp:

> Try not to be too overly violent. I love you. Just try to smile a little bit and do your best to convince them that you're sane. I know you'll do all you can and it'll all work out because I said so and since I'm so naïve, everything has to work out right. I love you. It's such a great feeling to be loved.
>
> I love you more than purple and chocolate and Pixy Stix and Robert Fulghum.

The whole time Dan was in the hospital, Lisa was constantly writing him. It's almost obsessive. Some letters were ten pages long, front and back. It's enough writing to imagine that this became a significant portion of Lisa's days, that last summer of 1990. She became frustrated that Dan wasn't writing as often. She described falling into great big depressive moods as specifically as she described commercials that came on the TV as she wrote and wrote and wrote. Sometimes she simply transcribed entire Shel Silverstein poems. During a family trip she wrote a twenty-page letter that was a play-by-play of the car ride.

At one time Lisa wrote:

I don't ever want to forget anything about Germany, ever. Both those nights in Berlin were just wonderful. I was so scared. I'm not anymore.

I had an awful dream last night that you finally came home and told me that you didn't love me anymore. It was terribly upsetting. It was a yucky dream. I didn't like it at all.

Dan eventually wrote back:

I wanna hit you with a really big stick. I wanna poke your eyes out with my favorite pocketknife. Cuz you're poison, runnin through my veins. I can't stand the sight of your brains, poison, and you smell bad too. I hate you.

Lisa wrote:

As soon as you get home, I'm going to fix you a great huge meal. And you can sit in the kitchen while I make it and make male chauvinist comments all you like and I'll just smile and put on an apron . . . and you'll kiss me and tell me you love me and life will be cool. If you don't leave that place I'll be in there soon. I'm about to go take a walk in the rain.

Dan wrote back on a clinic timesheet he'd swiped:

Lisa Lee,

It's Friday the 7th. 10:45 p.m. A whole fuck of a lot has gone down since whenever the last time you heard from me. Thanks for calling, sorry I couldn't talk. Lisa, this place has changed me. Hopefully I'll change back once I'm out. This place has gotten rid of my sense of humor,

> my happiness. I tried to fucking kill myself. They've got me thinking I'm fucking crazy but they think I'm "almost cured." What the fuck was wrong with me?
>
> After I get out, give me some time to return to normal. I don't want you or I to make any poor decisions because of this place. I love you.

Later, Dan sent her lyrics to a song:

> *I'm sorry now I killed you*
> *For our love was something fine.*
> *And till they come to get me,*
> *I shall hold your hand in mine.*

Dan wrote:

> I make every fucking decision for you. What we do, what you say, what music you listen to. None of it's right. I've changed you.
>
> Someday I'll go too far and do something very bad and you'll yell at me and be serious and I won't be able to handle it. But you can't let me get away with murder.

Years later, Dan created a personal blog online, before anyone really knew what a blog was. Part of his bio was supposedly written by his mother, but it's possible that Dan wrote it in the voice of his mother as a character. The entire blog is satiric. The bio reads: *He is extremely loveable. Only three major faults come to mind at the moment: he can't spell, sometimes he threatens us with nonsupport in our old age, and the last is a dark secret known only to the immediate family.*

Come on.

It had to be Dan, right?

I mean, nobody else was there.

Chapter Forty-Nine

SOMEBODY ELSE WAS THERE

WHEN I GOT TO THE polygraph documents, tucked into the thousands of records from the prosecutor's office, I found something unexpected. I discovered that besides tests for Kevin, Dan, and Mr. Dreifort, the police had also given a polygraph to a young man named David Branagan.

Who the hell was David Branagan? I went back through all the reports, searching for any mention of his name.

David's name first appears during Detective Klima's interview with faculty members at Shaker Heights High School. German teacher Lynda Mayer had mentioned him to the detective, even though he was no longer a student: "She described David Branagan as a student from a couple years ago. She stated that he was a lot older than these kids, but she recalled he lived in the area of the murder. She felt there were serious problems with Dave Branagan."

Sal Fabrizio, the economics teacher, also mentioned Branagan's name. "He describes David Branagan as somewhat of a con artist," the detective wrote in his report. "He was someone who screwed himself up royal with his drug and alcohol involvement. He stated that David Branagan was clearly intellectual when he participated but only participated when he wanted to." Fabrizio told the detective that Branagan was a user of everything: people, drugs, anything. "He was always preying on younger girls," he said.

Terry Sheridan, DeVan's private investigator, heard David Branagan's name when he interviewed Stefan Ravello, who worked at Arabica. At the time Sheridan had been building out a timeline. He'd asked Stefan who else had been present at the coffee shop that night.

"David Branagan and Holly Robinson were there," Stefan had said. David had been present when Tex told Kevin that Lisa was sneaking out of her house to visit Dan.

IT WAS DAVID BRANAGAN who initiated contact with the detectives working Lisa Pruett's homicide. This was on September 15, 1990, the day after the murder. A Saturday. David came to the station with his girlfriend, Holly.

"I heard about the Lisa Pruett murder," he told the officer who took his report. "I have some information that might be helpful. Around one P.M. today I was at a Rapid shelter. The Green Line. Westbound. On Shaker Boulevard, at Lee Road. There was a Black guy there and he was talking about her murder."

David thought the Black man was involved somehow.

As good detectives do, Detective Tim Ward asked him where he was the night of the murder.

He explained that he was out late that night with Holly, his girlfriend, who was the assistant manager at Arabica. They left the coffee shop around midnight. He escorted her home and then he walked back to his parents' house on Sedgewick, the street directly behind the Dreifort residence, which runs parallel to Lee. He lived a few doors north of Kim Rathbone. David said he walked past the crime scene at about 1:20 A.M. A police officer stopped him as he passed by, he said. The cop questioned him and then let him walk home.

Detective Ward checked up on that detail later. He asked every officer at the scene if they'd stopped the boy. But nobody had.

Ward noted in his report that David Branagan had also been a witness in the murders of Philip and Dorothy Porter. He had told police he'd seen a Black man running away from the Porter house. Same man. Same story. Three murders.

Detective Mullaney asked David back for another interview on November 7, 1990. This was well after Kevin's interrogation at Ohio State, and the police were reviewing all the loose ends in their case in anticipation of the indictment. Mullaney asked David to tell him his story again, from the top.

"Holly and I met at Arabica at approximately seven P.M.," he said. "We took the Rapid downtown and went to Gershwin's for dinner. I believe we had an eight-fifteen reservation, which we were early for.

"After dinner, maybe around nine-thirty or ten o'clock, we walked around downtown, along the lakefront. Then we took the Blue Line to Shaker Square. We walked to Arabica, which was closed for business. There were still people cleaning up, so we went in. Holly went downstairs to go to the bathroom. I went upstairs."

David didn't mention it here, but this was when Tex Workman and Kevin Young were there, talking about Lisa's plan to sneak over to Dan's that night.

"We left Arabica and walked up Van Aken to Holly's house, which is at ***** Winslow. We talked outside for a while. I watched her go inside and then I walked home. I turned right on Avalon, to Aldersyde, and took the circle to Parkland, then to Andover to the intersection of South Woodland and Lee Road. I saw two police cars in front of the Dreifort residence. I saw two officers with either one or two dogs. They were walking east on South Woodland.

"I walked down South Woodland to Sedgewick, turned right, and walked to my house, which is the eighth house on the right side of the street, went inside, told my mother what I had seen. She asked me what time it was. It was about one-fifteen or one-twenty A.M. I took a shower and went to bed.

"The next morning I woke up, got a phone call from Holly. She told me that Lisa Pruett had been murdered and raped. I took a shower, got dressed, made macaroni and cheese, and ate it while I watched TV. Flipping the channels, I saw a report on Lisa's murder. I went to the Rapid stop at Lee and Shaker on my way to Arabica. There was a Black man at the stop, had a pretty dark complexion. He asked for a cigarette and we started talking. He said he hadn't been in the area for about five or six years. He commented, 'That was *some* thing that happened to that girl down there,' and he pointed to Lee and South Woodland. I asked him if he meant the girl who had been raped and murdered. He told me she had been murdered, not raped. Then he made reference to the Porter murders, and that they hadn't caught the person who did that murder. The Rapid came and we both got on. I got off at Shaker Square."

David told Mullaney that he went to Arabica then and sat with Tex, Debbie Dreifort, and Stanley Kramer, who were all discussing the murder. That's when Kevin Young's name came up. David told them he thought that Kevin could have done it.

"Kevin left Arabica in enough time to cut off Lisa on her way, to approach her," David said. He told Mullaney that was all he'd heard about the murder, until he left to go into the hospital for long-term "treatment" on October 8.

Mullaney questioned David after he gave his statement. Much of the questioning had to do with what he knew about Kevin Young. He was only too eager to regale the detective with a couple stories: David claimed Kevin had offered him $50,000 to kill him so Kevin wouldn't have to commit suicide.

"Were you, in fact, stopped and questioned by Shaker Heights police the night of the murder?" Mullaney asked later.

"No."

"Why did you say that you were?"

"To build drama," he said. "To pique people's interest in me."

"When you arrived home on the morning of September 14, was your mother really waiting up for you?"

"No."

"Do you normally carry a knife?"

"Not day to day, no." But David did, in fact, keep several knives at home. One was a four-inch stiletto. "The handle is fashioned so that when the knife is open, you can put the fingers through along the lines of a brass knuckle," David said.

OUT OF CURIOSITY I brought the printout of David Branagan's lie detector test back to the company that had reviewed Kevin's polygraph in 1993, Poly-Tech Associates. Their main office was located in Akron, not far from my house. Bill Evans, who questioned Kevin back then, is still there, but it was Ken Butler who reviewed the old records, so he could provide a fresh assessment. Butler is a former marine who, like Kohanski, had worked as a police detective before turning his talents to the lie detector machine. He is the current board chair of the Ohio Association of Polygraph Examiners.

I pulled off Main Street into a squat parking lot beside a low brick building in the shadow of the Firestone factory. I rang the buzzer. A voice came on and instructed me to put on my mask and walk to the side door, where Butler would let me in. I turned the corner and there he was, a thin, older man with a long face under his own mask. He nodded and held the door for me, then ushered me into his small office, where a nice leather seat waited for the next unlucky subject. I took the chair beside it.

Butler sat behind his desk, which was piled high with cardboard boxes and got right to business. "I have to tell you that I support the analysis done on Branagan by the original examiner," he said. Meaning that, according to the data, David Branagan did not show deception in his answers. "But, with a caveat—this is not a test we use anymore because it's only about seventy percent accurate."

The method Kohanski used on all the suspects in the Lisa Pruett case in 1990 was a version of the Positive Control test. Back then, if you were an Ohio cop and you wanted training in lie detection, you took a class from a guy named Silvestro Reali, a retired police officer from Philly. Reali taught the Positive Control test. Butler surmised that Reali, or one of his disciples, had trained Kohanski.

Using the Positive Control test, nearly one in three sessions would result in a false positive or a false negative. Polygraph examiners in the State of Ohio now use better tests that have been studied and vetted over time. These current tests are believed to be over 90 percent accurate.

Regardless, David Branagan's results—as well as the results of every single suspect Kohanski interviewed—are worthless. He simply didn't do enough of them to make a fair assessment. Butler explained that the minimum number of exams needed for a true and accurate assessment is three. Kevin was the only suspect given three tests, and the last two had been conducted after the detectives had kept Kevin up all night and loaded him with caffeine and nicotine.

"The number one rule is you never give a test after an interrogation," said Butler. If you try to conduct a lie detector test after an interrogation, the suspect's charts are going to be all over the place.

We pulled out David Branagan's chart. It's a long sheet of paper, just like you picture, with those lines that go up and down like an earthquake meter. Butler pointed to little hiccups in the straight lines, places that, he said, indicated when a question was asked.

"Before everything was computerized you had these old printouts," Butler explained. "A polygraph examiner had to mark the paper by hand as it came out of the machine. Three marks with a pen. One mark for when the question was asked, a second mark for when the question ended, and a third mark for when the suspect gave his answer."

The reason for this is that some suspects can show deception as soon as a question is asked. Others may show deception after giving their answer. For that reason Butler typically evaluates the entire seven- or eight-second window from the question to the answer. However, Kohanski only made one mark, and only at the moment when the suspect, in this case, David Branagan, gave his answer.

As it turns out, the lie detector tests conducted during the investigation of Lisa Pruett's murder were conducted improperly. Stuff like this happens all the time.

I asked Butler if he'd ever been pressured to conduct a lie detector test after a suspect had been interrogated by police. He nodded, recalling a time when he was still working for the Akron Police Department. Homicide detectives once asked him to question a guy they'd brought in for murder, after they'd already been at him for hours. Butler, at first, refused, but his boss was adamant: He needed to do the test so they could use it to elicit a confession.

Butler, though, understood that if he was going to present expert testimony as a polygraph examiner, his credibility would be fair game. He wouldn't do the polygraph. So he tried to get the confession a different way. He decided not to hook the suspect up to the machine. He just hung out with him. Butler asked the suspect if he was hungry.

"I got him a cheeseburger, a smoke, anything he wanted. Who cares?" said Butler. "After I got him that cheeseburger, he told me in detail about how he beat this kid to death. I got my confession without giving him a bad test."

It dawned on me then, what a strange and difficult job Butler and other polygraph examiners have. They're the ones in the room when the criminals unload their darkness. This is the evil he hears every day.

"Do you take it with you?" I asked.

He gave a short laugh. “It’s hard not to,” he said. “It just eats you up. My wife was a nurse in the pediatric intensive care unit. Sometimes she’d get a kid in there . . . severely beaten, abused. Come home, tell me about it. Then I’d get a call to come down and give a test to the man who did it.”

He shook his head and looked away.

Chapter Fifty

THE LONG AND WINDING ROAD TO CHIPOTLE

HOLLY ROBINSON WANTED ME TO know right away that Lisa Pruett was a darling. "She was just nice to everyone," she said. "Lisa didn't fall into any of the cliques. She interacted with everyone."

Holly was David Branagan's girlfriend back in 1990 and she was anxious to share what she remembered. She started off by explaining that she hadn't seen him in many years and didn't know where he was now.

Holly was actually good friends with Debbie Dreifort when this all happened. She'd gotten to know Dan through his sister. "I thought it was interesting that Lisa and Dan were a couple," Holly said. "He was kind of with the stoner kids. Lisa was good for him. You could see it. He seemed chill, grounded, around her. And I can tell you he was absolutely devasted by her murder."

"How long were you with David Branagan?" I asked.

"About a year," she said. "He asked me to move in with him. He had moved out of his parents' house that year and he had this apartment on the west side, in Tremont. It was cool when we were together. But he could be strange. He gave me this expensive ring one time. It had this sapphire in it. I asked him, 'Where did you get this?' And he told me this story about how his mother had given it to him to give to a girl one day. I found out later he'd stolen it. He got drunk and told me."

"Who'd he steal it from?"

"David used to break into homes in his neighborhood," Holly said. "He got the ring during one of these break-ins. He showed me this box once. It's where he kept the stuff he took. It was full of jewelry. A pearl necklace. Earrings. It looked like old-lady jewelry."

At the time Holly was confused about why David was breaking into homes and stealing when his family was so well-off. It didn't make sense. "He was so privileged," she said.

"You know, he was kinky in the bedroom," she added. "He used to tell me, 'You should do porn. I could take pictures of you.' He was very experimental. And sometimes he went too far. We were in bed one day and he went to the window, opened it, reached out, and snapped off an icicle. He wanted to put it inside me. I told him no. But I never felt threatened by him."

"Do you think there's any chance that David killed Lisa Pruett?" I asked.

"I've wrestled with it," Holly said after a moment. "Back when the police interviewed me, I was a very different person. There were things I didn't know. Like, he always carried a knife. This penknife. I didn't tell that to the police. Then, later, I started catching him in all of these lies." It was cheating, mostly. But she noticed that lying seemed to come easy for him. She'd go to his apartment and he'd pretend he wasn't there, but she could hear that he was inside with another woman.

"Then the DA starts his case against Kevin," said Holly. "They were really far down the road with Kevin by then. They call me into the office, at the Justice Center downtown. It was in Carmen Marino's office. I think they just brought me in to tell me why they were going after Kevin, but I told them, 'Listen, I've come to learn some things about David Branagan. Things you should know.' But his body language—I could tell that wasn't what the prosecutor wanted to hear. They said Branagan had an alibi. But I was his alibi. And so I didn't think that was true."

The night of the murder, David walked her home. That part was true. They made out on her porch for a couple minutes and then he left. But Holly believed he had plenty of time to get to South Woodland and Lee before Lisa was murdered at 12:30 A.M.

She also recalled David bringing up the murder of Philip and Dorothy Porter. "Do you think the same person is involved?" he once asked her.

Holly remembered Kevin well, from the times he used to come into Arabica. "He had that kind of beautiful mind, like the guy in that movie."

After she caught David cheating again, they broke up for good and she didn't see him again for several years. Then, around 2005, Holly stopped at the Chipotle in Independence for a meal. The guy behind the counter was David Branagan. They didn't say anything to each other. She thought he was embarrassed about where he'd ended up.

"David had the ability to go anywhere, be anything," she said. "Instead, he ended up making me a burrito bowl."

WELL, FUCK.

This was not supposed to be part of the book. The story was supposed to be the cautionary tale of Kevin Young's arrest and acquittal, and a brief glimpse at the evidence that pointed to someone inside the Dreifort house.

Now, here was an entirely new suspect, another young man who had the means and opportunity to commit the crime. The motive was fuzzy, still. But this man, a self-professed serial burglar at best, placed himself at the scene of the crime. And I knew David Branagan had really been there because he'd been able to describe Drill, the scent dog, a detail that wasn't mentioned in the newspaper. That also meant that David had seen the policemen, but they had not seen him, which suggested to me that he had hidden somewhere and watched the detectives at the crime scene. Those officers hadn't seen him and they had been on high alert that night, looking for anyone in the vicinity. Looking for a suspect in a homicide.

Several people near the crime scene had also been victims of burglaries in the weeks leading up to Lisa's murder: Someone had slashed the Rathbones' screen door trying to get in, and the same night someone had snuck into their neighbor's house through a skylight.

And then there's the statement of Hollie Bush, the old woman who lived in the house on the property at Lee and South Woodland, where Lisa's body was found. She told police that she'd heard what sounded like someone breaking into her brother's car just before the screams started.

I asked my friend Mike Lewis, a private eye with Confidential Investigations, who helps me from time to time, to find a working number for David Branagan. He got back to me quickly with a phone number and a Twinsburg address. I was hesitant to call. I wasn't sure that this man was a murderer. I didn't want him to be, really. It didn't fit with my narrative. But what if he was? If I called him, what might he do to keep his old secrets from seeing the light of day?

I sat on it for two days. Eventually my curiosity won out. I dialed the number and a woman answered.

"Sorry for the strange call," I said. "I'm a journalist and I'm writing a book on the Lisa Pruett case. I was hoping to speak to David Branagan."

"David died in 2017," she said.

Chapter Fifty-One

THE SAID DAVID BRANAGAN

At 10:30 a.m., on October 14, 2017, Dr. Todd Barr, the deputy ME of Summit County, cut open the body of the forty-seven-year-old man on the table before him. He'd been found on his kitchen floor by his common-law wife that morning. His death appeared natural, even though the man was still young. David Branagan had not been kind to his body.

His coronary arteries were clogged; one had narrowed by 99 percent. That alone could have killed him. And his liver was shot—it was large and scarred due to years of alcohol abuse. Dr. Barr noted two tattoos: one on Branagan's right hand (a circle with two lines and an arrow head), another on his left thigh (a wizard).

Official cause of death was "hypertensive arteriosclerotic cardiovascular disease." And "cirrhosis of the liver" had contributed.

Tracy Warner never married David Branagan, but they had a child together and she called herself his wife. I drove out to her apartment in Twinsburg, a narrow condo amid dozens like it. She greeted me at the door and invited me in. She was younger than I expected, with curly dark hair and a friendly face. The only furniture in the living room was a small couch. We sat together there and she told me all about David.

"When we first met, in 2004, he was a raging alcoholic," she said. "I was working at this convenience store at the time, on 266th, over on Lakeshore, in Euclid. He lived in Watergate Towers. He used to come in every day and buy a twelve-pack of beer and he'd always come in already drunk."

Then one day in November 2004, David came into her store and bought soda instead of beer. "I asked him about it and he said he'd just done thirty days in rehab and was doing the twelve steps." Tracy asked him out a couple months later. "He was sober till the day he died."

The man whom David viewed as his dad was actually his uncle, Tracy told me. Jim Branagan was an attorney in Cleveland. Jim's sister had become addicted to drugs and booze and then she had a little boy. So when David was four or five, Jim took his nephew in and raised him as his own. David's biological mom overdosed and died when he was still a teenager.

Tracy and David eventually moved in together and Tracy got pregnant. Not necessarily in that order. They had a little girl. Over the years David had several jobs, mostly in restaurant management: Chipotle, Maggiano's, Pizza Hut. Not long before he died, he got a decent job as a dietary manager at a local nursing home.

He was a good father, Tracy told me. But not the best partner. She caught him cheating.

Toward the end David started acting stranger than usual. He started obsessively stockpiling guns. "There were twenty-two guns here when he died," Tracy said. "And ten thousand rounds of ammunition."

"Did he ever talk about the Lisa Pruett case?" I asked.

"He drove me through the old neighborhood one day," said Tracy. "He said, 'That's where Lisa Pruett was murdered.' I knew he broke into homes around there when he was younger. He told me that's what he was doing that night, the night Lisa was murdered. He told me that he and his friends were breaking into homes. And yes, I remember him telling me about the Porters, too."

"Do you think he could have murdered Lisa?"

Tracy sighed. "Let me tell you a story he shared with me. When he was in preschool, a boy picked on him. He waited until lunchtime and then he put Comet cleaner in the boy's sandwich. Do I think he did it? Sure. I wouldn't be surprised."

AFTER DAVID BRANAGAN got sober, he befriended a young man named Calvin Mitchell, whom he'd met working at Pizza Hut. Calvin was just seventeen and David looked out for him. They worked together five days a week, for nearly six years.

"He was real good at reading people," said Calvin during a break from the cell phone store where he works today. "He was great at managerial shit. He knew how to interact with employees. He was good at defusing arguments. And he became overprotective of me. I can tell you, he really loved his daughter. Loved Tracy, too."

Sometimes, when business was slow, David would share stories from when he was still a drunk—crazy stories about DUIs and how he'd experimented with hallucinogens; how when he tripped, the whole world felt like a video game. Sometimes the older man would take Calvin fishing out on Punderson Lake, take a little boat on the water and toss in a line.

"I told him I'd go, but I ain't taking a fish off the hook," said Calvin. "I was a Black dude in nature, you know? I had to take it in stride. He was more or less like a dad."

What bonded them, Calvin believed, was their troubled childhoods. Calvin understood the foster care life. The only time he saw David upset was when David got a call at work one day and found out his adopted father had died. It was around that time that David started collecting guns.

"It was definitely an obsession," Calvin said. "He was prepared in case something happened. What? I don't know. He showed me how to clean them, break them down. But he never went hunting. I think he wanted to be ready for the end of the world."

WHEN I WAS still researching the Maura Murray disappearance, I would sometimes post a note on my blog, asking for anyone who'd known her to contact me for an interview. I got some great pieces of information that way from people I otherwise would never have found. So I did the same for this case. I posted a message on my blog asking anyone from Shaker Heights who remembered David Branagan to email me. That's how I was contacted by a woman who knew him through her boyfriend, back in the early 1990s. She wished to remain anonymous: *I remember sitting in the house one day, everyone hanging out, and David was talking about stuff he did as a kid. He said, "I killed this family's dog one time." After that, I avoided him like the plague. But it stuck with me all these years. I thought about calling the police but never did.*

I asked Rebecca Workman if Tex had ever mentioned Branagan. She knew the name well. "Tex always thought David did it," she said.

I SAT WITH David's autopsy report for some time, reading through the details of how he had wrecked his body. Lisa Pruett, Kevin Young, Tex Workman, David Branagan . . . they'd all met the leichendieners before they should have. I reached out to former Cuyahoga County coroner Dr. Elizabeth Balraj to help me understand some of the medical jargon in the reports. She was a great help to me in the Amy Mihaljevic case when I was still a reporter.

Dr. Balraj is a slight woman of Asian Indian descent, the second woman ever to become board certified in forensic pathology. She was the first Indian-American woman to hold elected office in Ohio. For fifteen years she studied under the coroner Sam Gerber, a brilliant, bombastic blowhard of a man, known for his relentless pursuit of Sam Sheppard. And when Gerber died, Dr. Balraj stepped out from his shadow and ran the entire office until she retired. She is a force of nature.

In the autopsy room Dr. Balraj was a servant of science, perhaps the only completely unbiased professional in these investigations. She provided the *how* of a murder, unconcerned about the *why.* But that doesn't mean she wasn't affected.

"She was such a tragic case," Dr. Balraj said of Lisa Pruett. "So young, so much potential. Those cases were always the most difficult."

"I'm curious," I said to her. "You know what happens to a body after we die, but what do you think happens to us? What happens to who we are?"

"I think we go to God," she said. "I believe in what the Bible tells us. I believe we go to God."

Chapter Fifty-Two

THAT GROWING UNEASE

WE'RE COMING TO THE END now, and while I've referenced the Porter murders, I've not really told you much about them. I didn't want to bog you down with another crime that didn't have anything to do with Lisa's murder. In fact, I had avoided researching them because I didn't want to be tempted into thinking there could be a connection. The Porter murders were solved years ago. The case was closed. What would be the point of subjecting you or me to those separate horrors?

But it bothered me to learn that David Branagan was a witness and the one commonality in both the Porter murders and Lisa's murder. And in both instances he had implicated an unidentified Black man. And everyone knows, if you want to blame a guy for a crime in Shaker Heights, pointing to a Black man is bound to get the cops' attention.

I pulled up David's old address on Sedgewick and compared it to the location of the Porters' house, which was on the same street where the Dreiforts had lived. He had lived on the lot to the southwest of the Porters' property, separated by a thin strip of shrubs and trees. Pretty damn close. I needed to learn the details of what happened to the Porters, if only to settle my growing unease.

The impact that Philip and Dorothy Porter had on the history of Greater Cleveland is hard to quantify, but there's no doubt the city is better because of them. Philip was just a junior at Lakewood High School, in 1917, when he walked into the offices of the *Cleveland Leader* and asked notorious editor A.E.M. Bergener for a job. Normally, such bravado would have been met with a swift boot to the backside, but the paper's best journalists had left to fight in the Great War and they were short-staffed. Bergener hired the young Porter as an office boy, making eight dollars a week. Philip was born blind in his right eye and it was something a person noticed right away when talking to him. I have this theory that the best reporters are kind of funny-looking. A lazy eye or a generally rough mug are disarming to people. It makes the interviewer sympathetic and engenders this urge to open up as a kind of favor. Maybe that was the source of Philip's magic.

After he graduated high school, Philip enrolled in classes at Ohio State University. In the summers he wrote crime articles for the *Plain Dealer*. The paper hired him on full-time, in 1922. When World War II broke out, Philip became a PR officer for the Army Air Forces. As a reporter he covered the atomic bomb tests. In 1963, he was named executive editor. During Philip's tenure at the paper, Philip helped foster the journalism of some of the best writers Cleveland ever produced—people like Joe Eszterhas, Roldo Bartimole, and, yes, Terry Sheridan.

By the way, I managed to track down wily old Sheridan. His book editor had an email address that still worked. He's an expat living in Belgrade, watching us destroy ourselves from afar. I asked him why he'd left. *Long and convoluted story, James,* he wrote back. *Suffice to say I came for a war and stayed for trout fishing.* He still remembered Philip fondly.

Dorothy Porter, Philip's third wife, was an accomplished artist. Her specialty was aquatint, her images stark representations of urban life before the Second World War. Collections of her work have been displayed at the Cleveland Museum of Art and the de Young Museum in San Francisco.

Philip and Dorothy Porter were not simply that lovely old couple who lived down the way. They were goddamn royalty living in quiet retirement in the city they helped to shape.

On May 19, 1985, Dorothy's daughter, Joly Arnos, became concerned that she had not heard from her mother in several days. She sent her son, James, to check in on her. When he arrived at his grandparents' house, he found the day's paper—a Sunday *Plain Dealer*—still sitting in the driveway, unread. All the doors were locked. The lights were on inside. But nobody came to the door. So he went home and told his mother. They both returned to the house and Joly used a spare key to get inside.

"Mother?" she called. Nobody answered.

She told James to go next door and get the neighbor. She knew something was very wrong. James returned quickly with the neighbor and the two men went upstairs while Joly stayed put. They found Philip in bed. He'd been stabbed twice in the back. He lay facedown, still dressed in pajamas, his fingers grasping his eyeglasses. A thermos of milk and a plate of crackers sat on the nightstand. They found Dorothy's body in the basement. She'd been stabbed, once, and strangled to death with the cord from her iron.

Peter Gray was chief of police in Shaker Heights back then. Remember him? He was one of DeVan's investigators for a time. Chief Gray told the media that the Porter murders appeared to be a burglary gone wrong, but they had no leads. Philip and Dorothy had last been seen alive on May 17, a Friday night. They'd hosted a cocktail party at their house. Their guests left around 7 P.M. It appeared the break-in had happened between 7 and 9 P.M., when it was still light outside, an odd time for a burglary. The point of entry was a kitchen window; someone had cut through the screen and climbed inside.

Chief Gray told the *Plain Dealer:* "Nothing appeared to be disturbed. It doesn't appear to be a regular burglary, with things shuffled around. There was none of that. There wasn't even a real sign of a struggle. If it weren't for the two dead bodies, you wouldn't know something had happened."

Dorothy's purse and wallet were sitting out in the open. Her milk and brandy nightcap were found nearby. The working theory was that a burglar had come in as the Porters were preparing for bed and Dorothy had come down and interrupted the crime.

This was in the days before DNA. Long before the magic of genetic genealogy. Their only suspect was an unidentifiable Black man that fifteen-year-old David Branagan had seen running away from the house. And the case went cold.

Buckle up. This is where things get complicated.

In 1989, a young con named Donny Soke confessed to killing Karen LaSpina, a mother of three, whose bloodied body had been found in her Eastlake home, in 1985. She'd been stabbed fifty-five times and bled out on her kitchen floor. He told his story to Eastlake detective Tom Doyle. When Doyle pushed him for more info, Soke said his father had participated in the crime, too. Ted Soke was a member of the Hells Angels biker gang and known to local police.

Donny Soke was just twenty years old when he started talking to Detective Doyle. At the time Soke was serving a three-to-fifteen-year stretch at Pickaway on a burglary charge. He'd been in trouble all his short life, in and out of the boys' home as a juvenile. He'd gotten pinched on the burglaries only a couple of months after he'd turned eighteen. Ever since, he'd been sitting in stir. Soke told Doyle that he would testify against his father on two conditions: one, that he'd get a reduced prison sentence for the burglary; two, that Doyle would take him to see his mother, who was dying of cancer.

For weeks Doyle would pick Soke up from prison, take him to see his mom, maybe get him a pizza or a burger, and then drive him back. Each time Soke divulged a little more information about his father's role in the LaSpina homicide, like some hillbilly Scheherazade.

Ted was indicted for the LaSpina murder. But charges were dropped after Donny had a change of heart and admitted he'd made up the whole thing. None of it was true. But he soon discovered that it was too late to unring the bell. Because of his prior confession, Donny himself was convicted of the LaSpina murder. And now he was in the slammer for life.

What did Donny do after that? Like any gambling addict, he went double or nothing on another deal. He contacted Doyle again and said he had information on another murder, this one involving a "newspaperman." Doyle deduced that Donny meant Philip Porter and his wife, Dorothy. Soke said sure, that was it. He told Doyle that he, Ted, and another man, named Danny Crawford, broke into the Porter house and killed them.

According to later statements by an appeals panel, Detective Doyle gave Donny confidential police reports from the Porter homicides with all the information he needed to fabricate his story.

"The fact that Donald Soke had in his possession an initial crime scene investigation is nothing short of astounding," they wrote in their decision. "Not one member of this distinguished panel can ever recall a report of this nature being produced at trial, let alone given into the possession of a witness."

Ted was convicted by a panel of three judges for the Porter murders. And Donny again recanted his testimony, admitting he'd made it up in an attempt to get out of prison. Ted had to be retried. A jury found Ted guilty in that trial, too, and he was sentenced to seven years to life. Ted Soke died in prison, in 2008, after suffering a heart attack.

There is not one piece of forensic evidence that links any of these men to the homicides of Karen LaSpina or Philip and Dorothy Porter. The only things that convicted them were Donny's testimony and testimony from other jailhouse snitches, who cut their own deals with police.

IT WAS SUCH bullshit. All of it. For instance, Donny's confession didn't work at all if you understood Shaker Heights. In order to believe that the Sokes killed the Porters, you must believe that around 9 P.M. on a Friday, when the traffic on Lee Road is busy with people heading into the city to party, three small-time burglars rolled through and spotted papers piled up on the Porters' porch. By the way, Philip Porter, a former executive editor, would never have let that happen. They saw that the lights were not on inside, figured the house was empty, and parked on the street. That's what Crawford, the getaway driver, said; he parked on Lee Road and waited in the car for a half hour while the Sokes climbed through a kitchen window and killed the Porters. The only problem, there was no parking on Lee Road. It's four lanes of traffic.

Get the fuck out of here.

But if Donny and his father didn't kill the Porters, who did? What about a troubled neighborhood teen who broke into homes and stole old-lady jewelry, someone who carried knives, and had no qualms with killing animals and poisoning classmates?

In the prosecutor's files on Soke, I found David Branagan's witness statement. I was surprised to learn that Branagan had been with two friends when he supposedly saw that Black man running away from the scene. I tracked them both down. I've changed their names to protect their privacy.

I found Sam first. "I remember the day well," he said. "I was fifteen. Somebody had a bunch of fireworks. We knew there was an abandoned house and we thought to go light them off there. Me and Charlie and Dave hopped the fence and we went to the house to the left of where the Porters lived. We broke into the garage and set off our stash."

After the fireworks Sam said he saw some movement at the back of the Porters' house. "I dropped to the ground. I watched this guy going around the house, trying to get in. We bolted. Hopped the fence behind us and ran back to Sedgewick."

Charlie's story was a little different. When he called me, he told me that he saw the Black man come out of the back door of the Porters' house. "I heard the screen door slam shut," he said. "I beelined straight to the fence. This guy chased Sam and Dave down Lee Road."

Later, Charlie realized he'd left his jacket at the scene and had to sneak back to get it. He said he was concerned that his name was in it and the police might find it. Though, why he was afraid that the police would think he had something to do with a break-in doesn't quite track. And if they really did witness a break-in, why hadn't they called the police? Why didn't they ask their parents to call the Porters? Also, if the murderer had come out the back door, who locked it behind him?

Charlie said that a couple detectives stopped by his house after Philip and Dorothy Porter's bodies were discovered that Sunday. They took the boys' statements. Later, one of the detectives came back to speak with Charlie's mother. He told her he thought her son was lying.

When Soke confessed to the murders, he never saw the detective again.

Sam said that David grew more reckless as he got older. He stole wine from Sam's parents and broke into the Millers' house down the street and stole a shotgun. "When people mention David Branagan, I get nervous," he said. "He always wanted to be bigger and better than you. He wanted the limelight."

If Dorothy Porter had interrupted David Branagan burgling her house, she would have recognized him. What would Branagan have done to keep his secret life from being exposed?

"I'm sure it was Danny Crawford I saw coming out of that house that night," Charlie told me.

"But Danny Crawford is white," I said.

I MET WITH James Arnos at the Panera in Independence not long after those interviews. James was Philip Porter's grandson. He was the one who discovered his body, in 1985.

He remembers his grandparents fondly: the games of bocce ball in the backyard, Dorothy serving lamb with mint sauce, the days of gardening. He was a kid then, barely out of high school. He's nearing retirement now.

After some small talk I told him about David Branagan. I expected him to get angry with me. Or maybe stand up and leave. Instead, what he said was, "That makes more sense than anything they ever told us."

Chapter Fifty-Three

THE STATE RESTS

ON THE LAST DAY OF SUMMER, I drove out to the west side to interview Carmen Marino, the lead prosecutor at Kevin Young's trial. He was back with his wife, living in a renovated carriage house above the Cuyahoga River. He's seventy-eight years old, and his knees won't allow for shooting hoops anymore, which, as far as I can tell, is his only complaint about aging. He loved basketball. We sat at a window overlooking his backyard and the statue of the Madonna propped against a centuries-old tree at the rim of the gulley.

You know who Marino looks like? He looks like a dad from a 1980s sitcom. Gentle demeanor. A little big around the middle. A sardonic smile. God, it's hard not to love this man right away. DeVan told me once that there are two kinds of lawyers: lawyers who have hard heads and good hearts, and lawyers who have soft heads and hard hearts. Marino had a good heart. DeVan's right. It practically radiated from him. Marino's a guy you want to pal around with. Any jury would be enamored.

We talked books a bit first. As it turned out, Marino was the technical consultant for mystery author Richard North Patterson.

Marino served in Vietnam before becoming a lawyer. I tell you this because I could sense how important that was to him. It's in his aura, that sense that he'd been to hell and back again, and this was why.

In 1992, Stephanie Tubbs Jones was appointed as the new prosecutor in Cuyahoga County, making her the first African-American prosecutor in the history of Ohio. She made Marino her first assistant. As he told it, "I asked her, 'Do you think it's a good thing, as the first African-American woman to hold this office, to make a white Italian guy your assistant?' She told me, I was the only one she could trust."

Here's the kind of prosecutor Marino was: He stayed in his office every day until his in-box was empty. He couldn't leave work without returning all the calls that had come in that day. Nowadays he doesn't even own a cell phone. While we talked, his landline rang constantly. An old answering machine clicked on and people left messages. He'd get back to them.

Many lawyers in Cleveland still regard Marino as a tireless champion of justice. But Marino's legacy as a prosecutor is, for lack of a better word, troubled. He reminded me of what Harvey Dent said: "You either die a hero, or live long enough to see yourself become a villain." I don't think Marino is a villain. But he is a very complicated man.

Marino retired in 2002, shortly before several of his old cases—cases that put men in prison for life—were overturned because of his conduct. Investigations and appeals uncovered instances where Marino cut deals with witnesses for testimony, and he allowed at least one witness to lie under oath. He withheld thirteen pieces of exculpatory evidence that would have kept a man named Reginald Jells off death row. Judges called for Marino to be criminally prosecuted for his behavior. The prosecutor's office even took his name off their annual award for integrity.

I talked with Marino for forty-five minutes about his memories of taking down mobsters in the early 1980s, before we ever got around to talking about Lisa Pruett. He shared his personal philosophies on crime and punishment. He's no fan of the death penalty, for one. And he understood the damage of overcharging suspects, a practice now rampant in Cuyahoga County, forcing first-time offenders to cop to pleas instead of rolling the dice on a single charge at trial. That practice only creates more criminals.

"Once you give a person a record, they're done," Marino said. "They go to jail, come out, find they can't get a job, then go back to committing crimes to survive. If you give a person a break, you'll usually never see them again."

Finally the conversation turned to the trial of Kevin Young. Marino said that he was warned time and again by other prosecutors not to seek an indictment. There was no evidence, they said. So he sat with the detectives from Shaker Heights and asked them if there was a chance the case could get any better if they waited. The detectives told him it could not. Marino decided to roll the dice. Even without evidence Marino was sure he could convince a jury of Kevin's guilt.

"Your degree of confidence should be based on what you can do," Marino explained. "I knew if I could get it in front of a jury, I had a real chance at a conviction. I can argue well. Whoever argues best, last, wins."

"So, why do you think Kevin was found not guilty?" I asked.

"My back," he said. He'd hurt his back. Slipped a disc or something. It hurt him too much to stand, so he had to give his closing arguments from a chair. If he'd only been able to stand and look natural, he'd have won, he believed. The pain threw him off his game. "I screwed up the closing. The pain was radiating down my leg the entire time."

I asked him if he was still sure Kevin had done it and he nodded.

Marino summed up his feelings succinctly. "I didn't waste time on cases where the defendant was innocent."

But then he paused. And Marino told me another story. It was about a young African-American man who was identified as a rapist by a white woman. She'd picked two photos of him out of a lineup. But that was all the evidence they had. Classic he said/she said. But this young man had no record of violence, and there was something about him that gave Marino doubt. He didn't believe he was guilty. Neither did the detective who investigated the crime. But it was Marino's case. It was his job to go after the man the woman believed to be her attacker. And he won. He won over that jury because he was skilled at creating a believable story.

But it weighed on him in his final years, because he didn't believe the man was guilty. Marino looked him up later. After his prison term, the man never had another problem. Went on to lead a decent life, started a family. And Marino had to live with the fact that he probably put an innocent man in prison for rape.

I TOLD DEVAN about my conversation with Marino. He had nothing but nice things to say about his old adversary. Water under the bridge. I laid out everything I'd found out about David Branagan, and DeVan found it compelling, but was not sure if it would have made a difference if he'd known about it back then. Marino had already made up his mind. It was DeVan's job to find doubt, and Dan Dreifort was the best way to show that, because of how the police had utterly ignored him as a suspect.

"Having multiple suspects works well for a book," he told me. "But in a criminal case, if you know your client didn't do it, you can't read through a list of suspects for the jury. They'll think you're throwing things at the wall. They'll get confused. You have to pick one. And Dan was a viable suspect for many reasons. Kevin never was."

Chapter Fifty-Four

A NEW MOSAIC

Lisa Pruett rests in an unmarked grave in Crown Hill Cemetery, in Twinsburg. If you'd care to honor her memory, her parents have previously suggested donations to the Girl Scouts of America.

Nobody is currently investigating Lisa's unsolved murder. The Shaker Heights police consider her case "inactive." It is as cold as a cold case gets. To this day, detectives still believe Kevin did it and got away with murder.

I don't know who killed Lisa—not for sure. For many years Dan seemed like the most likely suspect, for all the reasons listed in this book. But I've come to believe he's innocent, too. I think maybe he took Robo that night. I think maybe he even had sex with her—the evidence suggested she was the one who took off her clothes, and there was a condom nearby. But I don't think Dan was with her when she was killed. I just don't see it anymore. As far as I can tell, Dan hasn't hurt a soul in the thirty years since. And he didn't drink himself to death like so many of the others.

As I finished this book, I was left with a few unanswered questions concerning Dan and Lisa's friends. Why didn't Daniel Messinger get an invite to Dan's party that night? He snuck Robo into the hospital and secretly met up with Dan at a bowling alley, but he didn't know anything about the party? Seems hard to believe.

I find it odd, too, that Daniel Messinger and Chris Jones asked to spend time in Lisa's room, alone, the day of her murder. Were they looking for something? Were they hoping to steal those intimate letters between Lisa and Dan before the police found them? Or was it just kids being weird?

And don't forget about Drill, the only unimpeachable witness in this case, Officer Matsik's K-9 partner. Drill picked up a scent from Lisa's bike and followed it over to Sedgewick, where Kim Rathbone and David Branagan lived. The dog lost the scent in front of Rathbone's house on its way to the Branagans'.

I think of Marino's closing argument, about the mosaic, where the pattern of the circumstantial evidence, as a whole, points to one man. There's a mosaic that could be designed around David Branagan, for sure. He was at Arabica when Tex told Kevin about Lisa's plan to sneak over to see Dan. He lived on Sedgewick, near the scene. He was breaking into homes that night. He carried a knife that fits the type used to kill Lisa. And—this is most important—he had the time to clean up after the killing. He first told police that his mother was waiting up for him when he came home, but he later admitted to lying about that detail. He also said he took a shower that night, at one in the morning. And then you have all the weird things he did later in life and the years of self-medicating. He's also the only witness in the Porter murders, the old couple who lived behind his house, who were stabbed to death during an interrupted burglary, where nothing of value was taken.

I like David Branagan for all three murders. I do. The police knew about him. The prosecutor knew about him. But the public never did, because Shaker Heights detectives believed they had a better case against Kevin and they set about trying to get him to confess at all costs.

The stories about David Branagan's predilections continue to come in to me. Just last month I was contacted by a former girlfriend of his from high school, a woman named Kim Hurtt. She started dating him when she was a freshman and he was a junior. She wasn't allowed to be there if his adoptive parents weren't home, but he'd sneak her over, anyway, using a footpath only neighborhood kids knew about, a thin path that wound through backyards between Lee and Sedgewick from South Woodland, all the way to where the Porters once lived. There was a spare bedroom over the garage and he would take her there for sex. Sometimes he would bring out the knives he collected and use them during foreplay.

Kim didn't know that he robbed neighbors, but she did know he was skilled at breaking into places, because he would sneak into her house at night and her father was a Vietnam vet who listened for the lightest of sounds. Once inside, he would coerce her into doing things she didn't want to do. "If you don't, I'll make a lot of noise and wake up your dad," he'd tell her.

"Looking back, [I feel] he had episodes of darkness," she said that day. "These depressive episodes sometimes. Do I think he's capable of having killed Lisa? Yes, I do. But we had it in our minds back then that it was Kevin."

YOU KNOW WHO I think Donny Soke really is? Donny Soke is what Kevin Young would have become if Detective Gray had broken him during that interrogation in Columbus. Kevin Young could have invented a story, like Donny did, and made Gray happy the way Donny made Doyle happy. And if he'd done that, Kevin would have lived the rest of his life in prison, knowing the dumb made-up story he told a cop when he was a teenager was what did him in. Just like Soke.

Soke communicates with me often now. I asked him how he has survived in prison all these years, how he hasn't gone completely crazy from isolation. He survives by living in his memory. He wrote:

I love to daydream about the times I would stay with my Uncle Denny and Aunt Debbie for summers. I didn't have to be afraid of being placed in a big, dark, cold basement when I was a child while the other kids (my brother/sister) got to sleep in their own bedroom, in beds upstairs. I felt safe at my uncle's. My aunt Debbie and I would spend our days going to garage sales or to farms where we'd pick our own cherries and strawberries. I wore clean clothes and always had food to eat and didn't have to go to bed hungry.

IN NOVEMBER, DONNY SOKE called me one night and his voice sounded different. "Doyle is paying me to confess to murders," he told me. "He's put over one thousand dollars into my account this year. My life is so comfortable right now. You gotta understand, if I told the truth, I would lose so much."

"Did you kill LaSpina?" I asked him.

"No."

"Did you kill the Porters?"

"No. We were never there. Doyle gives me the police reports so I can get the details right."

Soke explained, as best he could, in a letter I picked up at the post office a few days later. He'd written out his story on the back of five interoffice memos from inside the prison:

> Why do I do this, James? Because of this—I feel as if I'm doomed. Ever since being in prison the first time I've felt that this is it for me. I gave up man, and I didn't care. Plus, Tom Doyle has given me a shit-ton of money. I've been locked up for a long-long-long time and most of that time I've had to struggle. With Tom, there's no more struggles. None! And he's guaranteed to continue to do this until his final day on Earth. I kept the emails and receipts.
>
> I'm tired, friend. Over thirty-five years I have been locked away for something I had nothing to do with.

> Ted actually went to Death Row then died an innocent man because of me and my fucking lies.

RECENTLY I REACHED out to a detective in Willoughby and offered the services of The Porchlight Project to help them solve the Nadine Madger homicide, which Doyle told me that Donny Soke had confessed to. If we can prove he lied about that murder, it will cast doubt on all his other confessions. And I think we have a good shot. They have DNA from Madger's killer. All they're missing is a genetic genealogist who knows how to use the data.

In the meantime the Cuyahoga County prosecutor could retest the evidence in the Porter homicides and the Lisa Pruett case to know for sure. There have been so many advances in forensics since 1990, things like M-Vac machines that can pick up trace DNA from old clothes, better sampling techniques, not to mention genetic genealogy. They still have latent fingerprints on some of the evidence in Lisa's case that were never matched to anyone.

Shaker Heights has a big decision to make, just like Donny Soke did. Will they risk reopening the case if it means they were wrong? Or is it better to stick to the story they made up so long ago?

Lisa was a writer. Always writing. And like with the best writers, it was a compulsion for her. I like this bit from one of Lisa's last letters to her boyfriend, that summer of 1990. It's a snippet from a lullaby her mother used to sing to her and she shared it with Dan because she wanted him to sleep peacefully:

> *And I'll sing you the songs of a rainbow*
> *Whisper all the joy that is mine*
> *The leaves will bow down when you walk by.*
> *And morning bells will chime.*

At the end she tells Dan: *Give this letter back to me after you read it so I can sign it so fifty years from now you can remember me.*

DISCUSSION QUESTIONS

1. The title *Little, Crazy Children* comes from a passage out of *The Crucible*, an allegorical play by Arthur Miller that uses the Salem Witch Trials as a stand-in for McCarthyism. How do the events in *The Crucible* relate to what happened in Shaker Heights? Could the case of Lisa Pruett also be used as an allegory for McCarthyism? Why or why not?
2. The early 1990s was a time of "latchkey children," a parenting style in which children were regularly left without adult supervision during a significant portion of the day. Do you think this style of parenting influenced the families of Shaker Heights involved in the Lisa Pruett case? Were you raised as a latchkey child? If so, how did it affect you as an adult?
3. We learn that the teenagers of Shaker Heights were up to all sorts of mischievous behavior—a lot of drugs, sex, and violence that happened when their parents were busy doing other things. What was the worst thing you did as a teenager that your parents had no idea about?
4. The city of Shaker Heights, Ohio, hired a public relations firm to help shape the case narrative in town. In general, do you think that procuring help from a PR firm is a good decision for cities facing controversy? Why or why not? Can you think of another instance where a PR firm was hired in a murder case?

5. The local media played a big part in casting suspicion on Kevin Young. Is there another case where the media's coverage of a crime greatly impacted its outcome? How do you think the media might act differently today? Would the coverage be better or worse?
6. If you had been a member of the jury for Kevin Young's trial, how would you have voted? What was the key piece of evidence, or lack of evidence, that inspired your decision?
7. True crime books require the participation of many individuals who were directly impacted by the crime. The author must maintain a careful balance of empathy, discretion, and candor. How did the author treat his subjects in this book? What, if anything, could he have done differently for the victim and the victim's family?
8. Who do you think killed Lisa Pruett? What evidence leads you to believe this?
9. If you are a parent, did this book change the way you look at your own children? If so, in what way?

ACKNOWLEDGMENTS

I WANT TO THANK a few of my "Irregulars" who helped me locate former students of Shaker Heights High. Specifically, Leslie Green, Valerie Bogart, and Samantha Hanlon. My intern, Stephanie Ijoma, was a great help with organizing the police reports and interviews.

Val Bogart also read an early draft of this book and provided some very helpful notes and research. Other early readers include my assistant, Carolyn Berardino, and my friend Brandy Marks. A shout-out to my former editor David Gray for helping me understand Shaker Heights better. Thank you.

When all else was lost, Mike Lewis at Confidential Investigations was there to help me track down valuable sources.

I also owe a debt to the talented journalists who reported on Lisa Pruett's murder over the years—most notably, Jim McCarty, as well as Eric Stringfellow, Grant Segall, Christopher Evans, and the enigmatic Terry Sheridan.

Special thanks to Mark DeVan, without whom this book would not exist. And to Maureen Young, who helped me better understand her brother Kevin and Shaker Heights itself.

I'm very grateful to Carmen Marino, who spoke as candidly about his mistakes as he did about his many accomplishments. And also Richard Mullaney, even if he wouldn't go on the record.

I was lucky to have an agent and friend in Yishai Seidman, who was a loyal champion for my stories these past ten years. And to my new agent, Joelle Delbourgo, for getting the manuscript across the finish line.

I'm honored to be edited by the one and only Michaela Hamilton. And a sincere thanks to everyone at Kensington, especially Michelle Addo and Jesse Cruz.

And finally—thanks to Donny Soke. Keep a good thought, brother. We're going to do our best to get you out.